christian family
guide to

Starting Your
Own Business

Series Editor: James S. Bell Jr.

by Edward Paulson with
Carol and Gary Wilde

ALPHA

A Pearson Education Company

International Standard Book Number: 0-02-864476-X
Library of Congress Catalog Card Number: 2002166801

05 04 03   8 7 6 5 4 3 2 1

Interpretation of the printing code: The rightmost number of the first series of numbers is the year of the book's printing; the rightmost number of the second series of numbers is the number of the book's printing. For example, a printing code of 03-1 shows that the first printing occurred in 2003.

Printed in the United States of America

Note: This publication contains the opinions and ideas of its authors. It is intended to provide helpful and informative material on the subject matter covered. It is sold with the understanding that the authors and publisher are not engaged in rendering professional services in the book. If the reader requires personal assistance or advice, a competent professional should be consulted.

For marketing and publicity, please call: 317-581-3722

The publisher offers discounts on this book when ordered in quantity for bulk purchases and special sales.

Outside the United States, please contact: International Sales, 317-581-3793 or international@pearsontechgroup.com

Contents

Appendixes

Introduction

You have an idea. You have a vision. Your enthusiasm about them borders on obsessive, and your family is starting to wonder if you have a chemical imbalance in your brain. Congratulations! You sound like an entrepreneur ready to start a business!

Over 150,000 readers have taken the step you just took. They opened previous editions of this book, flipped through the pages, and saw enough of value to purchase it and turn it into an important business tool. I am pleased to welcome you to the pages of *Christian Family Guide to Starting Your Own Business*.

The prior content has been updated and revised. But the end goal of this book is the same as the prior editions: I want you to succeed! And be blessed by God!

Within these pages, you'll find the most accurate information on the legal, financial, and operational requirements of starting a business. In addition, you will find important tips for dealing with your eventual success as an entrepreneur, a Christian, and a person dedicated to family. Success can put you out of business if you don't prepare for it and handle it properly. A special new chapter is added that deals specifically with personal financial issues confronted by successful business owners.

Starting your own business is a lot more complicated than any of us initially realize. It helps to know that you are not alone in your thoughts, desires, fears, and ecstasy. This book was written with the intention of guiding you through the pitfalls and sharing in your successes. Great pains were taken to distill the "mumbo-jumbo" of business down to the basic ingredients that everyone can understand. No critical information was left out and a lot of complicated information has been distilled into its understandable essence.

I start first with you and your motivations. You are the key ingredient in any successful start-up, scary as that might sound. You are your most valuable asset. Who else will work all those extra hours for free? The more you know about you and your motivations, the more likely you are to create a successful business venture.

I have been part of several start-up companies, including a few of my own, and I know there is nothing more exciting than seeing your idea become a thriving reality—and there are few things more painful than seeing it die. I learned a lot of lessons along the way, which I hope to pass on to you. You don't have to go through a windshield to learn to wear a seat belt. I've already been through several business "windshields." Treat the thoughts and ideas in this book as your seat belt. Take them to heart and apply them where appropriate.

In short, this book not only leads you through the business creation process, but also serves as your mentor as your business comes to life. Keep referring back to this book as you become more successful. You may find tips here that did not seem important when you read them earlier, but now have a greater significance.

Creation is a uniquely human trait—because we are the Creator's creatures, after all!—that is not limited to the arts. I had an artist in one of my seminars apologize for her narrow-minded view of business. She thought of art as creative and business as uncreative. After the seminar, she realized that a new business creates job opportunities that didn't exist before. It creates new products and services that perform useful functions. It fulfills dreams for those involved in its success, and each business is a unique reflection of its owner, just like a work of art.

You are on the verge of a wonderful roller-coaster ride where you decide the direction of the track and the speed of the cart. Use this book to pick the optimal track layout, and then apply our management philosophy to successfully steer the cart.

I want you to be successful in your new venture. It breaks my heart to talk with entrepreneurs who took the risk, put it all on the line, and lost. If I can talk you out of starting your company in a few chapters, then you really didn't want it badly enough. If you get through the first few chapters and still want to be a business owner, then finish the rest of the book, prepare your business plan, and make your business idea happen! You clearly have strong entrepreneurial tendencies.

If you knew everything that would happen in the future, you probably wouldn't do anything. Only God knows the future, so commit it to Him. You will certainly feel more of yourself come to life as your idea unfolds, and if you are *really* lucky, you will never have to worry about financial freedom again. It will be yours in abundance, and well deserved. There is nothing idiotic about that, is there?

How to Use This Book

The book is divided into five parts. The sequence is designed to lead you through the business plan creation and start-up management process step-by-step:

Part 1, "So, You Want to Start a Business," asks you to take a hard look at you, your motivations, and your personal situation. Are you ready to pay the price needed to get your business up and running? Is your family ready? Can you wholeheartedly support your particular product as a Christian in the world? If the answer is still yes, then get into things by comparing short-term gains with long-term wins.

Finally, this part includes a business plan outlined with references to a sample business plan included in Appendix A.

After finishing Part 1, you either will believe that starting your business is the right thing to do or will realize that you aren't ready yet. Either way is fine, but you will know what awaits you if you decide to take the plunge. You'll also understand the basic components of the business plan, and you will be ready to create your own plan.

Part 2, "Establishing the Framework of Your Business," presents the legal aspects of business formation. This part introduces various legal business structures, such as sole proprietorships, partnerships, and corporations, with special emphasis on corporations. It's kind of dry but critically important. Take the time to read this part because it truly lays the foundation upon which everything else is built. The benefits you get from this section alone will pay for the price of the book.

Part 3, "Marketing Magic and Successful Sales," talks about pricing, advertising, competition, and sales. These four chapters are a lot of fun and provide a welcome relief from the legal stuff in Part 2. I also added a special section dealing with the Internet so that you understand the valuable impact that this technology will have on your business. You really can't provide too much marketing and sales information in a business plan, so living with this information for a while is time well spent. Wear shorts and bring the suntan lotion: This topic area can be pretty hot!

Part 4, "Facing Your Financials," or delving into the structured mind of the accountant, presents the essence of financial management. These chapters introduce accounting and financial terminology in an understandable way (a really tough thing to do—trust me!) while making you credible in your presentation to bankers and other financial people. These chapters deal with banks, cash flow management, credit card sales, credit-oriented transactions, and avoiding payment delinquency with your clients. A special chapter covers the international business that you will receive as a result of using the Internet. Read this chapter and be prepared for the coming international explosion.

Part 5, "Growing Your Business," covers stuff you will need when you are up and running, along with a special chapter on outlining your production plans. When you add people to your organization and begin to move out of the "sink-or-swim" stage, all kinds of things change. Success creates its own set of problems that can also cause your undoing; reading these chapters will prepare you for the typical major crisis points. For sure, read Chapter 17, "Help Wanted: Adding Employees," and Chapter 18, "The Tax Files: Payroll Taxes," before hiring employees.

In addition, I included several appendixes to give you further sources of insight and information. Appendix A contains a complete business plan that I wrote but never used because it didn't meet my personal objectives. It's a real plan that some of you might choose to try. Go ahead! It would be great to see it making someone money. Most importantly, it presents you with a concrete starting point for your plan.

Appendixes B, C, and D offer you further resources to contact, references to read, and a handy glossary of business buzzwords.

Extras

To guide you through the minefields of starting your own business, this book also provides additional tips and bits of information from those who have been there. You'll find words of wisdom, cautions, and helpful tips in these boxes:

Business Buzzword

This sidebar defines technical business terms for you.

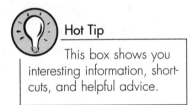

Hot Tip

This box shows you interesting information, shortcuts, and helpful advice.

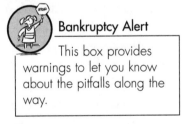

Bankruptcy Alert

This box provides warnings to let you know about the pitfalls along the way.

That's the Spirit

This box gives you Christian and biblical perspectives on business—and on your personal spiritual growth as you contemplate entrepreneurship with your family.

So, You Want to Start a Business

So you think you can be a successful entrepreneur? Well, you can do it. Yes, you read that right: I'm agreeing with you. You can be successful at starting your own business if you take the time up front to do some very important things.

One of those important things involves choosing the right kind of business to start. Each of us has different skills, interests, and abilities. To give yourself a fighting chance, you need to perform some honest self-analysis to determine what kind of business would be best for you. Once you know what kind of business you'd like to start, you need to figure out whether you can make money in this business of yours. You also need to create a plan for starting and running it. You also need to pray and both commit your business totally to the Lord and have a sense that this business is within his will.

Sounds like a lot of stuff to do, doesn't it? Well, don't worry; this first section is going to help you with all of it.

Why Start Your Own Business?

Bill and Mary Smith were walking through a mall doing some last-minute holiday shopping. In one store, on the second shelf in the back, Bill saw the dual-pronged, slotted trammel-widget-thingy that he had drawn on a napkin at a home study group three years ago. Everyone there had agreed that it was a great idea and that Bill should "make it happen."

Bill and Mary prayed about it for a while, but after three years, Bill still has that napkin in his desk drawer at work. Now the couple is looking at his great idea on sale at the mall! Somebody else had the same the idea and ran with it.

Have you ever had an experience like Bill's? Did it make you think that you should convince your spouse and family that it was just the right time to make the leap into self-employment—before missing out on another opportunity?

While many people have done just that—rushed to start their own businesses—I hope that perhaps you'll put off that decision for a short while, until after you've done an analysis of your own situation and goals to determine whether that's really the smartest move. For example, you can always make changes to your business once you start it, but you can't buy burning desire. It has to be there from the start. Otherwise, you're at a severe disadvantage.

If you're considering starting a business because you've had difficulty finding a full-time job that interests you or meets your financial goals, DON'T. Starting a business is not the same thing as creating a job for yourself. Starting a business means that you're ready to give up a regular paycheck, benefits, regular working hours.

A business is much more than a job; it involves a serious commitment to your customers, who will rely on you for your goods or services, and to your employees, who depend on you to provide their paychecks. Your success or failure doesn't just affect you and your family; many others will feel it, too.

If you're currently employed and thinking about quitting to start a business, don't give up the stability of your day job until you feel confident you'll be able to replace that income in the near future. Starting a business while you're still employed is an excellent way to "test the waters." Once you jump in, you have to be ready to work hard to keep your head above water. Be sure you have the interest and the stamina.

Why Do People Do It?

Running your own small business is tougher work than anything you have tried before, but it also offers rewards that are generally greater than your current employer can give you. Here is a partial list of common reasons why people decide to start their own businesses:

- **Adventure**   They like taking risks.
- **Bureaucracy**   They feel it's too hard to accomplish anything in their current job because every decision becomes a political issue.
- **Creativity**   They have a great idea for a new product or service that no one currently offers.
- **Competition**   They feel they can offer what their current company offers to the consumer, but for less money.
- **Control**   They want to be their own boss and make their own decisions about their family's financial future.
- **Earning potential**   They want to be paid for the extra effort they give to their work. They'd rather work more and have the chance to be paid more.
- **Flexibility**   They want a schedule that allows them to spend time with their families and work when they want to.

- **Fair wages**   They feel they aren't paid what they are worth in their current job, and if they worked on their own, they'd make more money.
- **Freedom**   They want to be able to decide for themselves when, how, and where they complete their work.
- **God-giftedness**   God has given you the traits and abilities of an entrepreneur listed above and is prodding you to move on.

Are these valid motivations? Yes. The need to exercise your own judgment, take your own risks, and create something from nothing can be profound. You may want financial independence to provide the freedom to do things with your family life that you couldn't do otherwise. You may have an idea that nobody at work supports or thinks is a good idea. You may want to serve God by improving the quality of life for others. If you believe in the idea strongly enough, you have to try it yourself or you will always wonder how it would have turned out.

That's the Spirit

Many workers in the modern marketplace feel increasingly bored with their jobs and with life. This is the subtext of all the glitzy commercials that show hardworking laborers building America and solving its problems. They portray the workplace not as it is but as we wish it could be—an engrossing, challenging, even uplifting human drama in which each of us performs our strategic role and fulfills a personal mission. Instead, for many work is "just a job." Its value begins and ends with a paycheck. —Doug Sherman and William Hendricks

Understand that although you might not report to a supervisor, you will still be working for someone else: your clients and customers. But you will also be working to achieve your own family's dreams, not those of your employer. You provide the energy, vision, and sustenance that keep the dream alive and strong. You also need determination and dedication to keep going when the going gets tough.

People who start their own businesses, or *entrepreneurs,* are a strange breed. They will give up almost anything to have the right to make their own choices, decisions, opportunities, and mistakes—even when they know that many of those choices and decisions may turn out to be bad ones. Hey, at least they had the power to make them!

When an entrepreneur starts to talk seriously about getting a job working for someone else, you know things must be pretty bad. But business owners who are committed to reaching their goals don't throw in the towel so easily. What often happens at those low points is that entrepreneurs come up with a really creative solution that helps turn things around. The need for money often forces those creative juices to flow!

If you don't feel a deep level of passion about your venture, then you should reevaluate your plans to become a business owner. If you have doubts about your motivations, then this is probably not your time to take the plunge. Wait until the need to work on your own becomes unbearable; then you know you're ready to start your own business.

Do You Have What It Takes?

Before you start your business, you'll want to be sure that you have a solid foundation in every major aspect of business management, or make friends with good people who do. (Pizza and Pepsi, is often a form of entrepreneurial currency.)

In their book, *Do It Right: Essentials for Success,* written and designed by Marcia Rosen of Rosen and Associates LTD and Lucy Rosen of The Business Development Group, the Rosens provide a number of checklists to help you, the potential business owner, learn more about your strengths and weaknesses. But what you'll also find is that the skills and personal characteristics on their list are also traits of successful entrepreneurs. Take a look at the following lists to see how you do. How many of these traits do you already possess?

My work style is:

Action-oriented

Highly organized

Energetic

Steady

Goal-oriented

Decisive

Hard-working

Determined and persistent

I'd describe myself as:

Dependable

Sensitive/perceptive

A calculated risk-taker

Self-motivated

Cooperative

Outgoing

Flexible

Resourceful

Dynamic

Curious

Alert to problems and opportunities

I have the following interpersonal skills:

Good leader

Good in a crisis

Intuitive/insightful

Supportive of others

Good communicator

Good boundary-setter

Able to compromise

Willing to ask for help

These are my practical skills:

Smart about money

Good problem-solver

Street-smart

Good troubleshooter

Possess sales ability

Possess bookkeeping ability

Able to juggle many tasks

Able to see both the big picture and small details

Good writer

Good at follow-through

Creative/artistic

Original thinker

Possess research ability

Possess computer know-how

Strategic thinker

If you find that you have 50 percent or more of the personal characteristics or skills on these lists, you have a solid foundation for becoming a successful entrepreneur. And just finding that you may be lacking in some areas doesn't mean you have to give up your dream. It does mean that you have to surround yourself with other people—partners, consultants, or employees—who can help you out in those areas.

That's the Spirit

There are all different kinds of voices calling you to all different kinds of work, and the problem is to find out which is the voice of God rather than of Society, say, or the Superego, or Self-Interest.

By and large a good rule for finding out is this: The kind of work God usually calls you to is the kind of work (a) that you need most to do and (b) that the world most needs to have done. If you really get a kick out of your work, you've presumably met requirement (a), but if your work is writing cigarette ads, the chances are you've missed requirement (b). —Frederick Buechner

Setting—and Reaching—Your Goals

Starting and running a business involves continuous learning. A lot of learning occurs from mistakes that you make along the way and vow never to repeat. Other learning comes from interactions you have with customers, fellow business owners, and friends who lead you toward success. You set the pace at which you want to learn based on how open you are to new ideas and suggestions you hear from employees, clients, and colleagues. The faster you can adapt, and adopt, what you've learned, the sooner your business will meet your goals. Remember to consider how your goals may affect your family, as well.

Some goals you might set for yourself involve:

- How much money your company will make each year
- How much money you'll earn as the owner
- How many hours you'll work each week, and how many hours will be spent with your family
- What percentage of your time will be spent traveling
- The number of customers you'll do business with the first year
- How fast your company will grow
- The number of employees you'll have on staff
- At what age you'll retire to a Caribbean island (or maybe serve God full-time)

As you begin to make decisions about becoming a business owner, you'll want to think about setting goals such as these to help you.

Keep in mind that committing your goals to paper will actually help you reach them. Once your targets are on paper, you can refer to them regularly to track your progress, change them as your company's situation changes, and use them to help keep everyone on your staff focused on what's truly important for your success as a company. Make writing down your goals a top priority, and review them regularly with all the members of your family.

When setting personal goals, be as specific as possible. Don't say that you want to earn "a decent living." Instead, state that you plan to take home $75,000 your second year in business. The more specific you can be, the easier it is to design a plan to reach those goals.

For example, you can plan several ways to earn that $75,000. You can calculate approximately how many customers you'll need to win, or how many products you'll need to sell, as well as how many employees you'll need to hire.

How is this for a great goal? "To reach $200,000 in sales with a profit before tax of 20 percent within 18 months."

So what will it mean if you don't meet the goal? Well, that depends on how much you are off. If you exceed your goal early, pop the champagne and congratulate yourself. If you are at $160,000 in sales with a 25 percent profit before tax, then you still took home some money and you are doing something right. Set your next goal and move on.

If you are at $65,000 in sales and $20,000 in the red, it may be time to reassess your goal, or even consider returning to your day job. Assess, too, how the debt affects your family's morale.

Start with a goal you feel is realistic and work backwards, developing smaller goals along the way that will help you hit your target. Be realistic and optimistic or you might get discouraged if you don't reach your goals. Set goals you can win.

In the following sections, we'll look at specific goals you can set for yourself and your business.

Financial Motivations and Goals

How much money do you *want* to make, and how much money do you need to make? Understand that these two amounts are not the same. I've never met anyone who made as much money as they wanted, but most people make as much money as they need. It all comes down to how well they manage the money they make.

Wealth is a relative term. If you make $100,000 per year and spend $110,000, you are living beyond your means. Most people would consider you poor. However, if you make $65,000 and spend $50,000, then you're saving or investing $15,000 a year. Over the course of just a few years, you would be considered very wealthy.

> **definition**
>
> **Business Buzzword**
>
> **Wealth** means consistently having money left over after you pay all of your bills.

In short, don't just calculate how much money you want to bring in; look also at what it costs to live your current lifestyle. Calculate how much money you need to cover all your living expenses. You'll also have to account for the expenses associated with your business—federal taxes, state taxes, health insurance, life insurance, tuition assistance programs, vacation time, and so on. (I'll cover these expenses in more detail in Part 4.)

The total of your minimum living costs and fixed business expenses is the amount you need to earn to live as comfortably as you are living now. You have to make at least this amount of money or one of the following three things must happen:

1. You decrease your expenses.
2. You figure out a way to make more money from your venture.
3. You stay with your current job until your finances are in order.

Look at your finances both on a short-term (12 months) and long-term (2 to 5 years) basis. First, you need to get through the short term to make it to the long term. If you do not have the money to support yourself for at least 12 months (some say 18 to 24 months), then you should hold off starting your venture until you have the needed savings. Or you can look for outside sources to provide the money you need, such as family members, friends, or banks and government agencies. You need to be able to support yourself during those initial lean months when your business probably will not be making enough to pay your rent or your mortgage. So start saving those pennies now.

You should also consider how much money you're willing to invest before you pull the plug on a business that is a cash drain. Realize that not everyone who starts a business becomes wealthy. Statistics suggest that only 20 percent of all new businesses will be around in five years. Generally, when a business fails, the owner doesn't make a lot of money on the deal. The average business owner makes somewhere around $30,000 to $40,000 a year in salary. That may not sound bad to some of you, but just keep in mind the number of hours entrepreneurs have to put in to make that money. It's hard work!

Family Motivations and Goals

If you are the type of person who cannot leave your family alone for the evening or weekend without having intense feelings of guilt, then you should examine your intentions and your family's needs before you begin a new business venture. Without your family's support, it will be difficult for you to succeed. There will be times when you will need to work at night, on weekends, and on holidays. At these times, you will have to choose between family involvement and business commitments. Your family needs to accept your commitment to your business without being hurt or angry.

So communicate openly with your spouse, children, parents, and friends about what you want to do and what kind of a time and energy commitment it will take. It's a good idea to prepare them in advance for some of the sacrifices that you and they may have to make. And make sure they're willing to make those sacrifices! Remember in the long run you need balance. Christian priorities mean God first, your family second (obligations as spouse and parent), and your business third. Jesus did say you can't serve both God and money. So if in order to have a successful business you put these two relationships after it, it's better to work for an employer.

If you sense from initial discussions that your family may resent your directing attention away from them and toward a business, think about ways that you can involve them in the company. Instead of thinking that you have to choose between business and family, talk with them about what you can all do together to run a business. Putting your children on the payroll may be a savvy tax strategy to consider. In addition, making your spouse an employee may enable you to pay for your family's health insurance through the company. It's definitely something to look into.

> **Hot Tip**
>
> Set specific goals. With a specific goal as your target, it's often easier to move ahead—you have something concrete that you're working toward. Now you just need to figure out *how* to achieve that goal you've set for your business.

> **That's the Spirit**
>
> If one part suffers, every part suffers with it; if one part is honored, every part rejoices with it. Now you are the body of Christ, and each one of you is a part of it. (1 Corinthians 12:26–27)
>
> George has a company that makes metal stamps. It was the Christmas rush, and he had been working a steady 7 A.M. to 11 P.M. day since before Thanksgiving. In fact, his final sale day was Christmas Eve at 11 P.M. His wife was attending the craft shows with him, and the children often came along for the ride.
>
> He looked vibrant, healthy, and happy. So did his wife. Imagine how different this scenario would be if the family waited at home grumbling about how their Christmas was being disrupted by dad's obsession. Instead, the various members of this family acted as on body, just as church members ought to do.

Families can suffer when they sense that the business is more important than everything else in the business owner's life. Be sure your family knows that this is not the case. Typically, just telling them won't do it; you have to show them by setting aside time to be with them.

Spend the time to get your family involved from the beginning. Set their expectations properly to best avoid having recurring ugly scenes later. Your family can become a source of strength if they understand the importance of their support in your and the business's success. Nobody is an island, and you may end up alone, snuggling your checkbook if you don't handle your family situation with respect.

What Are Your Spiritual Goals?

For some of us, a business helps us achieve spiritual goals through the belief that by providing a valued service to our clients, we are improving their lives. Spiritual goals can also be reached by creating an organization to perform social service work, such as a food kitchen or a halfway house. Some entrepreneurs want to create an organization where their employees can realize their full potential while contributing to the Kingdom.

That's the Spirit

Sally wants to bring new attention to the plight of people in recovery for alcohol or substance abuse. She believes that by creating products to better meet the needs of this group, she can draw attention to and help support them. Like many other entrepreneurs, Sally is dedicated to her business idea; she just happens to be doing it for spiritual reasons.

"Whoever wants to save his life will lose it, but whoever loses his life for me will find it. What good will it be for a man if he gains the whole world, yet forfeits his soul? Or what can a man give in exchange for his soul?" —Jesus (Matthew 16:25–26)

If you have a suspicion that making money is bad, there is a strong chance you won't make enough, and your business will fail. If you believe that computer automation is the root of all evil, you should probably avoid becoming a personal computer dealer. However, if you believe that training people is the most important way to contribute to the quality of their lives, then starting a training business would be a viable option.

In essence, don't neglect the nonbusiness side of your soul when deciding to start your own business. In fact, you should probably look there first.

What Is Your Ultimate Motivation?

Ultimately, it all comes down to your sense of God's will for you and your family. What do you want and why do you want it? How will this new business contribute to your life's purpose in Christ? How will it grow and shape every member of your family? How will it witness to your faith in the community at large? And will this new venture indeed give you the fulfillment that's been missing in your current job? Finally, are you willing to earn less money for a while as you try to establish your company?

If you like the stability of working 9 to 5, wake up! Owning your own business means that you don't have set hours because you'll be working close to 24 hours a day to get things going. If this paragraph alone is enough to talk you out of pursuing your own business, then send me a thank-you card. You are not ready yet to make that kind of commitment. It doesn't mean that you never will, just that right now is not your time.

On the other hand, if after reading this chapter you feel that starting your own business is still the right thing to do, then congratulations! If you feel that you were born to be an entrepreneur and are willing to do just about anything to succeed, you have the energy and the drive typical of entrepreneurs. I am privileged to be your tour guide on this journey of planning, legal structuring, and daily managing. Next stop: What type of business is the best for you and your family?

What Kind of Business Should You Start?

There are so many factors to consider before you launch a business that you may become overwhelmed before you even start. But if you take it step-by-step you can carefully weigh all your options—and there are a lot of them. Use this chapter to develop a list of possible businesses you might want to start and to begin to find the type of business that's perfect for you.

Developing Your Business Idea

Even though you may have decided that you want to own your own business, it's very possible that you have no idea what type of business to start. You'll find familiar types of businesses, such as franchises for fast-food restaurants, quick oil-change garages, and maid services, all available to you. You'll also see some businesses that have cropped up in response to changes in the way we live and work, such as meal-delivery services to help time-starved families, child chauffeur services, and recycled products for our homes and offices.

So, in light of the many options available, there is no simple answer to the question of what, exactly, you ought to choose. It really depends on a number of different things:

- Your interests
- Your experience

- Your abilities
- How much money you have to invest
- What else you could be doing to make money

You must have a clear picture of what you will sell in order to make money. This can be either a product or a service. In many cases, people stick with what they know; they choose to sell products with which they are familiar, such as computers, flowers, or kitchen appliances, or to offer services they are already trained to offer, such as accounting, plumbing, or repairing cars.

The following questionnaire should help you brainstorm some potential businesses to start. Take your time. Jot down your answer to each question in the questionnaire and complete the lists and exercises provided in the next few sections of this chapter. Be honest; these exercises will provide you with insight into what kind of business you will most likely succeed at.

Questions to Ask Yourself in Choosing a Business

1. Based on your education, your current or past jobs, and any special interests and hobbies, what three things do you know the most about? This experience could be the basis for a business.

   _____

   _____

2. What other experiences in your background could you draw upon for a business?

   _____

   _____

3. What do people tell you that you do well? Think about the times you've heard someone say, "You know, you really ought to start a such-and-such; you're so good at that." Maybe they're right. Maybe they would be your first customers.

   _____

   _____

4. What things do you like doing most? Think, for example, about these questions: What do you like to do on your days off?

   _____

What kinds of things do you leap out of bed for?

_____

What magazines, books, and newsletters do you enjoy reading?

_____

What headlines catch your eye?

_____

What things did you love doing most when you were a child?

_____

What is it you've always said you were going to do someday?

_____

If this were the last day of your life, what would you say you wished you had done?

_____

5. How much do you want to be involved with people? All the time? Sometimes? From a distance? Not at all? The answers can help you to start or avoid businesses that have a lot of people contact.

_____

_____

6. How many hours a week are you willing to invest in your business? Do you want a full-time or a part-time business?

_____

_____

7. How much money do you need to make? How much money do you want to make? Each week? Each month? Each year?

_____

_____

8. What resources do you have available to you in terms of property, equipment, and know-how? These resources could become the basis of a business.

_____

_____

9. Do you want to start a business from scratch, or would you prefer a franchise or direct-selling organization, such as Quixtar or Avon, that will train you?

_____

_____

This information is taken directly from Paul and Sarah Edwards' book, The Best Home Businesses for the 90s, *Second Edition,* 1994, *Jeremy P. Tarcher/Putnam Books, ISBN: 0-87477-784-4, page 20.*

Remember that taking a long look at how you like to spend your free time is a good place to start in deciding what kind of business is right for you. Make a list of all the things you like to do in your spare time. Include formal hobbies, such as drawing or stamp collecting, as well as informal activities, such as creating family scrapbooks, reading, or cooking. Don't forget to add your spiritual commitments of church, small group fellowship and activities, and personal devotions.

Along with reviewing your hobbies, consider the kinds of skills you've developed in your current job. Could you begin offering them as services on a freelance basis? Now may be the time to go out on your own and offer others the same services and know-how you've been giving your employer.

Begin by making a list of your major responsibilities at your current job. Think about what you do on a daily basis and also what big projects you have worked on recently. Are there types of activities you enjoy most? What kinds of things do people ask you to do most often?

In addition to thinking about what you do in your current job, also think back to past jobs you've held, what you did there, and what you enjoyed most about those positions. Add these responsibilities to your list. Make your list as long as possible to be sure you don't overlook any type of work you've enjoyed in the past.

What Are Your Strengths?

This question might sound silly at this point, but of all the activities and interests you've listed so far, which ones are you good at? No, really. Which ones do you really excel at? There may be things you like to do in your spare time but that you know could never be the basis of a business, and there may be other interests of which you have an in-depth knowledge that you could apply to a company.

That's the Spirit

Doing what you *like* improves your quality of life as you work toward that success. Before you commit money, energy, and time to your venture, make sure it's something *you really delight in doing*. Long ago, Israel's King David put it this way in the context of life's ultimate priority:

Delight yourself in the LORD and he will give you the desires of your heart. (Psalm 37:4)

Gather all of your completed questionnaires and read them through again. What kinds of activities come up repeatedly? Are there some types of things you like doing more than others? Do you see similarities among some of your abilities, skills, and interests? Could they be combined to form the basis for a business? This is the process you'll need to go through as you read and re-read the worksheets you've filled out.

Look at what you're good at, and what you enjoy, and combine them into a kind of business you could start. Here are some simple, yet effective, exercises to go through to determine where you may have the greatest success. (These exercises are adapted from *Job and Career Building*, Chapter 4, "Setting Objectives," Richard Germann and Peter Arnold, 1980, 10 Speed Press, ISBN: 0-89815-048-5.)

1. Take out a piece of paper and number it from 1 to 15 on the left side of the page. Now, write down a minimum of 10 and a maximum of 15 accomplishments. These events can be from your recent professional past or from your childhood.

2. Take out 10 to 15 sheets of paper (depending on how many accomplishments you listed) and write an accomplishment from Step 1 at the top of each sheet and divide the rest of the sheet into two vertical columns. Mark the left column "Successful Skills Applied" and mark the right column "Successful Personal Attributes Applied." You should have a separate sheet completed for each successful project or event you listed in Step 1.

3. Now, take out two other sheets of paper and rewrite all of the "Successful Skills" on one sheet and the "Successful Personal Attributes" on another. Cross out items that are on the lists more than once, and mark the number of times a skill or attribute appeared (on your sheets in Step 2) next to each skill or attribute. Reorganize the lists in decreasing order from most to least frequent. Some items may appear on both the attributes and skills lists; that's okay. At this stage, you should have a pretty good idea of what makes you tick when you are successful.

4. Group the skills and attributes into clusters that describe a general type of work or activity. For example, typing, filing, and detail work may be grouped under administrative skills. Coordinating people and events may be more managerial in nature.

5. Put these clusters into your perceived order of importance from most important to least important.

6. Write a sentence that describes your top skills and attributes so that anyone reading it would clearly understand the type of environment where you work best.

There you have it. You should now have a clearer idea of the type of job, work, and business environment in which you stand the best chance of success.

Your Personality and Abilities

In addition to your interests and experiences, your personality and abilities also play an important role in determining what kind of business is best for you.

Take a look at the list of activities in the following table and circle the ones that you like to do. Focusing on what you're good at can lead you toward a certain type of business.

Your Skills and Abilities

Information-Oriented	People-Oriented	Thing-Oriented
Working with words	Advising	Cleaning
Working with numbers	Caring	Making
Analyzing	Communicating	Organizing
Compiling	Helping	Repairing
Creating	Informing	Working with animals
Information-Oriented	**People-Oriented**	**Thing-Oriented**
Evaluating	Organizing	Working with food
Finding	Negotiating	Working with plants
Keyboarding	Performing	Working with tools
Organizing	Persuading	
Synthesizing	Planning events	
	Teaching	

This information is taken directly from Paul and Sarah Edwards' book, The Best Home Businesses for the 90s, *Second Edition, 1994, Jeremy P. Tarcher/Putnam Books, ISBN: 0-87477-784-4, page 21.*

Look at each of the forms you've completed and find the commonalties. What types of activities keep coming up over and over? Can you envision certain kinds of businesses that you would like to start? Are there others you now know are of absolutely no interest to you? Keep coming up with new ideas and refining them according to some other factors I go over in a minute.

What Does the Market Need Now and in the Future?

Up until this point, you've been focused solely on what you like to do, what kind of work experience you've had, and what types of products or services you could offer clients. Now you need to consider whether there is a demand for what you have to offer in the way of products and services.

It may be easiest to start this process by looking at recent trends in the market to give you some ideas for where you should focus your attention. To figure that out, you need to do some research. This doesn't have to be the typical, tedious, lengthy process you may be used to; it can be done in short spurts over time.

Researching Opportunities

You can learn about what people and businesses need by turning to the media. Newspapers, magazines, reports, websites, and radio and television stations reflect all our interests and concerns. By studying what kinds of things they've been writing about or talking about, you learn a great deal about products and services that everyone needs.

The best way to undertake this research is to read the following:

- National and trade business magazines.
- Local newspapers (and local news programs).
- Publications about subjects you're interested in.
- National news and business publications.
- Related materials and websites on the Internet.

Keep an eye and ear open for topics that everyone seems to be interested in or that everyone is talking about. Collectibles, as well as electronic games, are all the rage now. The Internet is always in the news as a new means of communicating, gathering information, and marketing. And don't forget any major, recent news events. Are there related products or services you can imagine that would tie into events such as these? That's how you have to start thinking.

That's the Spirit

In your search for what kind of work is just right for you, keep your life's priorities constantly in mind. The biblical Job, who suffered much for maintaining his integrity, is a great role model here:

If I have put my trust in gold or said to pure gold, "You are my security," if I have rejoiced over my great wealth, the fortune my hands had gained, if I have regarded the sun in its radiance or the moon moving in splendor, so that my heart was secretly enticed and my hand offered them a kiss of homage, then these also would be sins to be judged, for I would have been unfaithful to God on high. (Job 31:24–28)

If you already know what you want to sell but don't know whether people will pay you for it, narrow the focus of your research to similar businesses in your area. Study them, read all the recent articles about them in your local library's clipping files, and talk to the owners about how their businesses are going.

In your conversations with business owners and their families, ask them what they would be willing to pay for the product or service you intend to sell. Keep track of what price they tell you is reasonable. After several such conversations, you should have a pretty good idea of what people want and what they'd be willing to pay.

Your Employer Could Be Your First Customer

One of the first things to consider is whether you currently do something for an employer that other individuals or businesses may also need. You've probably heard about the new trend toward outsourcing, which is pushing companies to keep their full-time staff small and pay others to handle short-term projects or work unrelated to the company's main business. Essentially, instead of hiring more full-time workers, companies are relying more and more on short-term workers with a certain talent or skill. Outsourcing may provide opportunities for you to secure some new clients.

What outsourcing can mean for you is the chance to continue doing what you do for your employer, but as an outside consultant, *independent contractor*, or *freelancer*. When companies lay off workers, they typically don't eliminate the work that person was doing; they just shift the burden to someone else. That can work in the short term, but after a while, employees get overburdened and downright irritable about having to do everyone else's work in addition to their own. A potential solution for many companies is to hire people on a per-project basis when the workload is too great or to turn over responsibility for a particular type of activity to an outside company that specializes in that area.

To determine whether your current employer might consider paying you to do what you do now as an independent contractor, freelancer, or consultant, consider your boss's point of view. What are the advantages for your employer?

- As an independent contractor, you do not have to be paid benefits or have taxes taken out of your pay.

- In some cases, you may be able to be paid on a flat fee basis for individual projects rather than an hourly wage, potentially saving the company money.

- You don't need an office or workspace at the company. Equipment such as a computer, telephone, copier, and fax machine are not provided.

If you have a good relationship with your boss and your employer and you believe that there is a way for you to continue to work for them as an independent business owner, it might make sense to suggest that your employer become a client. I suggest having this discussion with your boss when you are sure that you want to leave and are ready to start your business. If your employer becomes angry that you want to leave, you may find yourself on your own soon than you expected to be!

Will You Make Money?

Before jumping in with both feet, wouldn't it be nice if you could get a better idea of whether your business will succeed? This is where some basic financial analysis will be helpful. Don't worry; you don't have to be an accountant to do this stuff.

Start-Up Dollars and Your Business Choice

Enthusiasm, skill, and fortitude will take you far, but combining these traits with cash will get you much closer to your goals. The reality is that service businesses (those that offer services such as accounting, consulting, or massage) generally cost less to start than product businesses (those that offer products, such as computers, clothes, or widgets). You could start a dog-walking company on little money as long as you keep your expenses on a short leash. (Sorry; the pun was too good to resist.) Seriously, though, leashes, collars, a phone line, and business cards are all you need to get into your own dog-walking business.

On the other hand, starting a product business often requires major machinery and equipment, office space, employees, and more. Maybe a lot more. Each of these items translates into more dollars and more delay before sales start rolling in.

Due to this fact of life, many companies start as service businesses and move on to include products as their cash and sales situation improves. For example, a computer programmer can start by offering software consulting (a service) and eventually develop and sell her own software programs (a product). Starting on a small budget doesn't mean you necessarily have to stay small, but it does help to keep expenses down when sales are lower.

How Much Can You Invest?

You don't have to have millions of dollars to start a business—far from it. Many people start small, often on a part-time basis, spreading their money between living expenses and business start-up costs. Other business owners get loans for thousands and thousands of dollars. For example, some fast-food franchises cost more than $100,000 just to open. You have to decide for yourself how much money you and your family are willing and able to set aside to start your business.

Only by estimating how much money you can make and how much it will cost to run your business will you know whether you should continue to pursue your dream. If there is no money to be made by starting the business, then you should probably drop the idea. After all, you need to provide for your family if you are the bread-winner of the household. On the other hand, if your spouse is providing the family income, and you just want to stay busy, then make sure he or she knows that your new "business" is actually mostly a fun hobby for you. Do not give the impression that it will be a significant money-making concern if that was never your intention in the first place.

Bankruptcy Alert

When calculating how much money you need to start your business, you must include the cost of your living expenses during the start-up phase. Don't assume you can live on bread and water until the business kicks in. Your family will start to resent the business if you find yourselves lacking a decent meal several nights in a row. This can cloud your judgment and significantly dampen everyone's enthusiasm.

Consider Your Start-Up Costs

As you think about your earnings potential, determine how much money you need to start the business, and how much money you need to pay yourself during that time to cover your basic living expenses. For example, if the business requires $50,000 to start and you need $48,000 to cover your personal living expenses until the company is on its feet, then the initial investment required is $98,000, not $50,000.

Use the following figure to estimate your start-up costs.

It is either your money or your investors' money that funds the business. It will definitely be your time, and time is also worth money. Professional investors require a formal business plan before they will invest. Even if you don't need outside financing because you have the cash to invest yourself, be as serious about evaluating the opportunity as an investor would be. (Check out Chapter 4 to learn more about creating a business plan.) Make sure that this is an investment you believe is going to pay off for you.

Business Buzzword

Opportunity cost is the profit that you could have gained by pursuing another investment instead of the one you currently have.

What else could you be doing with your money? How could it be spent if not working to start your business? All those other ways that you could have spent your money is what the financial pros call the *opportunity cost* of starting your business. Investors frequently look at situations in terms of opportunity cost: What other investment options are they giving up by investing their money here, rather than there? If the return from your business idea is lower than their next-best option, then they will not give you the money.

Startup Costs

Equipment to be purchased	$_____
Office rental	$_____
Inventory	$_____
Renovations	$_____
Supplies	$_____
Marketing	$_____
Utilities	$_____
Other: _____	$_____
_____	$_____
_____	$_____
_____	$_____
_____	$_____
Total	$_____

Living Expenses

Rent or mortgage	$_____
Food	$_____
Car payment	$_____
Utilities	$_____
Insurance	$_____
School tuition	$_____
Credit card	$_____
Other: _____	$_____
_____	$_____
_____	$_____
_____	$_____
_____	$_____
Total	$_____ per month
	= $_____ for 6 months
Total start-up cost plus 6-month living expenses	$_____

How Much Do You Give Up and When Do You Make It Back?

There are worse fates than having a business fail miserably. One of them is having it fail *gradually* so that it slowly bleeds your family's reserve funds and energy. For this reason, I suggest that you set some guidelines for when you will evaluate your company's performance. These milestones should include desired, or even required, levels of personal income and time investment required to keep the business running. If you exceed these goals, then you and your business are successful. (Note: Get your family involved in this goal-setting process. It is important that they know the sacrifices on their part are only in place for a set period of time, after which things will be reevaluated.)

The hardest question to answer is, "How long do I keep investing in the company before I can expect a profit?" This is a tough question, but you can expect to lose some money for at least 18 to 24 months, and you should be making a decent living at between 36 and 48 months. (These are simply rules of thumb based on discussions with other business owners and do not represent scientific findings.)

Hot Tip

Assume that you need to cover at least six months of living expenses—including your tithe to the church—before the company becomes profitable. It may take 18 to 24 months, but use 6 months as an absolute minimum.

When Do You Break Even?

One way to get a rough idea of whether your business can make any money is to do a *break-even analysis.* In a nutshell, a break-even analysis tells you how much you have to make in dollars or products sold to cover all your costs. Obviously, your goal is to do much better than that, but start first with ensuring you can at least pay for the products or services to be produced.

A break-even analysis takes into consideration three pieces of information:

- The average price of what you sell, which can be either products or services. Just estimate how much your typical sale will be.

Business Buzzword

A **break-even analysis** is a calculation of how much money you need to make to cover your basic costs of doing business. Above that, you're profitable.

- The average cost of what you sell, or how much it costs to produce your typical sale.

- Your total fixed costs per year, which are your total expenses for the year that you have to pay no matter how much you sell. This includes things such as rent, your phone bill, insurance, tax, employee salaries, and utilities. (See Chapter 11 for a more detailed discussion of fixed expenses.)

Your break-even price in dollars is calculated by dividing

Fixed costs/(1 ÷ average cost of products/average price of products)

The average cost of producing your products can be calculated by adding all of your expenses associated with manufacturing, such as raw material costs, labor costs, and waste and dividing it by the number of products produced. That's your average. Some individual units may have cost more than others to produce, but over time the cost evens out.

Similarly, the average price of your product can be determined by adding your anticipated sales for the next year and dividing by the total number of units you expect to sell. While you may make more per product when you sell through some channels, calculating the average takes those differences into account.

For example, if I have annual fixed costs of $30,000 and sell software programs that are priced at an average of $100 and cost me $20, my break-even in dollars is $37,500:

$$\$30,000/(1 \div 20/100) = \$30,000/.8 = \$37,500$$

This means that I have to have sales of $37,500 a year just for my business to break even. To calculate the number of software programs I have to sell, I just divide $37,500 by the price of the program, which is $100:

$$\$37,500/100 = 37.5 \text{ or } 38 \text{ units}$$

These numbers by themselves may mean nothing to you, but if you put in some estimates of your average sales price, cost, and total fixed costs, you see what you can expect. Once you figure out the break-even in dollars and units, think about whether those figures seem high, low, or reasonable.

If you're not selling a product, there are other ways of estimating your break-even point. If you are thinking of becoming a consultant, for instance, you determine your hourly rate and divide your fixed costs by your hourly rate. That tells you the minimum number of hours you need to bill each month to break even. If you come up with 10 or 11 hours a week, or 40 a month, you're doing well. The average number of hours that a new consultant bills weekly is around 14; this number should get up to around 24 to 30 hours a week once the company gets up and going. If you're having trouble choosing an hourly rate, call some of your competitors and ask what their rate is; that is a guide for what local clients are willing to pay.

If you come up with a break-even number that is much higher than you think you could ever achieve, your business may have serious problems. Are there ways you can reduce your fixed costs, such as by setting up a home-based office or putting off hiring employees until later?

Starting a business is exciting, exhausting, and expensive (the three Es). Just be sure, well ahead of making the plunge, that it is indeed the best option for you and your family. If so, go for it—and get involved in some exacting short- and long-term planning. That's what Chapter 3 is all about.

Chapter 3

Plan to Win the War

Jake's company had started out as a small beverage manufacturer; it now sold millions of dollars a year in fruit-drink products. It had recently introduced two new lines of frozen fast foods. The response to the new products had been tepid at first, but was slowly improving.

The company's real moneymaker, the main beverage product line, was doing well and supporting the new ventures, but Jake had reservations about how long it could last without the new frozen food lines carrying their respective part of the profits (which was just starting to happen). It seemed a good time to maintain the status quo. However, the company product developer had just introduced several new projects. Jake was calling a meeting to talk things over.

As the president and founder, what would you do if you were Jake? Would you listen and take your product developer's advice? Would you thank him for his input and say "no"? How you respond to questions like these will determine how your company grows, and whether it grows in the right direction. That's why, in this chapter, we'll talk about the importance of strategic and tactical planning when starting a new business. You are the leader, and you need to set a course your company will follow.

Comparing Strategic and Tactical Actions

Don't let the terminology scare you. A *strategy* is a careful plan or method, the art of devising or employing plans toward a goal. *Tactics* are small-scale actions that serve a larger purpose, such as a strategy. Strategic and tactical planning are a part of everyday life, though you may not think of every decision you make as strategic or tactical. For instance, have you ever said:

"She won the battle, but lost the war."

"Don't throw out the baby with the bathwater."

"He can't see the forest for the trees."

Each of these quotes refers to a short-term event or situation and its affect on the overall results of something else. Each quote suggests that by focusing too much on the short term (the battle), or on what's right in front of us, we lose sight of the bigger picture (the war). This is the essence of strategic and tactical planning.

That's the Spirit

Even Jesus urged his followers to think about strategy and tactics when seeking to "win the war" of Kingdom-building:

Suppose a king is about to go to war against another king. Will he not first sit down and consider whether he is able with ten thousand men to oppose the one coming against him with twenty thousand? If he is not able, he will send a delegation while the other is still a long way off and will ask for terms of peace. —Jesus (Luke 14:31–32)

A strategic plan is made up of many tactics, or short-term actions, that together help you reach your goal. For example, winning the battle may have been a tactical success, but if it contributed to losing the war, then it was a strategic mistake. Introducing a new advertising program is a *strategy* you might use to increase sales, but if your products aren't manufactured yet, you'll wind up with irritated customers who may not want to buy from you even when the products are available. That would be a strategic mistake. Your efforts to bring in immediate sales caused more harm than good because your company simply wasn't ready to handle the sales.

Every decision you make in your company either moves you closer to or further away from reaching a strategic goal. It is the responsibility of the company's management (you) to determine the strategic direction for the company and to ensure that all employees know what to do to achieve those corporate strategic goals.

Taking the time to create an overall strategy is time well spent because it provides a road map for future decisions. Your business plan should be contained in a larger plan encompassing goals for your family and relationship with God.

Short- and Long-Term Planning

Nothing happens in the long term without *short-term* actions that move you toward your desired outcome. Short-term actions cannot help achieve any particular goal if no goals have been set or no plan has been developed. You have to know where you're going before you can figure out a route to get there, right?

Taking the time to determine your own goals and your company's *long-term* mission and objectives will guide your daily actions. Without this framework, you and your employees may be busy, but the business will not move forward because everyone is pulling in separate directions. Making sure everyone knows and understands the goals and objectives of the company will make life a lot easier—for you and your employees. Defining the company's goals will minimize employee frustration because they will know what they're working toward. You can minimize confusion by identifying and eliminating activities that don't directly support the goals of the company.

That's the Spirit

A famous journalist abandoned a lucrative position for reasons of conscience. A friend asked, "Can you afford to do this?"

Said the journalist, "Well, I have a very wealthy partner—God Almighty." A person in partnership with God can afford to lose his own independence, to surrender it to the interests of the Kingdom of God, to accept the divine dictates, because the wisdom and spiritual resources of the heavenly Father are at his disposal. —Spiros Zodhiates

It all starts with you. Take the time to learn more about yourself, your personal motivations, and your long-term goals to ensure that you take your company in the proper direction. For example, if you like the idea of working alone from a home office, make sure that you're not setting your business up to grow to a point where you have to hire employees or get an office outside your home. If your business starts to grow in a direction or at a speed that makes you uncomfortable, you may start to resent the business and eventually unravel what is otherwise a good thing. You can avoid this by simply deciding up front what kind of business you want to have, both short term and long term.

You Are a Key Part of the Strategy

Businesses, like people, develop *momentum.* Once they get moving in a particular direction, it is difficult to reorient the people and procedures to a new way of thinking and doing business. Businesses also develop *inertia,* or resistance to change. The larger the organization, the longer it takes for change to occur, even with total support from top management. This means that your business may be nimble when there are only a few employees, but you can expect it to become harder to turn around as it grows in size.

Beware. You, the owner, also have momentum and inertia that may take you and your business in directions you may not have intended. The rallying cry "We can do anything!" may be true, but on limited resources, you can get yourself and the company into a lot of trouble. Sometimes big risks are explained as large faith in God, but can actually border on presumption—telling God he better come through. Be careful not to try to do too much too quickly. Like the food and beverage company example at the beginning of this chapter, you have to pick your battles and fight them well, or your company can become spread so thin that it loses its focus and competitive advantage. The essential value of strategic planning and goal-setting is that it …

> **def·i·ni·tion**
>
> **Business Buzzword**
>
> **Inertia** refers to a resistance to motion, exertion, or change. **Momentum** is a force that propels us in one direction and makes it difficult to change course or stop.

1. Keeps your own personal inclination on track with the business goals;
2. Provides you with the freedom to go with your instincts while giving everyone else in the company a framework for decisions.

Synchronize Your Goals with Company Goals

A part of your job is to ensure the company's survival—not just meet your own job satisfaction needs. This is important to know, because if you are the type of person who enjoys the start-up phase of business, then the daily routine of running the business will probably bore you to tears after a while.

Some entrepreneurs unconsciously create change within the organization just to feed their need for the excitement of solving real-time problems. Others come up with endless ideas for new products and services, new markets to go into, new distribution channels to conquer—anything to bring back the excitement of a new venture. Unfortunately, change and new directions may not be what your young, or even mature, company needs. With the limited resources associated with smaller companies, small doses of change are the best prescription unless market forces mandate a higher level of change.

That's the Spirit

Someone with a *start-up temperament* thrives on new and exciting challenges. Someone with a *maintenance temperament* thrives on keeping established systems running smoothly. The key operative term here is: "thrive." Do you thrive on your work? The famous Anglican crime-writer Dorothy L. Sayers, who was known for immersing herself in her work day and night, lends some insight here:

"Work is not primarily a thing one does to live, but the thing one lives to do. It is, or should be, the full expression of the worker's faculties, the thing in which he finds spiritual, mental, and bodily satisfaction, and the medium in which he offers himself to God."

If you are a person who dislikes change and who prefers routine, you may go to extremes, once again unconsciously, to avoid disrupting the status quo. This is also not the best situation, because business life is never static, no matter how much you may want it to be, and treating it as such is a guaranteed death knell to your dreams of success. Ignoring opportunities for expansion or product improvements that everyone is clamoring for is very dangerous.

A blending of the two types of temperaments—start-up and maintenance—is required for success, and the first step is knowing where you sit on the mayhem-to-routine continuum. Then surround yourself with people who have different temperaments than you have. Having that kind of balance in your organization will help keep the business running smoothly.

Look for the ideal where the company's goals and your goals are in sync and have the best of both worlds. For example, let's say you decide to start an Italian restaurant because you love to create new pasta dishes and you can get your whole family involved. Let's also assume that people start coming to the restaurant because they love your pasta recipes.

As more people come to the restaurant, you will be required to keep making the same old pasta recipes day after day because that is what your customers want. If you get bored with this repetition, you might decide to modify the existing recipes a little to see if your customers like them. Notice that you are now feeding your own need for variety at the expense of the customer's need for consistently good food that they can rely upon.

If you love creating new recipes but not cooking existing ones, you have a potential problem.

Solution: Plan to hire someone to do the daily cooking while you go off to create new dishes that are introduced in a way that complements the existing business flow. This is best done gradually: If you become enthused for Chinese food and force that inclination on your restaurant, your customers might get confused by a Chinese/Italian menu and take their business elsewhere.

> **Hot Tip**
>
> As a first attempt at delegation, consider using an outside consultant. (For example, if the company financial books are getting too complicated to manage, you might hire a professional accountant to do it for you.) You free up your time while still ensuring a high-quality output. You also make time to generate more revenue by getting rid of responsibility for activities that don't directly create sales.

Changing the focus of your business can jeopardize your relationships with your customers and put your business at risk no matter what products and services you're offering. There is a big difference between adapting to meet customer demands and reengineering your whole business to meet your own needs. Make sure that you spend your time on areas that complement the strategic direction of the company as defined in your initial plan. If you must try other things, do it in a way that does not interfere with daily business operation or sacrifice family goals.

Grow Beyond Your Own Capabilities

Once you've developed enough business to exceed your own personal capacity, you'll face some tough decisions. Do you now need to turn over your favorite accounts and routine activities to somebody else? You may find effective delegation difficult at first. But the business will eventually stagnate if you just can't let go.

Employees can become frustrated if they think you don't trust them. And your clients can become frustrated because they are no longer getting the level of service they expect from your company simply because you are too busy to respond to their needs in a timely manner. You can become frustrated because you are paying your employees to work for you so that you can improve the quality of your life—here you are working 60 hours per week when they only work 40 to 50. What are you paying them for, anyway?

This is a common situation and one that has strangled more than one small company. The need for more people is a sign that you are doing something right. Trusting your employees enough to delegate responsibility to them, while continuing to keep a close eye on the important things, can make or break your company.

Plan from the beginning to grow beyond your own abilities, or know that you will always need to live within the resources you alone provide. Plan to grow not only in the day-to-day *logistics* (paperwork), but also in the strategic areas.

Business Buzzword

Logistics are those activities that make the daily routine effective. You will probably need clerical help, once you become successful, to hand off the daily routine paperwork so that you can have time for other activities.

Adding people to your company in either an employee or partnership capacity (see Chapter 5) opens up new opportunities that were previously not available due to your limited expertise. That's right! You can't do everything, even though you think you can. Let go of the things that do not make the best use of your time and give them to people who want to do them well. Spend your time doing what you do well, and use your team to balance the other areas.

Your Mission: Defining Your Mission Statement

If this next section turns you on, check out *The Essence of Small Business* by Colin Barrow. Before you can even begin creating your business plan, which outlines how you will run your business on a daily basis, you must identify the strategic direction of the business you're about to create. You need to define the overall company direction in a *mission statement.* This simple statement covers, in just a few sentences, the reason for your company's existence. It provides the overall umbrella under which all other goals and actions fall. It says what your company does and who it does it for.

A typical mission statement for a clothing retailer, for example, might be the following:

> "To provide trendy, natural-fiber clothing to health-conscious women between 18 and 35 years old, at reasonable prices in an environment where buying is fun."

Notice that the mission statement is brief and to the point, determining the overall direction of the company. It also sets limits. If a vendor tempts you with a hot men's clothing line, you can see that men's clothing would clearly be in violation of the mission statement. Either the company's prescribed mission statement needs to be changed or the idea to add men's clothing needs to be dropped so that the company can stay focused on its core mission.

When you create your company's mission statement, consider the following:

- What do you plan to do? For example, "We will sell second-hand office equipment."

- Who do you plan to do it for? For example, "We will focus on price-sensitive customers in the local geographic area."

- What best ensures success? For example, "We will target sale prices of products to be at 60 percent of new retail price for comparable products."

You can embellish these simple objectives with more specific points that add more details to the mission statement frame. Additional items might include the following:

- The time frame within which it will be done, such as within the next 18 months or the next five years.

Business Buzzword

A **mission statement** is a written document that explains why you're in business.

Business Buzzword

Features are the different characteristics of a product or service. For example, the features of a drill bit may include its size, length, and the type of material it is made of. **Benefits** are what the customer gains by using your product or service. One benefit of the drill bit is that it makes holes of a specific size.

- How your company will deal with changes in the marketplace (such as technology advancement, new competition)—for example, by investing in new equipment or hiring more staff.

- The *benefits* (not the *features*) of your product or service, which will persuade customers to buy from you (such as free delivery within 24 hours of purchase). By focusing on benefits, rather than features, you will concentrate on the true value of your product to the customer.

- How following the mission statement will contribute to the company's short- and long-term success, such as by keeping the company focused on a high-growth market or keeping expenses down.

It may take you days to write these simple sentences. But it is these sentences that define everything else that occurs within the company, so defining these statements is time well spent.

Business Buzzword

Action plans are the detailed activities you do to help the company achieve its goals. These include meetings, proposals, visits, or creations you make. **Tasks** are individual assignments given to people to help the company reach its objective. Each task is broken down into action plans. **Objectives** are large projects that affect your company and involve several people.

After defining your company's mission statement, you can now define the company's overall *objectives*, or *goals*. These are projects that comply with the mission statement and have specific time frames and measurable results. A typical objective may be to "add three new products to the line over the next 12 months."

You can then break these goals down into individual *tasks* that you assign to individuals for completion within specified time frames. These tasks all contribute to the completion of a particular objective. A task in our scenario may be "review the new product lines for 15 potential vendors within the next six months."

Tasks give rise to *action plans* that literally define who is doing what on which day. For example, "Visit XYZ Dress Company on Tuesday from 1 to 3 p.m.," would be a typical action item that helps complete a particular task. Completing the task moves the company closer to achieving its objectives and continues to support its mission.

Action plans, tasks, and objectives are related to each other in the same way that tactics and strategies are. Action plans make up tasks, which make up objectives, just as tactics are components of a strategic plan. Different words, same idea. The following figure shows how they all stack up.

All actions ultimately support the mission statement by achieving short-term and strategic (long-term) goals.

Once you've got your business up and running, you should periodically take a look at the specific actions you are performing (say, within the last week) and then read your mission statement. Do your actions support that mission statement and further its overall intent? If so, congratulate yourself on your focus. If not, then you should evaluate how you spend your time. Have you gotten yourself into areas that do not correspond with your initial intentions? Does your initial mission statement need modification, or does how you spend your day need modification?

Aim for Tomorrow's Goals—Today

So here is the challenge (like you needed another one at this point): Keep one eye on the long-term opportunity while taking care of today. As Jesus said in Matthew 6:34, "Don't worry about tomorrow, for tomorrow will bring its own worries. Today's trouble is enough for today." This is where focusing on your goals is so valuable. The daily "fires" that erupt can look critically important when, in fact, they are irrelevant to the long-term objective. Actually, some of those fires can be left alone to burn themselves out while you focus on those objectives that lead to your desired strategic goal.

But what things are likely to hinder you? Consider:

- Bogging down in action without prioritizing. Spinning your wheels? Time-management techniques are available to help keep you on track. One technique that I use is to assign a priority (A = high, B = medium, C = low) to each task and then assign a payoff (1 = high, 2 = medium, 3 = low) to the same task. The priority sets how important the completion of this task is to the company. The payoff sets how much I expect to enjoy the task as it is being completed. If a task is a high-payoff, high-priority task, it will probably get done.

- Waiting until you have every piece of information. Evaluating a lot but doing nothing is called *"analysis paralysis."* In this mode, you never know enough to make a decision or take any action and, consequently, nothing gets done. The truth is, you'll never have all the information you need; so in many cases, you have to just make a *"best guess"* and proceed.

- Failing to set deadlines for your goals. Specific actions make the company's mission become a reality. Deadlines and time-frame commitments drive action. If you do not have a time frame attached to an action, objective, or task, you will probably never achieve it. If your objective or task is important enough to track as a project, then it is important enough to have a time frame attached.

def·i·ni·tion **Business Buzzword**

Best guess is making a decision based on the information you have available right now as to the right step to take.

- Always avoiding risk. Remember that risk and reward go together. We all know that few valuable things come without risk. Accept the fact that you will need to make risky decisions with incomplete information, and do everything you can to minimize the uncertainties while choosing your risks properly to ensure that you use your company resources to their best advantage. Your family will thank you!

From Small Tactical Wins to Major Strategic Victories

Many of your projects and objectives may take months to complete. The middle of a project often looks like the inside of a tunnel with darkness behind and in front of you. At times like this, as when reading the middle chapters of a long book, you simply need to keep moving forward until the light at the end appears.

That's the Spirit

Sometimes a business associate can keep you out of trouble—but also keep you out of business! He or she may be so cautious that creativity is stifled.

But Christians don't need to live that way. They recognize that all of life is in God's hands; therefore, they're willing to venture out as he leads them. It's called living by faith.

Faith is being sure of what we hope for and certain of what we do not see. (Hebrews 11:1)

What, then, shall we say in response to this? If God is for us, who can be against us? (Romans 8:31)

Keep yourself going by creating a set of "small wins" and celebrate them with your family. For example, I may treat my wife and kids to an expensive sundae when I hit specific milestones, such as making a certain number of sales calls. On occasion, I will throw an unexpected office party for my staff to let them know I appreciate their accomplishing a particularly important project.

Add up enough small wins and the strategic objective is ultimately met. There is nothing like winning, and the small-wins technique leads to the big wins that count. So ... now that you're feeling like a winner, it's time to devise your business plan. On to Chapter 4!

Preparing Your Business Plan

Most families plan more extensively for a vacation than they do for a new business. Big mistake! Don't quit your day job until you research the type of business you want to start and feel confident that your family is behind you all the way.

Your eventual success means creating a business plan, which is a document about 40 to 50 pages long that outlines your plans and intentions for running your business. It serves as your guidebook for managing your business as it grows, as well as being a reference manual for your management team.

Researching Your Plan

God bless libraries and the librarians who run them. Virtually all the information you ever need to research your business idea is out there. You just have to know where to look for it.

Before you can begin to write your business plan, you must first learn more about your business: the market you're working in, the types of products or services you're offering, and the needs of your customers. (Check out Chapter 2 for more about developing your business idea.) Although you might have years of experience in the type of business you want to start (perhaps you've been working in your family's printing shop for decades), investors want to feel confident that your instincts are correct.

To show them that your ideas are on target, you have to give them proof in the form of reliable published articles, reports, and other statistics. Saying that you know the market for printing is growing exponentially each year is nice, but being able to back up that statement with a report from the Department of Commerce gives you a lot more credibility—and that's what you need at this point. To accomplish this, all you need to do is turn to reliable experts, such as publications, reports, and market gurus. All are available by phone, fax, Internet, or at the library.

> **Hot Tip**
>
> Almost anything is easier to do when you have a picture of how it's supposed to look when it's done. For this reason, I've included an actual business plan in Appendix A.
>
> Take some time right now to read through the Kwik Chek plan because I frequently refer to it throughout this chapter.

With the growth of the Internet, it is likely that you can find all the information you ever need in cyberspace. If you or your spouse are gifted at Internet searches, you might be able to avoid trouping off to the library. However, I still find that trained librarians are often able to point me in just the right direction.

Some of the most useful databases available to help you in learning more about an industry, a company, or a group of target customers include:

- Lexis/Nexis
- ProQuest
- Dow Jones

The following are some helpful websites you can turn to for assistance:

- www.fuld.com—A competitive intelligence resource
- www.thomasregister.com—The Thomas Register
- www.dnb.com—Dun and Bradstreet

You may find that more information exists than you could ever use in your business plan. Chances are good that somebody, somewhere has compiled exactly the information you want. The challenge becomes finding it. Once you find it, you also might need help getting it in the form you want. The point is: Somebody, somewhere, is working to find an answer to your questions.

> **That's the Spirit**
>
> Suppose one of you wants to build a tower. Will he not first sit down and estimate the cost to see if he has enough money to complete it? For if he lays the foundation and is not able to finish it, everyone who sees it will ridicule him, saying, "This fellow began to build and was not able to finish." —Jesus (Luke 14:28–30)
>
> Notice that Jesus used a business analogy to highlight the importance of counting the cost of a new endeavor. Though our acceptance with God is a free gift, the call to a life of discipleship will involve some sacrifice.

Public and university libraries contain a gold mine of information. General information is available from books, and more up-to-date information is found in magazines, newspapers, and industry newsletters. Using the Reader's Guide to Periodicals or the online search services in the library, you can get your hands on articles that relate exactly to what you're interested in. I talk more about the online services available to you for your research in Chapter 10.

It is unlikely that you'll find all the information you need in a single article. You might need to piece together information from several sources to get a complete picture of the market or industry you're considering entering.

Using the Kwik Chek used-car evaluation business plan as an example, assume that you need to know the number of used cars in service today, along with the expected growth in used-car ownership over the next five years. In one article, you might find the percentage of households in the U.S. that own used cars, and another article might contain the growth rate expected, by household, in ownership of used cars over the next five years.

Census data can tell you the total number of households in the U.S., and with some simple math, you can calculate the number of used cars and the expected increase over the next five years. You now have the total available market information needed to estimate market size and potential sales revenues. For example, the market demand evaluation data found in the Scarborough Report (see the "Market Analysis" section of the Kwik Chek Plan) shows that 14 percent of car buyers in Austin, Texas plan to buy used cars.

Getting Help

You are not alone when you prepare your plan, even though it might feel that way. Organizations out there have a vested interest in helping you succeed at starting your own business. These include the local Chamber of Commerce, entrepreneurial associations, and the Federal government. That's right! Here are a few resources that can help:

- The Small Business Administration (SBA) works with a group of retired executives called SCORE (Service Corps of Retired Executives) to help you create a business plan and acquire funding. These are people who have already been where you plan to go; they can help you assemble the plan. Better yet, their services are free! Simply contact your local SBA office (see Appendix B) and ask for the phone number of the local SCORE office.

- Small Business Development Centers (SBDCs), which are collaborative programs developed by the SBA and local colleges and universities, also provide free counseling help to people starting a business. There are more than 750 SBDC locations across the country to assist you. You can find a local office by calling 202-205-6766.

- Women- and minority-owned companies can also turn to Minority Business Development Centers (MBDCs) for low-cost assistance. Centers across the United States help minority and women-owned companies write a business plan, develop a marketing campaign, and pursue government contracts for hourly rates typically under $20. See Appendix B for more contact information.

The Pieces of Your Plan

Effective business planning is a lot like assembling a jigsaw puzzle. All these stray pieces need to be put together in a logical order for the puzzle to work. You need to arrange the various pieces of business information you've collected and organize it so that it tells a story. Once you've developed an outline of the major pieces of information about the business you want to communicate, you can start to write, fitting all the bits of information together.

The business plan is essentially a document that is broken into chapters. Each chapter deals with an important part of the way you manage the business. Your business plan should contain the following basic elements:

I. Table of Contents

II. Executive Summary

III. Market and Industry Analysis

IV. Business Description

V. The Competition

VI. Marketing Strategy

VII. Operations Plan

VIII. The Management Team

IX. Funding Needs

X. Appendixes or Supplementary Materials

Take a look at each of these sections in detail.

Table of Contents

The Table of Contents is not a major element of your business plan, but it helps show the reader what information they will find in the coming pages. Because tables of contents are generally found in well-organized documents, you can make a good impression by including one at the front of your plan.

Executive Summary

Although this section is the first in the business plan, it is much easier if you write it after you write all the other sections. Write up one paragraph to describe each section of the plan. Finish the Executive Summary by listing the amount of money required, the projected return on investment, and the major advantages your company will have over the competition.

The Executive Summary should be one or two pages long and is often the only section a potential investor will read. Based on those few paragraphs, he or she will decide whether to continue to read the rest of the plan. If the investor doesn't proceed to read your plan, you've just lost a potential investor. For this reason, your summary needs to catch and hold the reader's attention.

Bankruptcy Alert

Make sure that "Company Confidential Information" is marked on every page of the plan (in the header or footer), including the Executive Summary. This alerts readers that the information should not be shared with outsiders.

Take a look at the Executive Summary provided in the sample plan in Appendix A. It is short and concise and describes the Kwik Chek concept and the amount of investment required for the business to make a profit, explains the potential market penetration, and includes a brief explanation of why and how it will be a successful business.

Market and Industry Analysis

The Market and Industry Analysis section presents information describing the market need for your product or service. This is where you detail all the information you gathered regarding the size of your market, the number of potential customers for your product or service, and the growth rate for your market or for the industry as a whole (which usually means worldwide). This section not only relies heavily on the results of your research, but also on your ability to compile the information into a simple, concise, and easy-to-read format. See Chapter 7 for details regarding creating market estimates.

You must make a number of assumptions when completing your market analysis. For example, the percentage of available customers that you expect will pay for your product or service, called *potential market penetration,* is a key estimate in determining the amount of money you will make if every potential customer bought from you (your potential sales revenue).

---

def·i·ni·tion | **Business Buzzword**

Market penetration is a measure of the percentage of total customers who have bought from you. If there are 1 million people in your market and 500,000 have bought your product, you have captured 50 percent of the market.

Potential market penetration is your estimate of how much of the total market you can capture over time.

Your **potential sales revenue** is the dollar value of sales you would achieve if everyone who is a potential customer bought from you.

You can come up with some decent projections of potential market penetration through information from other companies who did what you plan to do or from "guesstimates" from people experienced in the field. No one expects you to know exactly how many sales you will make during the first year, or even the first two years, but you can provide fairly accurate estimates by making some educated assumptions.

Looking at the Market Analysis section in the Kwik Chek plan, you notice immediately how I used facts and figures to support my belief that there was a market opportunity. These facts were summarized from all the information I gathered when I researched my business concept.

Business Description

The Business Description part of the plan explains your product or service idea and how it meets the needs of your market. Describe exactly what it is you will be selling and why people, or businesses, will buy it. How is it different from similar items already on the market? If it is a revolutionary concept, explain why the world needs this new breakthrough.

 Hot Tip

Your local computer store should have, for instance, Biz Plan Builder (under $100) from Jian. For more information on Biz Plan Builder, call 1-800-346-5426 or go to www.jian.com.

Take a look at the idea described in the Kwik Chek plan in the Description section. For this business concept, you see a real-world scenario that explains how the Kwik Chek service will benefit a customer.

In this section, you'll also want to briefly touch on how your company has been organized, such as whether it has been structured as a corporation, partnership, or sole proprietorship, whether any stock has been issued, and who invested money to start it and how much. If you intend to use your plan for financing, these questions will come up immediately as you start to talk with investors, so you may as well take care of some of the questions right away.

The Competition

Who are the established companies already selling products and services similar to yours? How will they react to your company? Depending upon your idea and how long your product or service has been available, your competition might consist of other new and aggressive companies just like yours or established companies from whom you intend to take business.

Bankruptcy Alert

We all think our business idea is unique, but the customer might think it's like dozens of others. Rely more on the market data you've collected rather than your opinion about whether there is a similar idea already in existence.

At this point, it's a good idea to provide a list of the other major players in the marketplace to show that you know exactly who your competition is. You should also indicate your impression of their strengths, weaknesses, and overall success in the market. By learning about your competition, the reader of your plan can better understand how you will succeed: either by going after a market opportunity that no existing competitor is addressing or by doing what everyone else is doing, but with a different twist.

Marketing Strategy

If nobody buys your product or service, you're out of business. Period! Nothing ends a business faster than no customers. In this section of your business plan, you need to explain to the reader what you intend to do to get customers.

As part of your marketing strategy, you should describe how you intend to let the public know that you're in business, such as through a number of marketing methods that I cover. You should also explain your sales approach, such as selling by direct sales representatives, with a mail-order catalog, or through a retail storefront. You'll find a detailed discussion of all the different ways you can market your business later in the book, but start to think about how you'll describe your plans to the reader of your business plan.

That's the Spirit

As you develop your business plan, don't forget to make plans for the new dynamics of family life that you'll face. Self-employment will bring unique opportunities and challenges to every member of your household. Do not neglect an ongoing dialogue with your children about what this will mean their daily routines. Be sure all expectations are thoroughly aired. Pray with them to seek God's guidance for your business plan.

[Parents], do not exasperate your children; instead, bring them up in the training and instruction of the Lord. (Ephesians 6:4)

In the Kwik Chek plan, I outlined the major approaches I will take for getting word to my target audience about the benefits of the Kwik Chek service. Notice that to effectively bring in customers, several methods are used to increase public awareness of Kwik Chek.

Operations Plan

This section describes operational procedures, manufacturing equipment, the level of production required, locations, international arrangements, licensing arrangements, and any other aspects related to providing the product or service defined in the idea section.

Check out the Operations Plan and the assumptions outlined in the financial statements in the Kwik Chek plan for one way to address operational issues for a service business.

The Management Team

One of the most important elements of your business plan is the section telling the reader why you and your partners are the most qualified group to start and run this business.

That's the Spirit

In only three years Christ defined a mission and formed strategies to carry it out. A staff of 12 unlikely men organized Christianity, which today has branches in all the world's countries and a 32.4 percent share of the world's population, twice as big as its nearest rival. Managers want to develop people to their full potential, taking ordinary people and making them extraordinary. This is what Christ did with His disciples. Jesus was the most effective executive in history. The results He achieved are second to none. —James Hind

In this section, you need to briefly describe the backgrounds and experience of your management team to show the reader that you know what you're doing. If you have an associate with 25 years of experience in the business who's going to be working with you, be sure to mention it; it makes your company much more credible.

Define each of the major jobs that will be held by the people who will be working with you. If you have three people who'll be working for you at the start, describe what their titles are, what their responsibilities will be, and why they are qualified to have the jobs. You're going to put their resumés in the Appendix at the back of the plan (in case anyone wants to read the specifics), but also write a paragraph or two about each person in this section (nothing too lengthy).

If you have advisors or consultants who have been working with you and giving you advice, mention them if they are fairly well-known or if they have a lot of experience. If you've set up a board of directors, briefly mention the members of your board. The point of mentioning other people here is to show the reader that you're not trying to do everything yourself and that you recognize you don't know everything and rely on professionals in those instances. Many business owners think they know everything and don't need advice from other people. These are usually the ones who don't last very long.

> **Business Buzzword**
>
> The **break-even point** is the point where you are making just enough money to cover your expenses.

The Management Team section in the Kwik Chek plan describes a very small management team consisting of two people. One person will provide the marketing and technical expertise for the company; the other person will be the bookkeeper and office manager of the company.

Funding Needs

Now, it's down to the bottom line. Everything else up to this point was presented as the foundation for the financial analysis. This section spells out the actual investment required and when and how the business will make enough money to pay it back. You define the amount of initial investment and how much you will need in the future based on certain sales and operations projections. The investors really want to know how much money will be invested, how much they can expect to make, and the time frame in which they'll make it. Everything else is simply a teaser to whet their appetite for the financial feast that follows. You should also include a break-even analysis that covers the volume required to push the company from a deficit to a profitable operation.

You should include an *income statement, balance sheet, and cash flow analysis* that projects the first three years of operations. (You'll learn more about preparing these forms in Chapter 11.) This is sometimes called a pro-forma income statement. A *pro-forma balance sheet* for the next three years is also a necessary component. Pro-forma just means that the numbers are projections, or estimates, of future sales and expenses.

Your income statement summarizes how much money you made and how much money you spent for a specified period of time, which is typically one year. It allows you to look at the big picture of how much money you expect to make.

Use a balance sheet to determine the value of what you own (your assets) and what you owe (your liabilities) at a particular point in time, usually the last day of the year. Bankers are interested in this statement because it gives them an idea of what your business is worth and whether you can pay off your loan by selling all your assets.

Business Buzzword

The **income statement** reflects all income and expenses for a particular period of time (usually a year). The **balance sheet** shows your total assets and liabilities. The **cash flow analysis** shows exactly how much you received and how much you spent on a monthly basis. A **pro-forma balance sheet** estimates your future sales and expenses.

Now for the clincher: Estimate and show your actual cash needs for the first 12 months, broken out by month, and then for years 2 and 3 on an annual basis. The key here is figuring out exactly when you will receive payment for your sales, keeping in mind that if you do not receive payment when you sell your product (as you do in a fast-food restaurant), you will always be waiting for some customers to pay their bills. There is sometimes a time lag between when you make a sale and when you get paid that you have to account for. Putting together a cash flow statement ensures that you are always ahead of your expenses so you won't run out of cash to pay your bills. (Generally, that's called bankruptcy.)

The initial capital required to start the business, the funding sources, and how it will be spent is summarized in the "Funds Needed and Their Uses" section.

Appendices or Supplementary Materials

Most of the work that goes into building a house doesn't show, such as the foundation and the walls. However, without these "invisible" ingredients, the house wouldn't stand up on its own. The appendices and supplementary materials are similar in that you refer to them often throughout the plan, but they appear as detailed references at the end. Included are the charts, graphs, extrapolations, resumés, and pieces of literature needed to convince the investor that you have done your homework.

Remember that busy people, which includes most investors, won't take the time to read a plan that is much longer than 40 or 50 pages. They also won't figure out what you're talking about if you haven't been crystal clear. You need to do the work for them; spell out your information in plain English. Lead your readers through the plan, step-by-step, explaining your idea and how you intend to make money doing it. Present the information succinctly to that end, and keep the following Dos and Don'ts in mind:

- Do make a good first impression. Print the plan on bond paper, creating a nice cover, and binding it or placing it in a nice presentation package.

- Do create a financial section to organize the detailed financial charts and tables and other supporting information.

- Do get rid of typos; spelling errors, and grammatical gaffes are inexcusable. Hire a professional proofreader if you need to.

- Don't present an opinion as fact without any supporting information.

- Don't just present facts and figures without explaining why investors should care. Summarize the implications.

- Don't present conflicting information. Analysts will eat you alive if you present inconsistent information.

- Don't use obsolete data while analyzing a rapidly changing marketplace.

Keep the Plan Alive!

Congratulations! You've finished your business plan. Take your family out to dinner at a nice restaurant and celebrate your triumph. Enjoy the moment; offer thanks to God. Then get ready to make your business work according to your estimates.

Don't throw away your business plan now that it's done (or leave it on the shelf to accumulate dust). It is a working document that outlines your best guess on how to create a successful business. In a lot of ways, it becomes a friend who reminds you of what was important to you when you were just starting out. Use it as a barometer for determining your performance as compared to estimates (sometimes called performance to plan). Know that your investors will be checking your performance against the business plan on a regular basis!

A well-executed business plan provides milestones for determining whether your initial estimates and assumptions were accurate, which allows for midcourse corrections if needed. Once the plan is complete, you'll want to determine exactly how you'll structure your business—which is the topic of our next chapter.

> **def·i·ni·tion**
>
> **Business Buzzword**
>
> **Performance to plan** is a comparison of how well you thought you'd do (financially and otherwise) and how well you actually did.

Establishing the Framework of Your Business

Now that you have an idea of what you want to accomplish with your business, you need to make some decisions about its legal structure. Some people start a business and never incorporate. Others incorporate first thing. Still others simply hang out a sign and start selling stuff. People starting partnerships usually write up some sort of agreement, whether they file the paperwork to evidence that effect or not.

An entire chapter deals with the special issues related to corporations. The reason people approach the process of incorporating very differently is that there are a lot of things to consider. From taxes, to liability, to taxes, to raising money, to taxes … there are many things to think about. In this section, you can figure out what kind of business structure might be best for you, as well as receive some tips on setting up a corporation, if that is what you choose to do.

Structuring Your Business

Just as one house style wouldn't meet the living requirements of all families, no single business structure meets everyone's business needs. Depending on your current situation and future business aspirations, one business structure might meet those needs better than another. Take the time to determine where you want the company to go using the information provided in Chapter 3. This long-term perspective suggests the best structure for your specific situation. In this chapter, I'll review the different structures and discuss the pros and cons of each one.

Use this chapter as a general starting point. Understand the information presented and then apply it to your situation. This is your homework portion of the process. You should then run your assessment by the proper legal and accounting professionals to ensure that you are set up properly for your particular situation. Try to avoid the temptation to "go it alone" at this stage, because an error regarding your company's structure can have serious strategic consequences later on.

What Are the Various Business Structures?

The three basic business organizational structures are *sole proprietorships, partnerships,* and *corporations.* Under each category are subclasses that apply to specific situations.

def·i·ni·tion Business Buzzword

In a **sole propri-etorship,** you are person-ally responsible for all the business's obligations, such as debt, even though the business might have a dif-ferent name from you.

A *sole proprietorship* is the most common and easiest type of business to create. Anyone who performs any services of any kind, such as a gardener, caterer, or even baby-sitter, is by default a sole proprietor unless he or she specifically sets it up otherwise. A small company with only one employee is often kept as a sole proprietorship, but there are no restrictions on how big a sole proprietor-ship can become. It depends exclusively on the desires of the owner, or *proprietor.* The majority of small businesses in the United States are sole proprietorships.

A *partnership* is formed whenever two or more people decide to enter a for-profit business venture. Typically, each partner owns a portion of the company's profits and debts, which can be set up in a written agreement between you and the other partners. You do not need to file any special paperwork to form a partnership, but you should make sure you and your partners sign an agreement to minimize misunder-standings regarding each person's rights and liabilities. If you do not have an agree-ment signed by all parties, then any partnership-related disputes are handled under statutes based on the Uniform Partnership Act (UPA) used in most states.

A partnership agreement states the terms and conditions of the partnership. However, the UPA defines generally accepted standards on items not covered in the agreement. It is essentially a "gap filler." Any law library has detailed information on the UPA, but the best way to avoid UPA issues is to work with a complete part-nership agreement from the beginning.

def·i·ni·tion Business Buzzword

In a **partnership,** you and one or more peo-ple form a business mar-riage legally linking your debts and assets from the start.

Most larger bookstores carry books that cover creating partnerships for your particular state. These books are inexpensive and helpful in making sure that you and your partners dot the right i's and cross the right t's. Once you have done the grunt work, I suggest that you present it to an attorney to make sure all of the proper legal lingo is included and that everyone's interests are protected, in-cluding your family's assets.

For many people, forming a corporation is a sign of how serious they are about their business because it is more involved and more expensive to set up a corporation than to set up a sole proprietorship or partnership.

When you form a *corporation*, you actually establish a separate organization—separate and distinct from you personally. Some of you may ask why that's such a big deal; what's the advantage? The advantage is that if the corporation is sued, you are not personally responsible for any damages that might be awarded (unless, of course, you are also named in the suit). Paperwork and record-keeping is also more involved with a corporation, which is why some people decide it's not worth the hassles. There are other ways besides incorporating to protect yourself personally from liability.

> **def·i·ni·tion | Business Buzzword**
>
> A **corporation** is a separate legal entity created through the state where the business is incorporated.

Select the business structure that is right for you and your family, based on where you are today and where you want to wind up down the road. Consider the advantages and disadvantages of each business structure before making a decision.

Sole Proprietorship: Going It Alone

Judy woke up this morning, got the kids off to school, and finally decided to begin selling those little wooden dolls she makes and gives away every Christmas. She and her husband had discussed it for months. Now she has just become the head of a sole proprietorship.

> **Bankruptcy Alert**
>
> Guard against the dangers of the sole proprietorship and partnership forms. They can leave the owners personally open to any type of litigation filed against or debt incurred by the company. Years of work and personal wealth acquisition can be lost in a short period of time using these forms of business structure.

Once you begin providing products or services with the intention of making money from these activities, you become a sole proprietor. Your business expenses are deductible, all income is taxable, and you assume the liabilities of the business. (More on the tax implications later.)

Notice that Judy did not have to create a separate name to start her business. She simply started her business and began selling her product, using her own name. This is why the sole proprietorship is such a popular business structure.

However, if Judy wants to call her business "Dolls and Such," she must file a "Doing Business As" (d/b/a) form with the local authorities, usually the county clerk's office in the area where she plans to do business. The d/b/a filing is sometimes called a *fictitious name statement*. If no one else is using the name she chooses, after filing her d/b/a form, Judy can transact business as "Dolls and Such." Filing the d/b/a gives her legal rights to the name within the jurisdiction of the governing body, which is typically the county. If someone else later uses the name within the county, Judy can ask the courts to order that person to cease operations under the name she legally owns. The other business is then forced to rename itself.

Being a sole proprietorship does not limit whether you have employees, although many sole proprietorships are one-person businesses. You can hire employees as a sole proprietorship, but you, as the owner, become the target for any claims made against the business as a result of any of the actions of your employees. With employees, you must apply for an employer identification number (EIN) as a corporation does since this is the IRS' tracking mechanism for employers. (See Chapter 18 for details on obtaining an EIN.) Oddly enough, you as the owner are not an employee of the company even though you draw a salary.

> **That's the Spirit**
>
> "We can make our plans, but the Lord determines our steps." (Proverbs 16:9) Your business plan may not go exactly the way you want, but remember the Lord is in charge.

> **That's the Spirit**
>
> Be sure that your partners share not only your business goals but your values as well. Many partnerships break up because of differences in ethics and values. "Don't team up with those who are unbelievers. How can goodness be partner with wickedness?" (Proverbs 6:14)

Partnership: A Business Marriage

When two or more people form a partnership, they are essentially married, from a business standpoint. Either party can obligate the other via the business, and everything the business and the partners own individually is on the line. In essence, a partnership is like a sole proprietorship owned by several people. All liability is passed to the partners.

A special partnership type, called a *limited partnership*, provides certain partners with a maximum financial liability equal to their investment. To maintain this limited financial liability status, these partners, called *limited partners*, cannot participate in the daily operation of the business. The *general partner* is responsible for the day-to-day management of the business. Limited partners invest in the company and rely on the general partner to run the business.

Special laws govern the operation of a limited partnership, and if they are not precisely followed, the courts might hold that the partnership was general, not limited. The formerly limited partner might find himself as liable as a general partner for business-related debts. Be aware that you must complete and file special paperwork with the state to form a limited partnership.

Corporations: Share the Wealth

Creating a corporation is like creating a new business life. A corporation is a separate and distinct business entity that is responsible for itself. Upon formation, the corporation issues shares of stock to *shareholders*, the owners. The shareholders exchange money, goods, or expertise to receive their shares of stock.

A *board of directors*, elected by the shareholders, manages the corporation. This board then appoints *officers* of the corporation to handle the day-to-day affairs of the company. In essence, the board members represent the interests of the shareholders

in the company operations. Depending on the state in which the business is incorporated, the business owner in many small corporations may be the primary, or only, shareholder and only board member. This same person is listed as the president, secretary, and treasurer of the corporation.

The corporation pays taxes on its annual profits and passes the profits to the shareholders in the form of *dividends*. The board of directors determines the amount of the dividends.

The major benefits associated with a corporate business form is that the corporation is liable for its own financial and civil liabilities. The shareholders risk only the amount of money they have invested in their respective shares of stock.

Another major corporate benefit involves raising money for the business by selling shares in the corporation. Once the buyer and seller agree to a price per share of stock, the buyer simply purchases the number of shares needed to equal the amount of money needed. For instance, assume you need to raise $100,000. If you find a buyer who is willing to pay you $4 per share, then you sell them 25,000 shares of stock to receive the $100,000. Life is rarely this simple, but this example outlines the basic benefit associated with corporation finances.

To further illustrate the point, assume you still need $100,000 but don't know anyone with that kind of money on hand. Instead of selling 25,000 shares at $4 each to one person, you could sell 2,500 shares to 10 different investors for $4 each and still get the money you need. You now have ten shareholders instead of one, but you got the money you needed. Forming a corporation is the route to take if you eventually plan to sell a large amount of stock to a number of different people.

Public or Private?

There is a difference between a publicly held and privately held corporation. Publicly held corporations are traded on the various public stock exchanges, such as the New York Stock Exchange, American Stock Exchange, and NASDAQ. The shareholders are typically large numbers of people who never come in direct contact with each other. They trust the board of directors to manage their investments for them.

Privately held, or *close,* corporations are more common. The shares are held by a few people, often family members, who also sit on the board and participate as officers of the corporation. The shares are also not offered to the general public.

Business Buzzword

A **close corporation,** or privately held corporation, is owned by a small number of shareholders, often only one.

Unless you are planning to create a very large business, you will probably create a privately held corporation with you and a few others as the only shareholders. It is generally easier to form a small or close corporation in the state where the principal shareholders reside and work. Because state tax laws vary, be sure to check with an accountant before making this decision.

If the number of shareholders exceeds 75, you must comply with the *Securities and Exchange Commission (SEC)* regulations for publicly offered companies. People historically chose to form a limited liability company (LLC)—more on this topic later—that permitted more than the prior 35-shareholder limitation placed on S corporations, but this limitation has been raised to 75 shareholders which removed some of the motivation for LLC formation. You will definitely need legal and accounting services if any of this discussion applies to your particular situation.

def·i·ni·tion **Business Buzzword**

The **Securities and Exchange Commission (SEC)** regulates public offerings of company securities. The SEC mandates strict guidelines for the dissemination and content of company financial information to help assure investors that the information they receive on public companies is reliable and reasonably comprehensive.

When a company "goes public," it offers to sell shares in the company to the general public. This is a common way for the founding members of a company to make money from the large numbers of stock shares they received during the start-up stages. The founders often buy or receive this stock at the outset for a nominal price, sometimes pennies per share. When the company goes public, the shares might sell for dollars per share. (You don't need to be a CPA to figure out that several hundred thousand shares sold at a public offering can add up to a lot of profit. This opportunity alone keeps many people actively working for start-up companies, along with their associated risks, instead of working for larger, more stable companies.)

Subchapter S Corporations: A Little Bit of Protection

Suppose you want the legal protection provided by a corporation but want the income to pass directly to you so you can declare it on your personal income tax statement. You can thank the IRS and Congress because they created the *subchapter S corporation* for just this purpose.

Hot Tip

The Small Business Administration (SBA) set up the Procurement Automated Search System (PASS) to increase the number of government contracts awarded to smaller businesses owned by minorities and women. Any business owner can complete an application to be listed in the government's database of potential suppliers. When an agency needs a product or service, it can search PASS for the names of potential vendors. Call your local SBA for information on PASS or look at www.sba.gov.

In a *subchapter S* or *S corporation*, instead of the corporation paying taxes on its income, the business income is passed to the shareholders, who then declare the income on their personal income tax statements. Subchapter S corporations retain all the legal protection provided by a standard C corporation (any corporation that is not an S corporation).

Why opt for the S instead of C corporation? If you are personally in a lower tax bracket than the corporation, then passing the business income to you decreases the overall taxes paid. In addition, if the corporation loses money, you can use that loss to offset personal income earned from other investments you may have. You can also avoid double taxation if you use an S corporation, which can have a welcome tax-reduction effect as outlined in Chapter 23. However, if you don't plan properly or if the company does better than you expected, you can find yourself with a huge tax bill at the end of the year.

def·i·ni·tion **Business Buzzword**

A **subchapter S** or **S corporation** is a type of corporation with few shareholders. All profits are passed directly to the owners and taxed as income, which avoids double taxation.

If you think the S corporation is right for you, check with an accountant and an attorney before taking the plunge. (You first incorporate as you would any corporation, and then file IRS Form 2553 to establish your S corporation tax status.) A little prevention goes a long way to avoid unforeseen problems down the road. Notice that the decision is heavily based on how much revenue you anticipate the company will generate. This is why the strategic planning aspects of business are so critically important.

Limited Liability Company (LLC)

How would you like the advantages of a corporation or partnership without some of the restrictions regarding shareholders? That's what a new form of business organization, called a *limited liability company (LLC)*, can provide.

Limited liability companies are now authorized in most states, and the remaining states are expected to approve a similar structure soon. The reason for their new popularity is that LLCs provide business owners with personal liability protection, just as corporations and partnerships do, and still provide tax profits at the individual level only, as subchapter S corporations do.

What sets LLCs apart from the popular S corporations is that LLCs do not have the same restrictions regarding shareholders. S corporations limit the number of shareholders to 75 and require that they be U.S. citizens; foreigners, domestic corporations, and co-owners of partnerships may not participate. LLCs, on the other hand, have no limits on the number of shareholders and do not place restrictions on the makeup or citizenship of shareholders. In addition, LLCs can have more than one *class* (*kind*) of stock and can own stock in another corporation. An LLC allows you to avoid double taxation as with a standard C corporation but provides most of the legal options regarding liability protection and stock sales that a C corporation has. For most small business owners, setting up an LLC may be overkill.

Because of these advantages, some people expect that LLCs will exceed subchapter S corporations, regular C corporations, partnerships, and limited partnerships as the preferred organizational structure. Others feel that the added complexity associated with setting up an LLC will diminish their popularity. Only history will know the outcome. Increasing the S corporation shareholder limit to 75 will reduce the need for LLC formation, which now tips the argument in favor of the S corporation for many new businesses.

Because conversion to an LLC from another type of business structure can be costly, LLCs are generally recommended more for start-ups instead of established businesses.

Business Buzzword

A **limited liability company (LLC)** is a new type of business structure available in almost every state that has many of the advantages of a partnership or subchapter S corporation but fewer of the disadvantages.

Business Buzzword

Corporations can sell different **classes of stock**, such as preferred stock or common stock, at different prices. The various classes differ in when and under what circumstances dividends are paid.

One concern about LLCs, however, is that there is no unified set of tax laws because individual states created their own laws regarding LLCs, which were then copied by other states. The IRS has yet to provide a general set of national tax laws for LLCs. Check with your secretary of state to find out more about the laws governing LLCs in your state. If you are not careful, you might set up your LLC only to find out that the IRS will treat your company as a partnership for tax purposes.

Professional Corporations

A special corporation structure addresses the needs of professionals who share a practice, such as lawyers, doctors, and accountants. The *professional corporation*, as it was initially called, provided special tax-related benefits to the participants. Many of the benefits have been reduced since 1981, however, and the growth in the number of professional corporations has declined. If you are a licensed professional who falls into this special category, check with your accountant to determine whether a professional corporation provides you any special benefits. Professional corporations use the letters P.C. after the company name to indicate the kind of corporation.

Business Buzzword

A **professional corporation** is a special corporation sometimes used by lawyers, doctors, and accountants.

Franchises: Paying for Their Experience

Although a *franchise* is not technically a business structure, it is a way to start a business using the experience and training provided by an existing company. You are familiar with franchises if you have ever eaten at a McDonald's or had coffee at a Starbucks.

Business Buzzword

In a **distributor franchise,** the franchisee (the dealer) is licensed to sell the franchiser's products. In a **chain-style franchise,** the franchisee (the local owner) is licensed and required to prepare the food in accordance with the franchiser's standards. In a **manufacturing franchise,** the franchisee is licensed to create a product in accordance with the franchiser's specifications.

A franchise arrangement allows you to start your own business with strong expertise behind you. This improves your likelihood of success and might decrease the amount of up-front cash required because many franchisers assist with the initial funding. However, it might increase the up-front total investment required (cash and loans) because you are buying a share of a proven business franchise concept. Unless you are dead set on "doing it your own way," you should consider the purchase of a franchised operation as a business option.

When you purchase a franchise, you need to set up a company just the same as if you start it from scratch. You still need to evaluate which form of doing business is best for your situation: sole proprietorship, partnership, or corporation. Look to your franchiser for guidance regarding these fundamental decisions. If your franchiser does not offer assistance in these areas, you might reconsider whether the organization is the right horse to which you should attach your cart. Where will the franchiser be when difficult questions arise?

> **Hot Tip**
>
> When should you use a lawyer? *Before* you need one. Prevention is the best cure for legal problems. However, in some situations you might consider the numerous computer software packages that can automatically generate a wide variety of legal documents for you. Most packages even modify the documents to suit the state in which you do business. They usually cost under $100 and pay for themselves with one use. Check out *PC World, MacWorld, NOLO* Press, or *PC* magazine for an assessment of the software.

Dealing with the Tax Man

The impact of taxes on your choice of organizational structure is worth checking into, even though a full discussion is beyond the scope of this book. I'll simply present a comparison chart here to illustrate that individuals and corporations do not pay taxes at the same rate.

Typical Personal and Corporate Taxable Income Rates

Single		Married Filing Jointly		Corporate	
Income	*Tax Rate*	*Income*	*Tax Rate*	*Income*	*Tax Rate*
$0-25,750	15%	$0-43,050	15%	$0-50,000	15%
$25,751-62,450	28%	$43,051-104,050	28%	$50,000-75,000	25%
$62,451-130,250	31%	$104,051-158,550	31%	$75,000-100,000	34%
$130,251-283,150	36%	$158,551-283,150	36%	$100,000-335,000	39%
$283,151+	39.6%	$283,151	39.6%	$335,000-10M	34%

You will find that the break points between tax levels differ. Depending on your situation and the company's income levels, you might be better off leaving the money in the company and paying corporate taxes instead of paying yourself a large salary and paying personal income tax.

> ### That's the Spirit
>
> The Bible recognizes that two kingdoms must co-exist until the day when Christ returns—the secular government and the not-yet-fully-revealed Kingdom of God. Therefore, Christians faithfully pay their taxes!
>
> Give everyone what you owe him: If you owe taxes, pay taxes; if revenue, then revenue; if respect, then respect; if honor, then honor. Let no debt remain outstanding, except the continuing debt to love one another, for he who loves his fellowman has fulfilled the law. (Romans 13:7–8)

However you choose to structure your company, realize that taxes are a legitimate means of raising funds for government on earth. As a Christian family, you'll want to be conscientious in paying your fair share. However, if you think that incorporating would help keep your tax (and other) liabilities more reasonable, move on to Chapter 6.

Chapter 6

The Implications of Corporations

My company started out as a sole proprietorship, but I decided to incorporate a few years ago. When I tried to incorporate under the sole proprietorship name, I learned that the name was already taken by a business in another city. We now have two operational names: one for the local community, Applied Concepts, and one for outside the local area, Technology and Communications, Inc. We retained the local name due to its local recognition, but the headaches associated with having two business names should not be ignored.

In fact, when incorporating, you create the potential for all kinds of headaches. Hopefully, this chapter will help you avoid them all! Just realize that your corporation has the ability to make commitments, incur debt, hire employees, flourish (if successful), and go out of business (if not). You are the principal avenue through which this entity is created, and the responsibility for performing the proper legal steps involved with the corporation's birth is in your hands.

Corporations are created under guidelines established by the state in which the corporation will reside. Each state has its own regulations that govern the creation and operation of a corporation. The secretary of state's office defines these guidelines and is your contact point for initial information. In this chapter, I give you a general overview of the process.

Creating a Corporation

First, determine who is going to be a shareholder in the corporation. How many shareholders will there be? Almost always, you need a minimum of one shareholder or officer of the corporation before the state allows you to incorporate. Some states require a minimum of two officers. You are asked for the names of the president, treasurer, and secretary. These can all be you. Just like the general store owner in a small town, you might have to wear several hats in your corporation.

Next, determine the states where you intend to do business. Many states allow you to incorporate in that particular state but locate your main offices and operations in another state. (Delaware is one state that permits this situation.)

Bankruptcy Alert

Check the laws of your home state carefully. If you incorporate in another state, your state might charge stiff taxes to out-of-state corporations, negating a lot of the tax advantages of incorporating elsewhere. If you do business in more than one state, you might have to file tax returns and pay taxes in all of them. You must also track and pay applicable sales taxes for the states where you have sales or operations offices.

The corporation filing fees you have to pay to the state to set up your corporation vary widely, from as low as $40 to as high as $900 or more (in California, for instance). Unless becoming a national company immediately is important to you, you are probably better off keeping the process simple and incorporating only in your home state. Start-up life is complicated enough without adding more complexity than is necessary.

Your corporation must have a name that serves both a legal and marketing use. The name must comply with the state's legal requirements and should also convey something about your offerings to your customers.

Public relations firms and advertising agencies often assist companies in finding a name that works for their situations. You might want to get a bid from a company that specializes in naming. After all, you usually keep your name for life. Once you find the name you want to use, you must reserve it with the state for a period of time (usually two to six months) by filing a *fictitious name form* with the secretary of state's office.

There is a nominal fee for reserving the name. The office performs a name search and tells you whether the name you want to use is still available or some other company is already using it. I suggest giving the secretary of state several names to check at once so that you don't have to keep going back to the drawing board if your top choice is already in use. You must incorporate within the two-to-six-month window or the name is forfeited.

Finally, you must file *articles of incorporation* with the state. The articles outline the basic characteristics of the business and become the legal framework within which the corporation must operate. The business's purpose, planned duration of existence, and capital structure, such as how many shares of stock have been issued and who owns what, are defined in the articles. (You'll learn more about articles of incorporation later in this chapter.) Once you file the articles and the fees are paid, you are incorporated.

> **That's the Spirit**
>
> The Christian faith enables us to face life—including all the uncertainties of our new ventures—not because we can see all that lies ahead, but because we know that we are seen. It's not that we know all the answers, but that we are known.

Congratulations! You have just given birth to a business with a life and identity all its own. The secretary of state will send you the official "birth announcement." Establishing a trusty board of directors is a natural next step. Later in the chapter, I show you how to do just that.

Laying Down the Law: Articles of Incorporation and Bylaws

How do you establish the articles of incorporation and the bylaws for your company? These two documents spell out the overall intent of your corporation. You file the articles of incorporation with the state as part of the corporation formation procedure. The board of directors creates the bylaws and determines the company operating procedures.

Articles of Incorporation: The Basic Ingredients

The articles of incorporation need not be lengthy. They just need to be accurate and to provide the state with the necessary information for incorporation. Most of the articles are easily created. Try this basic structure as a starting place. In the following articles, type the bold sentences and fill in the italic requests.

- Article One: The Company Name

  The name of corporation is (*enter your company name*).

- Article Two: The Period of Duration

  The period of the company duration is (*enter the number of years your company will be in existence, which is usually assumed to be PERPETUAL*).

---

def·i·ni·tion Business Buzzword

The total number of shares of stock the corporation is permitted to issue is known as the number of **authorized shares.** For instance, if 1,000 shares of stock are authorized at the start of the corporation, a total of only 1,000 shares can ever be sold to shareholders—no more than that. **Issued shares** are the number of shares that are actually issued. **Par value** is an accounting term used by bookkeepers in tracking the shares issued. Its value is usually set very small.

Bankruptcy Alert

Don't issue all authorized shares of stock to yourself when you first start and capitalize your company or you might limit how you work with and sell shares of stock later.

- Article Three: The Company Purpose

  The purpose of the company is to (*enter the basic reasons why the company exists; most people simply use FOR ANY LEGAL PURPOSE*).

  You can also be a little more specific and mention the types of products or services the corporation will be selling. However, if you ever decide to change the purpose of the corporation, you might have to alter or amend your articles of incorporation. For this reason, it is best to be somewhat general.

- Article Four: The Capital Structure

  The total number of shares that the company is authorized to issue is (*enter the number of shares*) **at a par value of** (*enter the par value of each share*) **dollars each.**

  For example, you can assume that the company is authorized to issue 100,000 shares at a par value of $.01 each. (Don't confuse *authorized shares* with *issued shares*. Issued shares are actually in the hands of a shareholder. Authorized shares are shares that can be sold by the company but need not be.)

  You can even authorize and issue different classes of stock, but this is certainly overkill for the vast majority of businesses at your current stage of development.

Get big and profitable enough to make worrying about multiple stock classes important, and then hire some financial wizards to help you put it together.

Keep this section simple unless you have specific reasons for creating a more complicated capital structure, and be sure to verify your capital structure with your accountant and lawyer before finalizing your articles. You need to file amended articles of incorporation if you ever decide to change your capital structure. In addition, if you sell shares and then change your capital structure, you need to convert the old shares to new ones.

Business Buzzword

Consideration is a legal term for "something of value." That something could be money or the right to do something. Many contracts are not valid until some form of consideration has changed hands. In some cases, that consideration can be as little as $1 to make the transaction legal.

Bankruptcy Alert

If you do not handle all financial transfers between you and the corporation as you do those with either a standard investor or employee, then you might place your corporation status and protections in jeopardy. You would document a loan made to or received from a third party, and you must do the same between you and the corporation.

- Article Five: Initial Capitalization

  Most business transactions are not considered binding, or final, until money has changed hands. For this reason, your corporation might require some form of *consideration* to officially start.

  The corporation will not commence business until it has received for the issuance of its shares consideration of the value of (*enter the desired amount of money or valued services amount; usually not less than $1,000*).

  Notice that this initial capitalization must be paid for by corporate stock and that stock currently has a par value of whatever you set in your articles of incorporation. For example, assume that you invest $10,000 in your corporation and that your articles of incorporation authorize 100,000 shares at a $1-each par value. This means that the corporation must issue 10,000 shares of $1 par value stock, or 10 percent of authorized shares, to you in exchange for the initial capital investment. Check with your particular state's authorities to determine whether a minimum percentage must be issued to validate the corporation existence.

- Article Six: Address and Registered Agent

  The address of the corporation's registered office is (*enter the address*) **and the name of its registered agent at such address is** (*enter your name or the name of the person who is the primary contact for all company-related business, including legal matters*).

The address must be a street address, not a post office box.

- Article Seven: Board of Directors Information

  The number of directors is *(enter the number of directors, typically 1 to 3),* **and their names and addresses are** *(enter the names and addresses of each board member).*

  Some corporations have a *board of directors* consisting of only one or two people, such as the owner and the owner's spouse, but then also establish an *advisory board* to give business advice and guidance. An advisory board works in the same way as a board of directors in counseling the president, helping identify new opportunities, and giving feedback on the direction of the company.

  The difference is that the members of the advisory board have no financial interest in the company; they are not shareholders, and they assume no liability for the corporation's actions. In some cases, you might find that successful business people are more likely to agree to serve on an advisory board than on a board of directors because they don't want to be held liable for the consequences of the corporation's actions. This decision protects their family from any negative financial issues.

- Article Eight: Name of the Incorporator

  The name and address of the incorporator is *(enter your name, assuming that you are the person forming the corporation).*

  This can be a third party with no interest in the company at all who is simply completing the paperwork for you, such as an attorney.

  The incorporator must sign the articles in front of a notary public. Then, you file the articles, or a copy of them, with the state.

> **def·i·ni·tion** **Business Buzzword**
>
> The **registered agent** is the official person to contact for all legal matters. The registered agent may or may not be located at the official corporate address, also called the **registered office**. In some states, the registered agent must be an attorney, and in others, you can serve as the registered agent.

> **def·i·ni·tion** **Business Buzzword**
>
> An **advisory board** counsels and guides the senior management of a company, much as a board of directors does. However, an advisory board has no financial stake in the company and assumes no liability for the corporation's actions.

Bylaws: The Basic Ingredients

Your corporation now exists. What is it going to do and how will it conduct itself on a daily basis? The bylaws should explain. They are the internal rules that govern employees' and officers' actions when the directors are not there to supervise. Violation of the corporation bylaws is usually treated as a grievous offense and can be grounds for dismissal in most companies.

Hot Tip

Pull out your bylaws every 6 to 12 months to remind you of the direction in which you initially intended to steer the company. Daily work pressures and family concerns can take you off track, and this review will help you to keep company operations consistent over the long term.

Of course, when you're both the president and the board of directors, you can fire yourself whenever you want. If you have outside shareholders—investors other than you and a spouse or close family member—be aware that they can use a violation of the bylaws as a reason to bring in someone else to run the company if they hold a majority of the shares. If you own the majority of your corporation's shares, they probably can't fire you, but they can still cause problems for you. The moral of the story: Set up bylaws that you should have no problem living by.

The first board of directors meeting is used to adopt the corporate bylaws. The bylaws can cover any areas of conduct deemed necessary and generally include company policy in areas such as ...

- When and where shareholder meetings are held
- When and how the board is formed
- How frequently meetings are held
- Voting rights of shareholders and directors
- Procedures for hiring and dismissing company officers and a description of their duties
- The overall handling of stock shares and dividends
- Usage of the corporate seal
- Internal approval procedures for legally committing the company
- Definition of the company fiscal year, which is frequently the calendar year for simplicity's sake
- References to the articles of incorporation as needed and procedures for amending the bylaws

The bylaws contain a lot of information that helps to maintain consistency in company policy in the midst of daily pressures. Make sure that the bylaws reflect the business and spiritual integrity of the organization; then stick with what you have or change the bylaws to better reflect your mission.

Software packages such as "It's Legal" by Parson Technologies give you the standard bylaws language for under $50. Many software catalogs and computer retailers carry these programs. But you should always consider having significant documents (such as contracts and official paperwork) reviewed by your attorney to make sure you establish your legal structure the way you intend.

Establishing a Board of Directors

It has been said that human beings are reasonable in that we can always justify and rationalize our desires and actions. Being "reasonable" in this way may be a dangerous trait when you run your own business. It is often helpful to have someone to report to, or you'll find reasons to take the company into business areas where no company has gone before—or where no company should go, leaving your family in jeopardy.

This is a wonderful reason for creating a board of directors. A board of directors is a group of people who are not involved with the daily operation of the business but who have a vested interest in keeping the company on track. Board members usually serve for one year, but three-year terms are not uncommon.

If you plan to keep your company small, you can act as your own board, perhaps adding family members as appropriate. This certainly keeps arguments between the board and upper management to a minimum. If you plan to grow past the "mom-and-pop" stage, you should consider a board of directors consisting of advisors from the business community.

Directors are required to act with the best interests of the corporation and its shareholders in mind. As long as they act with integrity and make decisions that any "reasonable" person would make given the same information, they are generally protected from potential lawsuits or claims as a result of their decisions. This is the *business judgment rule* designed to protect directors from claims derived from frivolous lawsuits filed by irate shareholders who may have lost money on their investments.

For example, if a board of directors decides to stop selling a particular product because it loses money for the company and a customer becomes upset at that decision, the customer may still sue the corporation. However, the members of the board of directors cannot be sued unless the customer can prove the decision was a poor one for the company.

That's the Spirit

Tempted to worry about how all of your business dreams are going to work out? Take some time today to remember who holds your life—and your business—in His hands:

I lift up my eyes to the hills—
where does my help come from?
My help comes from the LORD,
the Maker of heaven and earth.
He will not let your foot slip—
he who watches over you will not slumber …
The LORD will keep you from all harm—
he will watch over your life. (Psalm 121)

As you proceed with setting up your board of directors, keep these general guidelines in mind:

- Acquire board members with diverse backgrounds. This will bring different perspectives and contacts to the company. Adding board members with financial, legal, managerial, and political experience can assist the company greatly when fast decisions must be made.

- Gradually phase in the director stock ownership based upon participation and company performance. Doing so means that board members receive a small number of shares when they join the board. These shares increase over time, based on company performance and the time board members spend on company business. Gradual phase-in assures that the directors are motivated to make your company succeed.

- Make sure that all board members agree to disclose any potential conflict of interest situations that may arise. Most organizations require that all board members sign a disclosure form up front, either stating that there are no known conflicts of interest or explaining potential conflicts. Nothing breeds contempt and distrust faster than finding out that one of your confidants is cavorting with a competitor without your knowledge.

- Be sure to look into the subject of voting rights in a corporation. This topic can get pretty complicated and is beyond the scope of this chapter. But if you aren't careful, you can have a board of directors that steers you right out of the company! So plan to learn the pros and cons of corporation voting rights, perhaps by asking your lawyer to provide you with all the details.

Now you're well on your way to incorporating. Your next area of exploration is the wonderful world of marketing for your new business.

Part 3

Marketing Excellence and Successful Sales

Now that your business is set up and you've filed all the necessary paperwork, you need to get some customers. Customers will make or break you because customers bring in money. In this section, you'll learn how to use marketing to get customers and keep them. You'll also discover the basics of selling, along with information about—believe it or not—how your competitors can actually help you succeed. Finally, we'll take a look at the Internet and how you can expect to use it positively in your business.

If you thought that marketing and selling were the same thing, you're in the majority; but actually, they're not. In this section, you'll learn what the difference is, why you should care, and how marketing and sales are the keys to your success.

Masterful Marketing

Jamie, a wife, a mom, and the marketing director of her own small business, brought the whole family into the living room to ask them an important question. After all, her husband and teenagers were all hard at work in various parts of the company.

Problem was, Jamie's Stellar Products Company had seen a drop in its sales, yet it was spending more and more money on marketing activities. Jamie wondered whether Stellar was starting to do something fundamentally wrong. She had always believed that the harder you pushed something, the more it moved. For the first time in her company's history, the harder she pushed by spending more money and energy, the less she got back.

"Okay. It seems like Stellar has a loyal customer base, but I'm afraid to keep depending on our same old customers for our livelihood. That's why we've been targeting new markets. Yet our dismal sales figures in those new areas are pulling us down, big time. What do you think, guys?" asked the smiling, yet nervous, entrepreneur.

Jamie, like most small business owners, was facing one of those occasional crossroads of marketing decision-making. Like her, every owner must regularly ask this key question: "How do I make sure my product or service is targeted to the people who can use it most?" Especially when sales are slipping, the question is crucial. This chapter introduces you to some of the basic concepts of marketing as the foundation for a wise response. It should also provide you with a good background for the next chapter, which focuses on sales.

In general, it is marketing's responsibility to identify the most likely customers, design the best product or service offering, set the product or service's price range, and choose the overall advertising message and presentation content most likely to get customers to buy. Specific marketing activities include market research, product or service development, analysis of pricing levels, creation of marketing materials and sales aids, targeting cost-effective sales channels, advertising, public relations, and sales support.

Who Is Your Market?

We human beings like to believe that we are all different and that we are each unique, and on some basic level, we are. However, in other areas, we fall into certain groups that think, act, buy, and react alike. We're not all lemmings who jump off a cliff at once, but we do have certain characteristics that bind us as a group. These characteristics are often called demographics and include such things as age, income level, educational level, and marital status.

Breaking down your target customers by demographic characteristics is called *market segmentation*. When marketing people discuss the *demographic profile* of their ideal customer, they are looking for the common characteristics associated with their most likely customer.

Business Buzzword

A **demographic profile** refers to a specific set of demographic characteristics that sales and marketing people use to target likely sales prospects.

Market segmentation refers to dividing the total available market (everyone who may ever buy the product) into smaller groups, or segments, by specific attributes such as age, sex, location, interests, industry, or other pertinent criteria.

A bank, for example, might segment its customers by age because people's banking needs change during different phases of their lives. People over the age of 50 are more likely to be interested in retirement-related products than 18-year-olds, and 18-year-olds are more likely to be interested in college loan details than 30-something couples who want to buy a home with a bank mortgage. Market segmentation helps the bank to group similar customers together and develop products that they will be interested in.

Compiling information about potential customers is the challenge for market research companies. As a business owner, you can then buy and use this information to develop effective marketing programs to sell to these potential buyers. Here are some good places to look for market research reports:

- Your local library. Typically, the library purchases a wide variety of these reports and makes them available to the public.

- The federal government. It compiles information about the age, household size, and financial status of all Americans in the form of a national census every ten years.

- The Yellow Pages. Look under "Market Research & Analysis" for the research companies in your locality.

Target Marketing: Picking Your Customer

If you sell beef products, it wouldn't make sense to invest time and money displaying your products at a vegetarian convention. Obviously, people who don't eat meat aren't the best sales prospects for a meat product. Also, consider the ideal customer's economic or lifestyle demographics. Who can afford your product? Where do these customers shop?

 Hot Tip

There are a number of government and commercial websites containing useful marketing data. Check out some of these for help in researching your market:

American Demographics magazine   www.demographics.com

Census data   www.census.gov

Social statistics   www.whitehouse.gov/WH/services/

Business articles   www.reuters.com

Identifying your customer is an important part of the marketing process. If you don't know who will buy your product and why, you have no idea who to contact and how to present your wares. When you don't know who your likely customers are, the result is a scattergun marketing approach, in which you blanket the market with a general message and hope that someone sees it and calls. This is not a very effective approach because it is costly and time-consuming and results in few sales.

Target marketing, on the other hand, focuses your financial and personnel resources on the people most likely to purchase what you offer. Suppose a particular geographic area has 100,000 potential customers for your products or services. A direct mail piece sent to this group at $1 each would cost $100,000. From this mailer, you might get a 2 percent response (which is a typical response rate). That number translates into 2,000 people wanting more information from you. Of those people, assume 10 percent, or 200, actually buy your product or service. For a $100,000 investment, then, you've sold your company's goods to 200 people. A little statistics and customer characteristics analysis will probably show that these 200 people have similarities that propel them into a specific market segment (which I discussed earlier).

Although promotional methods such as direct mail are discussed later, I should point out that you just spent $500 per customer to get each sale. Now, if you're selling a $10,000 item, you've done well, but if you're selling a $20 item, you've lost big bucks.

To develop a target marketing approach, you first need to define which markets contain your best potential customers. This means that you need to know something about what you're selling and who needs it most.

Name Your Price

Ultimately, the customer pays a price that is consistent with his perceived value of the offering. If the customer perceives the name on the product as having high value (such as designer clothing), then he or she might be willing to pay a high price to wear those designer duds.

Other pricing strategies are cost-based and market-based. You can calculate cost-based prices by determining the costs of producing a product or delivering a service and then adding a profit margin. This means that you'd better know your exact costs or this can really "cost" you the farm. You might think that you're doing great, only to find out that your costs were wrong and you are selling for less than your overall costs.

You determine market-based prices by studying what similar products or services cost and asking a similar price. You need a lot of information about your product costs, your competitors' pricing, and how customers decide what and when to buy to accurately and comfortably fix pricing for your offerings.

def·i·ni·tion **Business Buzzword**

When your price is calculated using the cost to the company plus whatever profit margin is reasonable for your industry, you are using **cost plus profit pricing.** A widget that costs $1 to produce with a desired 50 percent profit margin would sell for $1+ (1 × 5) = $1.50. You're simply adding on your desired profit percentage to your costs.

When you price offerings at a level set by what everyone else is charging, rather than by costs, you are using **market-based pricing.** With this strategy, you can generally make more money assuming your competition is charging reasonable rates and you can keep your costs down.

Obviously, you can set your prices wherever you want, but your best price means more sales for you because you will have figured out what your customers believe is a fair price for your goods. In return, they buy more. Knowing what your competitors' profit margin is can help you adjust your own pricing strategy.

You must answer several key questions when determining a pricing strategy:

1. What are your competitors offering your potential customers in terms of their basic product or service price and the price of any add-on services?

2. How much does it cost you to supply the product or service desired by the customer (including those additional intangibles just discussed)?

3. What additional features do you offer your customers that your competitors do not, and are these features worth more money?

The costs associated with a product vary, depending upon where it is in the product life cycle. The next section provides a brief overview of a new product's typical life cycle. You can use this model as a guide in determining your pricing, distribution, and marketing message strategies.

That's the Spirit

Do not take advantage of each other, but fear your God. (Leviticus 25:17)

The LORD abhors dishonest scales, but accurate weights are his delight. (Proverbs 11:1)

The verses above remind us that setting prices isn't merely a business matter. It's also a matter of interpersonal relationships. The key, for the Christian, is to make sure that prices aren't "gouging" a fellow human being in any way. Yes, make a profit. But do it with wise, legitimate, and reasonable pricing.

The Life Cycle

Every product or service goes through a *life cycle* from its introduction until the time it is discontinued or taken off the market. The life cycle usually refers to products, but services go through a similar evolution. The life cycle is divided into four basic stages:

> **def·i·ni·tion Business Buzzword**
>
> The **life cycle** is a set of four distinct phases every product or service goes through from the time it is introduced to the market to the time it is discontinued.

> **def·i·ni·tion Business Buzzword**
>
> When so many competitors enter the market that everyone has to keep dropping their prices to win sales, **price erosion** lowers the market price and profit margins.

Stage 1: Market development (a.k.a. embryonic) The product or service is new to the market, having recently been introduced. Sales are slow at this stage and customers take longer to make a purchase decision due to their lack of familiarity with the product. Only potential customers who have shown a willingness to experiment with new products or services are good prospects at this stage. That group of experimenters is often referred to as *early adopters* because they are the first to try something new.

Stage 2: Market growth Sales are increasing steadily and there is a general awareness of the product or service. Competition usually starts to show up at this point.

Stage 3: Maturity Overall demand starts to level off as customers purchase the offering as a routine part of doing business. Customers have a high degree of familiarity with the offering. *Price erosion* can happen at this point due to intense competition from what is now an established market for the product or service.

Stage 4: Market decline Customer demand for the product or service starts to decline due to improved variations of the product by other companies, new technology, or other market forces that make the product inferior or obsolete.

Although most products or services go through a life cycle in a matter of years or a decade, fad products such as novelty gifts (the mood ring or pet rock) might experience an entire life cycle in a very short period of time (such as a single Christmas buying season). Durable goods, such as microwaves, might have an extended life cycle caused by the level of technological sophistication and a high level of consumer acceptance.

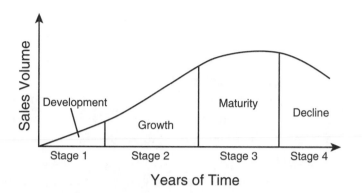

Product/service life cycle.

Notice that the perceived value of your offering changes over the life cycle. In the early days, when customers are just learning about what you are selling, only a small segment takes a chance by making a purchase.

In the growth stage, with demand for your offering increasing, you might be in the driver's seat. This means you can charge a premium price because you have something everyone wants.

By the time you enter the maturity stage, you probably encounter competitors who have developed similar products, which forces you to compete on price and service. For example, the personal computer industry is in the maturity stage of its development. Notice the rapid price erosion combined with improved performance that this industry has experienced. This is typical of an industry in the maturity stage of the life cycle.

The product life-cycle concept affects your pricing strategy. Once you determine where your product or service offerings fall in the product life cycle, you can make a better choice about your long-term strategy. The price you set for your rates as a new consultant, for example, is different from that of an experienced, nationally known consultant.

Use the three different strategies—cost, market, and perceived value pricing—to choose the price level that will generate the most sales. Then make sure that your price is consistent with your life-cycle position.

Your Marketing Message and Positioning

Take a moment and think about the hundreds of marketing-related messages that bombard you on a daily basis. How do you sift through the irrelevant ones and focus on the ones of importance to you? It depends on the way the product is presented and whether it communicates a message of interest to you. The marketing message, the essence of your positioning goal, is the key to customer perception.

Creating a positive image in the minds of potential and existing customers is called *market positioning.* The purpose of market positioning is to have potential customers perceive your product or service in a particular way that not only differentiates it from the competition but also makes them more likely to want to buy from you.

The message should be simple, easy to remember, and easy to understand. The only way you can effectively position your company or your product in your customer's mind is to understand his or her thinking and lifestyle. You must know your competition's marketing approach and …

1. Make sure that your company is seen as different from the others, or

2. Make customers more comfortable with your totally new company or product by making it look a lot like your competition, which adds validity to your company by association.

Here are some examples of typical positioning statements:

- Lower price with superior quality.
- More convenient and better-stocked store shelves.
- More fun at a lower price.
- Earn your college tuition in exchange for several years of training.

Spend a lot of time thinking about your positioning statement and try out several variations on colleagues. The marketing message will appear in almost everything you produce and will create the perception your salespeople work with during the sales process. If your message is off, you are in trouble because your customers won't even think of you when they need exactly the products or services you provide!

Promoting Your Company and Products

Getting the public's attention is crucial to marketing success. Here are some resources for bringing attention to your company's offerings (some are even free):

- Free media publicity. Newspapers, magazines, TV, and radio shows are always hungry for fresh stories. Once you find a situation where your company is a potential source of information for a reporter or editor, the first step is making contact with the media to let them know. It might take several contacts before the editors and reporters recognize your company or personal name and think of how to use it as a story.

- Public relations (PR) firms. Some companies specialize in making the desired media contacts for you. Many PR firms in your area already know the editors, which often makes it easier for them to persuade an editor to profile your business or to quote you. Although it costs a lot of money to hire a PR firm, its services will probably help improve sales for your company.

- Self-generated press releases. To get started, create a written announcement (officially called a press release) and contact the business editor at the publication, radio, or TV station where you want to be featured. The press release must contain your company contact person's name, address, and phone and fax numbers. The release itself should be one page long. Make sure that you cover the 5 Ws of journalism in the release: who, what, when, where, and why.

All About Advertising

Advertising is good for increasing awareness of your company and its offerings. Unless you're in retail, don't expect to close many sales directly from your advertising. The point of advertising is to firmly plant your marketing message into the consumer's mind so that they think about you the next time they are looking for what you offer. Advertising also gets the company in front of a wide variety of people in a timely manner. Marketers (or marketeers) call this *mind share*.

The greater the mind share, the more likely people are to contact you when they are looking for what you offer. If you have no mind share, then they won't even know to call. You develop mind share by using advertising, publicity, promotion, and personal experience with your company.

> **def·i·ni·tion** **Business Buzzword**
>
> **Mind share** is the portion of a person's thought processes that includes perceptions of your company's offerings. One hundred percent mind share means that any time a person needs your type of offering, she thinks of your company.

Pushing and Pulling

Advertising is useful for creating a pull marketing strategy, which means that the customers "pull" your product through the distribution channel by asking for it. A pull strategy is expensive because it requires massive marketing to your potential customers to alert them to your product's availability.

At the other extreme is the push marketing strategy, which requires you to convince distributors to carry and promote your product, hoping that customers purchase it. A push strategy might show faster results but depends on the activities of the specific distributor. Some companies begin with a pull strategy, then they are lucky enough to build visibility through customer demand. This often raises distributors' interest level, and it transforms into a push strategy.

Keep the following points in mind when you consider advertising:

- Many companies provide money to distributors for cooperative advertising. If you mention their products in specific ways in your ads, they pay for a portion of the ad. Contact each of your suppliers for their specific restrictions.

- Yellow Page advertising is a must for any business trying to reach the general public, such as a restaurant. The phone book comes out only once a year, so you should plan in advance to be included.

- Placing an ad just one time in a paper or on TV or radio is generally useless. You need to repeat your ad on a regular basis to get the best results, so plan for six to ten insertions.

- Advertising firms specialize in making companies like yours succeed with advertising. They also have an art department that can design an ad for you.

- Contact each publication, radio, and TV station you are interested in advertising with and ask them to send you a *media kit*. The kit includes demographic information about the people who read each publication, listen to specific radio programs, and watch individual TV shows. Typical information includes age, sex, education, and marital status.

- Ask each media supplier if they have ever run ads like yours before and what type of responses they received. This might help you determine whether it makes sense to invest in advertising there.

There are a number of new advertising tools now available via the Internet, including banner ads, site ads, and search engine listings. For people using the Internet regularly, this can be a great way to get their attention. To explore how to use the Internet as one of your marketing tools, check out Chapter 10.

Your Selling Approach

How does your customer buy your product? That is the question. Is it better to pay commissions to independent sales representatives, sell products at wholesale rates, or to simply sell it to your customers with a direct sales force?

Using Distribution Channels

The *distribution channel* has a profound impact on your contact with the customer, the profit margin available, and the lead time for delivery.

The distribution channels you use to get your product or service into the hands of customers affect the markup and profit margin you can expect. Markup and profit margin are related but definitely different; be sure you understand each before pricing your products.

Business Buzzword

The **distribution channel** is how your product or service gets from your facilities into the hands of customers.

Markup is added to the cost of a product, whereas profit margin is a calculation of what percentage of a product's price is profit; the difference is the product's cost. Because there are many businesses involved in the process of getting a product from the manufacturer to you, there are also many different markups added at every step of the way.

A product typically starts at the manufacturer who actually produces the product. The manufacturer adds a markup to the cost of producing the product and sells it to a distributor. The distributor is responsible for getting the product to a wholesaler, who may sell within a particular city or region. Each adds another markup for their own business to make money. Retailers, who are the only members of the distribution channel to have direct contact with customers, also add a markup. From the manufacturer to the retailer, there could be several markups along the way, resulting in a retail price that is passed along to the customer.

The best part of using third parties, such as independent distributors or sales representatives, is that they are out selling your products while your employees stay focused on internal company activities, such as marketing and creating new products. A few minutes spent evaluating the positive and negative aspects of the various distribution channels should help you in deciding your course of action. Read more about sales and the use of sales representatives in Chapter 8.

Mail Order and Direct Mail

Do you want to take on the opportunities and headaches associated with mail order? With a mail-order system, you get the order along with its payment and then you are responsible for getting the product into the hands of the customer. You have 30 days from the time you receive the order to the time you have to ship it, which gives you plenty of time in many cases to produce or acquire needed products, instead of stockpiling a huge inventory.

A big down side is that customers can cancel the orders after you ship them. Credit card fraud is also a real problem with mail-order sales, which means that you might never get paid for the order. Accepting credit cards is crucial for mail-order sales because you risk having even worse collection problems if you rely solely on checks for payment. Many companies wait until a check clears before shipping the product to the customer as one way to combat bad checks.

You'll want to set up a marketing system that can run as smoothly as possible, day after day. That way, you'll have a firm foundation for increasing sales, year after year. To learn more about all sales you'll be making, move forward into Chapter 8.

Hot Tip

By law, you have to ship a prepaid order in 30 days or offer a refund to a customer who doesn't want to wait any longer. Although it might improve your cash situation to produce according to how many orders you receive, make sure you can deliver in 30 days or less.

Without Sales, Nothing Happens

Picture a salesperson. What do you see? A fast-talking nonlistener who is always looking at your pocketbook? A slick dresser who continually promises to do things in "your own best interest" but who is obviously only interested in selling you something—anything—whether you need it or not?

Of course, there are horror stories—those examples of poor salespeople who do their employers and their customers no good whatsoever. But you must raise the standard by approaching sales with integrity. After all, no matter how you feel about sales, there is one undeniable fact: Without sales, you are without a business. Furthermore, without integrity and honesty in your sales practices, your Christian witness and business reputation will eventually suffer.

Getting Close to Closing the Sale

If it turns out that the customer has a need for what you're offering, the sales process begins. Obviously, more satisfied customers result from professional selling than from manipulative types of selling. You don't need to be a business expert to understand that satisfied people buy more and tell their friends to buy from you. This is good.

True business and selling success usually comes from a lot of smaller successful clients instead of a single "killing." The huge deals make good press and media headlines but really don't reflect the reality of day-to-day business success.

In other words, the sales process takes place in a number of stages. Look at the way you buy anything. You go through your own set of questions and stages before actually forking over your money. You might evaluate the available information, read about the product in magazine or newspaper articles, and ask knowledgeable friends for their opinions before eventually deciding on a purchase.

Professional selling involves numerous small events and exchanges of information that must occur before the sale can happen. At each step along the way, the salesperson makes small requests for customer action or *closes*, which eventually leads to a sale. For example, asking to meet with someone face-to-face is a small close in that you are asking the customer to take an action that leads in the direction of the sale. If the customer agrees, you are one step nearer to getting him to make a purchase. Asking the customer to provide you with detailed information about his needs is another small close because you are asking the customer to take steps toward buying your product or your service. Once the customer is satisfied that buying your product or service is the right decision, he or she commits to a purchase.

Business Buzzword

A **close** (pronounced "cloze") is a request by a salesperson for a specific action on the customer's part. Asking for the order is the ultimate close, but smaller closes occur at each stage of the selling process to gradually move the customer toward committing to the purchase.

People expect to be asked reasonable questions that help them solve their problem, and they also expect you to ask for the purchase. If you don't ask for the order, you can't blame them if they don't give it to you.

Everyone Has to Sell, but Not Everyone Closes

It is important to ask for the order at the right time in the sales process, or the salesperson can alienate the customer. Nothing is more irritating to a customer than to be continually asked to buy something before she is ready. Eventually the salesperson's lack of sensitivity gets in the customer's way of making a rational decision. At this point, the customer might leave simply because it is too much of a hassle to buy from the salesperson.

> **That's the Spirit**
>
> As Christians, we may fail badly. However, Scripture tells us that tough times need never quite put us "down and out." The apostle Paul put it this way:
>
> Rather, as servants of God we commend ourselves in every way: in great endurance; in troubles, hardships and distresses; in beatings, imprisonments and riots; in hard work, sleepless nights and hunger; ... through glory and dishonor, bad report and good report; genuine, yet regarded as impostors; known, yet regarded as unknown; dying, and yet we live on; beaten, and yet not killed; sorrowful, yet always rejoicing; poor, yet making many rich; having nothing, and yet possessing everything. (2 Corinthians 6:4)

Everyone in your organization should support the sales process by providing information, support, service, and guidance when requested by the customer. When it is time for the final order to be placed, the salesperson takes care of writing up the sale. Everyone in a company needs to be part of the selling process, but only a few really need to close; beware of the difference.

Aggressive selling is closing when it is inappropriate to close and is rarely effective because it turns off the customer. Professional selling is closing when it is necessary to move the customer forward to a new sales stage, and the customer is comfortable moving ahead to the next stage. The moral of the story: Don't rush customers into making a decision, or you might lose them forever.

Is Your Offering a Special or Commodity Item?

Your company's approach to selling is largely determined by your market positioning and message. (These concepts were covered in Chapter 7.) Offerings with plenty of competition, where the products and services are pretty much the same, require that features and benefits such as price, delivery, warranty, and stability be emphasized to set your company apart. Specialty products and services, such as high-technology electronics or tailored clothing, require a higher level of personalized service and credibility as part of the sales process because each product is so different from the others on the market.

Where does your product fit? *Commodities* rely more on the distribution channel to effectively get products in the hands of customers, as well as established customers who use your product on a regular basis. There is little or no difference between commodity products, which include milk, white envelopes, and lead pencils.

Specialty products require a higher level of technical and sales sophistication because the product's competitive advantage must be explained well. The salesperson has to know about the benefits of the competitors' products and services and how they compare to his own company's offerings in order to sell the customer on why his is better.

Is Your Customer Qualified?

All the sweet talking and fancy brochures in the world will not close a sale from an *unqualified prospect* (someone who is not able to buy). I have seen more new, and even experienced, salespeople invest valuable time on prospective customers who were really never qualified to purchase in the first place.

A *qualified customer* is someone who is interested in buying from you and has the means to do so. If you don't know the answers to these five key questions, you haven't qualified the potential customer. Get the answers, or you might waste a tremendous amount of time and energy on a prospect who cannot buy from you.

1. **Does your customer need what you have to offer?** Would you buy something you didn't need just to make the salesperson happy? No way, and they won't either! Your challenge is to accurately identify your potential customers' needs and make sure your marketing message addresses them.

2. **Are you working with the decision maker?** Ultimately, a single person will authorize the purchase of your offering. If you are not dealing with the person in charge of the budget, who can say "yes" and sign on the dotted line, then you are only dealing with someone who has the authority to say "no" to the sale (or at best can only influence the outcome).

 **Business Buzzword**

An **unqualified prospect** is an individual who says that he needs your product or service but who has not yet confirmed that he is able to make the purchase decision.

3. **Is there money budgeted for this purchase?** It is perfectly okay to ask whether money is already in the budget for this purchase. You might find that the money is coming out of next year's budget and that the sale is on hold until the next fiscal year starts. You might also find that there is no money currently budgeted for this project, which should set off warning bells in your head.

4. **Is there a pending event?** A pending event is something expected to happen in the future that affects when a decision is made. Typical pending events include ending fiscal years (when budgeted money needs to be spent or is lost), management orders, moving offices, and mergers. If there is no pending event, the customer can, and might, take forever to make a decision.

5. **Is your customer politically open to using your offering?** Many companies have divisions and subsidiaries they are supposed to buy from, and if it is discovered that they are planning to buy from another company, someone might try to kill the deal. Not because the product isn't right. Not because you did a poor job of selling. Simply because they have a company policy that says all purchases must first be made from an internal business partner. Period.

Try to find out about potential barriers to your sales early and save yourself a lot of frustration and anguish later. You can do this by researching all the divisions of a large company to determine whether there are groups providing the same service or the same product that you are. It might also be useful to know who the company is currently buying from to determine whether you'll be able to win business away from them.

The Nine Stages of Selling

Baking bread can be a frustrating and exhilarating experience at the same time. It is an art form, and anyone who has failed in the bread-baking process can verify this. You must follow specific steps in precisely the right order and at precisely the right time. Reordering the sequence or trying to rush the process invariably leads to a poor-tasting loaf.

The sales process is similar; a sale will go through specific stages before the deal is either lost or won. Performing these steps out of sequence usually leads to poor results, and skipping a step usually leads to disappointment. Plan your sales strategy to include moving the customer from one stage to another, with small closes along the way, rather than rush them forward to the final close. I'll walk you through these stages and explain what occurs and what you should accomplish.

That's the Spirit

One of the classic baseball television shots comes from the 1975 World Series, in which NBC captured Carlton Fisk, jumping up and down, waving his arms, trying to coax his hit to stay fair. It did—for a home run.

That colorful close-up would have been missed had the cameraman followed the ball with his camera, as was his responsibility. But the cameraman inside the Fenway Park scoreboard had one eye on a rat that was circling him. So instead of focusing the camera on the ball, he left it on Fisk.

We encounter problems like that rat. We have no idea how they will be resolved, but because of them, we may see God work in a way we never would have without the problems. —Craig Brian Larson

The Suspect Stage

At this stage, you have heard from a friend of a friend that perhaps Company A needs your products or services. Suppose you provide business consulting services. This is the first stage in the process, and it usually occurs as a result of your marketing efforts, such as a direct-mail letter, advertisement, or phone call.

When you don't know much about Company A but you think they might need your services, they are considered a suspect or a lead. There really is no close at this stage other than to make contact with a person on the staff at Company A to verify that he has a need for your services.

The Prospect Stage

If you make contact with a representative of Company A and learn that they do indeed need the services you provide, you have just received confirmation and can move Company A to the next stage as a prospect. In the first stage, you just suspected that Company A had a need, and now after receiving confirmation, you know for a fact that they have a need. They are now a prospective customer.

Confirmation from a prospect can come in the form of a response to your direct-mail campaign, a request for additional information, or a phone call made by your salesperson. The close for this stage is to have Company A agree to an in-depth discussion about their business needs. Not your needs, but their needs! This discussion can occur in person or over the phone depending on geography and industry.

The Entrée Stage

In the entrée stage, you have your first major interaction with the prospect. This contact is often made in person. For technical sales in particular, personal contact is usually required to explain complex products and features.

Bankruptcy Alert

You do lose control when you use distributors or reps to perform the sales function for your company. Major problems can erupt when distributors make commitments or promises on your behalf. Be sure that you define up front each party's responsibilities to avoid such situations.

This stage enables you to learn more about the prospect's need for your services and lay the ground-work for the next stage. Here you qualify Company A regarding money, time frame, and the decision-making process. Your close for this stage is to have the prospect detail for you exactly what they intend to buy: how many, for what purpose, when, at what price, and so on. The more you know about their plans and needs, the better the job you can do in convincing them that you are the best choice for this project.

The Discovery Stage

In some cases, there is no need for a discovery stage because the prospect has already indicated its needs to you and has requested a specific proposal or quote from you. When this happens, you can proceed to Stage 5.

When you are dealing with larger companies, you might find you have to speak and meet with several people before being ready to send a proposal. Often, this is because many layers of management need to give their "okay" to whatever business you might be trying to win. This might mean many presentations, meetings, or visits just to be sure you've spoken with everyone involved in deciding which vendor company the prospect should use. When you're meeting with numerous people, you have to repeat the process of learning each person's needs and concerns.

If you haven't already collected this kind of information in Stage 3, determine the prospect's situation, what they think may be the best way to improve the situation, the kind of budget they have, how quickly they want the work done, and the most important factors they use in picking a supplier. Armed with this information, you can write a proposal that shows you truly understand their situation and that you can provide a solution that's also in their budget.

The Proposal Stage

Once the prospect's needs are defined and the overall sales criteria are established, it is time for you to present your best solution: your proposal. This can be in the form of a formal written document or bid, or you can simply tell the prospect that the shoes cost $75. In either case, you now explain to the prospect that you recommend a specific solution to improving his situation, and the cost is such-and-such.

For a large-dollar sale, this stage might involve a formal presentation to a committee of people. Make sure that you clean the food stains from your shirt or blouse, leave the kids with a sitter, and turn off your cell phone!

> **That's the Spirit**
>
> Never knowingly give false information or impressions when you're trying to make a sale. It's just not worth it!
>
> A fortune made by a lying tongue is a fleeting vapor and a deadly snare. (Proverbs 21:6)

Initial Trial Close Stage

In the initial trial close stage, you ask the prospect for his reaction to your proposal, and whether he plans to buy from you. Don't take "no" as final at this stage. "No" might only suggest that you missed something or that the prospect needs time to consider your proposal. Ask for some feedback on your proposal and just listen to what the prospect tells you. You might be surprised by what you hear. Adjust your proposal accordingly and resubmit. Feedback at this stage is your friend if they don't accept your proposal as you presented it.

The Budget Stage

Many large purchases must go through an approval process at the prospect's company, which can take anywhere from a few hours to a few months, depending on the company and the offerings involved. This stage is often nerve-wracking and requires patience. Unfortunately, all you can do is maintain regular contact with the prospect to ensure that nothing stops the positive momentum toward the sale.

For a small purchase, this stage can be as simple as running a credit card through the machine and getting an approval code.

The Close Stage

The close stage is when you ask for the order and either get it, find out what is missing, or simply lose the deal to another company. All prior closing stages lead to this

Hot Tip

Start tracking and forecasting your sales as soon as you receive an inquiry from a potential customer. Monitor the prospect's progression through each of the sales stages so that you can better gauge when the actual sales transaction may occur. This gives you a consistent way of forecasting sales and predicting cash inflow.

point. If you read the situation properly and had valid information, you stand an excellent chance of winning the sale. This is an exciting and scary time for both you and your customer, particularly when the sale involves a large amount of money.

Many salespeople are very skilled at getting prospects to this stage but then lose a sale because they simply don't ask for it. Few prospects ask you if they can sign a contract on the spot or issue a purchase order unless specifically asked by the salesperson. Don't leave the prospect hanging at this stage; just ask for the sale.

If you get a "no" or a "maybe," return to the discovery stage to find out if you missed some crucial bit of information or if the prospect's needs have changed. Then go through the rest of the stages again.

The Post-Sale Stage

You've made the sale and the deal is closed. Everyone should be happy, right? Check back with the decision maker to make sure things are going okay. Make sure the customer is still happy with his choice and isn't having doubts or misgivings. This is an often overlooked and critically important stage to building long-term customer satisfaction.

Business Buzzword

A **distributor** is a company that purchases products from you at a reduced rate and then sells those products to its own customers. Money is made on the difference between the sale price to the customer and the cost of the materials as purchased from your company.

A **manufacturer's representative** is a person or company who sells your products on your behalf. Reps do not purchase the products; they only sell them to their existing customer base. They make their money on the agreed-upon commissions earned from successful sales.

It is much less expensive to keep an existing customer than to find a new one. Your most valuable assets are your repeat customers. Guard them jealously. To ensure that they continue to be repeat customers, check back with them after each sale to confirm that they are pleased with their purchase. Show your customers that you have their best interests at heart and weren't just after the sale.

A Commodity Sale Versus a Complex Sale

The sales process varies somewhat, depending on whether you are selling a CD player at a department store, a nice house on a lake, or a $500,000 computer system. Although the timing of each stage might differ, the sequence must be followed or the sale process gets disrupted.

For example, the department store sale stages are something like this: The customer walks up and asks for assistance. This handles Stages 1 through 3. You ask what she is looking for and how much she wants to spend. There are Stages 4 and 5. You find a unit that you think matches her needs and ask whether she wants to buy; end Stage 6. Her credit card is processed, and she signs the receipt and walks out the door with her CD player (Stages 7 and 8). Asking her how she likes the CD player the next time she comes into the store covers Stage 9.

The sales process becomes more complex when working with high-dollar items or services, but the stages of the sale are the same. Trying to charge a consumer's credit card for a CD player before she has agreed on a unit would definitely not work in this scenario. Why do you think that placing Stages 7 and 8 before the other stages would work when selling a $500,000 computer system?

Map out your sales cycle and expected stages to set realistic expectations about what is needed at each stage of the sales process and the time frames involved in moving a prospect from Stage 1 to Stage 8.

Your Sales Channels

Salespeople are important people in your organization. Just as important, in many cases, are the people who support the sales team, such as the customer service personnel. You might want to have a few salespeople responsible for finding new customers but also have a number of support people who are solely responsible for serving and selling to existing customers.

These two tasks, finding new customers and supporting existing customers, require different skills. The support person has a relatively routine job that revolves around meeting delivery deadlines and keeping account information up-to-date, but the new business salesperson must create opportunities on a daily basis.

Running an efficient and productive sales team requires focused attention, enthusiasm, and commitment. But you don't have to do it all by yourself. Hire the help you need to keep sales coming in.

There are a couple of different options for how your sales staff can reach new customers. You can use independent distributors to expand distribution of your product quickly through its own sales channels, or you can build a direct sales force that deals directly with customers. Both approaches have pluses and minuses.

Selling Services Instead of Products

Services provide an interesting sales situation. The customer is buying something of value, but when the project is completed, she might not have anything tangible to show for it. For example, the result of your service contract with a customer might appear in the form of a new organization structure, better-trained staff, a new logo design, or a piece of software. These items clearly contribute to the company's success, but they are less obvious to the customer.

You have to keep in mind that services solve people's problems through your expertise and experience. Because the customer doesn't walk away with a tangible product, he must walk away with the belief that he benefited from using your service. Benefit-oriented selling is an important part of any sale, but it is critical when selling services such as consulting or training.

Clearly defining the *scope of work* from the beginning is critical to success when selling services instead of products. Because the customer might not have something tangible at the end of a project, it is important to clearly define at what point the project is complete. More than one company has been left holding the bag when they submit an invoice that the customer feels is too high or should not be paid at all because the customer doesn't feel he got his money's worth. The company providing the service may have done everything they were asked to do, but if the customer thought he was getting something else, it becomes difficult to get paid.

To avoid such situations, the best policy is to get it in writing. In your proposal to your potential customer, state clearly what you are offering to do for them and at what price. Make the desired outcome as specific as possible, preferably including the delivery of a final report. If there is nothing tangible you can provide to signify the completion of a contract, such as with service contracts and warranties, set a specific time period during which your services are offered. After that period is up, your services stop.

> **def·i·ni·tion Business Buzzword**
>
> The agreement on exactly what services will be provided to a customer is the **scope of work.** For instance, the scope of a project might be writing a press release or painting a building. Mailing all the press releases or painting the business owner's house is beyond the scope of work, meaning that those activities were not included as part of the agreement and would have to be paid for separately.

Always avoid vague, ambiguous statements such as "We will edit the new corporate brochure until the customer is happy with it," which is a time bomb just waiting to explode. What happens after you've done 25 versions of the customer's brochure and he just can't make up his mind? Is your work done or do you have to continue to edit and re-edit until the customer is satisfied? If you state exactly how many rewrites you provide as part of the agreement, the answer is probably no—you don't have to keep working forever—but with vague statements, you will probably never get paid.

Instead, use carefully chosen and specific wording, such as the wording I used for a sales brochure design proposal: "We will provide an initial concept design followed by a professionally created first draft and then a second final version of the brochure that includes any requested customer changes from the first draft." Establish *milestones*—that is, measurable targets or events that demonstrate that you have provided the service and reached your objective.

Advance payments (retainers) or down payments are always good, but they are particularly valuable with contracts for service. A little cash on the line always seems to keep the memory of both parties active and on track. It's also an excellent sales qualifier. Any prospect who is unwilling to pay a percentage of the total project cost is not someone you want to do business with. A charge of 25 percent is the suggested minimum, and 35 to 50 percent is not out of the question. Submit invoices regularly (determined in agreement with your customer) if you are billing on an hourly basis so you receive regular payments for your work.

> **def·i·ni·tion Business Buzzword**
>
> **Milestones** are important target dates or goals that help you track how well you're performing against your long-term business goals.

So ... you know about selling. But how well do you know your competition? That's what Chapter 9 will help you determine.

Thinking About Your Competition

When you start your business, you are in the enviable position of having no major competitor take you seriously. This provides you with a tremendous amount of freedom because nobody will be aiming to eliminate you in sales situations. You know that you are doing okay when competitors start to know your name and change their marketing strategy to go after you. That's good news and bad news at once.

Because you are just starting out, you should be collecting as much information as possible about the companies in your particular market segment. People might not yet view you as a competitor and thus might be more open with their information. Sit down with the information and imagine the picture that your prospective customers have in their minds about each of your competitors. Your competitors' marketing message and positioning generally creates this image. (See Chapter 7 for more on this topic.)

How does your offering compare to your competitors'? If you were a customer looking at the two companies, would you see them as direct competitors or as two companies in separate market segments? Does this perception come from the fact that they offer different products or services or that their marketing message presents it differently? From this approach, you can get a good idea about who to treat as a competitor.

Accumulating Competitive Information

Information is everywhere, and all you need to do is keep looking for it, find it, collate it, and, finally, put it into some semblance of organization and order. It is amazing how fragments of information can give you an excellent overall picture of a competitor. Where do you start looking for competitive information? Consider:

Bankruptcy Alert

Beware of the tendency to spend a lot of money for market research that you can generally perform on your own.

- How about the Yellow Pages? Who is listed in the category you would choose for yourself? How many companies are listed there? How do they position themselves in the ad? Grab last year's Yellow Pages and compare it to this year's. Has the number of competitors increased or decreased? Did some of the advertisers advance to a display ad? Did their positioning change?

- How about newspapers and trade publications? Scour them for advertising, articles, and quotes from any of your potential competitors. Ask your friends to do the same. They might find something that you missed. Start a folder for each of the competitors.

- How about the library? It might keep files on local companies that you can scan for free. Every time you find a piece of information, write it down or photocopy it. Date and place the information in a folder.

- How about your customers? Ask them what they know about your competition. How do they like dealing with them? What do they like? Dislike? What is their satisfaction level?

- How about your competitor's advertising? Review a competitor company's own sales literature such as brochures and catalogs. Check out its website, which may tell you more about the people, sites, plans, products, services, policies, warranties, and pricing than you can get anywhere else.

- How about a clipping service? Some companies specialize in accumulating information about companies for a fee. You tell them which companies you want them to watch for and which newspapers or magazines you want them to read. They generally photocopy an article that appears and send it to you on a regular (usually weekly) basis.

> **That's the Spirit**
>
> There's an old story about two merchants between whom there was a great rivalry. One of them was converted to Christianity. He went to his minister and said, "I'm still jealous of that man, and I don't know how to overcome it."
>
> "Well," said the minister, "if somebody comes into your store to buy goods, and you cannot supply him, just send him over to your neighbor." The man did so and, sure enough, when he began sending customers over to his competitor, he in turn began to send his customers over to this man's store—and the breach was healed.

- How about calling? You can simply call your competitors and ask for information. A lot of times, they will send it to you. Don't use a fake personal or company name. If you misrepresent yourself, you are toying with industrial espionage, which is really scary. Penalties for fraud and misrepresentation can be severe and can damage your business and your credibility. Just give them your name, number, and address and hope that you're talking to someone who doesn't know who you are. This approach is probably a safe bet when you first start out and will become more difficult as your success builds along with your reputation.

Opened ears, focused attention, closed mouths, and organized details are the secrets to accumulating competitor information.

Comparing Yourself to Them

Now it's time to get into the trenches and start analyzing the information you've collected. How do you compare to the competition from your customer's perspective? When you find the answer to this question, you are on your way to determining your own position in the marketplace.

Here's an exercise that will help you find some answers. Take out a pad of paper or create a spreadsheet to automate the easy calculations that follow:

- Divide your sheet of paper or spreadsheet into four columns: A, B, C, and D.

- In Column A, write down the top ten criteria your customers probably use in deciding who to buy from. Characteristics can include technical competency, service, phone support, convenience, credit terms, years in business, depth of offering, price, and so on.

- In Column B, place a number that corresponds to the amount of importance you believe a customer places on this particular item, based on your experience. Make 1 stand for most unimportant and 10 stand for a must-have. Although these are your opinions, they are still worthwhile to note. Your chart should look something like the following figure:

In this example, Competitor #1 has a superior market position compared to your company, as indicated by the higher total (262). This higher total helps to justify the higher product price.

(A) Characteristics	(B) Importance (1-10)	Your Company		Competitor #1	
		(C) Effect (1-10)	(D) Result (B x C)	(E) Effect (1-10)	(F) Result (B x E)
Years in Business	4	3	12	6	24
Credit Terms	7	8	56	8	56
Hours of Operation	7	8	56	8	56
Depth of Offering	6	6	36	8	48
Prior Experience with Company	8	5	40	6	48
Certification	5	8	40	6	30
Ideal	370	**Totals**	240		262
		Sale Price	$75		$95

- Create individual columns for each of your competitors and your company. These columns will contain a number between 1 and 10 that gives your subjective assessment of how well each company meets customers' needs. (See Effect Columns C and E in the example.)

- Create another column for your company and each of your competitors. For each company and each of your competitors, multiply the subjective assessment column's number (Column C and E) by the importance number (Column B) and insert the result in each column you've just created.

- At the bottom of each column, total all the numbers in the column for your company and each competitor. This final number provides a relative weighting assessment of how each competitor compares against the others and your company.

How does the number in your last column compare with those of your competitors? Is your number higher or lower? The same? How does your price compare with the others when compared against the summary numbers, such as in Columns D and F in the example?

In general, you want your number here to be high because it indicates how close you are to ideal for your customers. Ideal is calculated by totaling the importance column and multiplying by 10—the perfect score for each item. For example, the sum of the importance column in the previous table equals 37, which, multiplied by 10, equals 370 points for the ideal.

Divide your rating (such as 240) by the ideal (such as 370) to see how close you are from a percentage standpoint (240/370 = 65 percent). What is the proper percentage level? It's a relative setting and one that is highly dependent upon your business and customer type. In general, you should strive to be in the upper 25 percent or have a percentage rating of 75 percent or higher.

Numbers are okay, but I think in pictures, so I plot price and Total Relative Weighting Importance Factor against each other for my company and my competitors (see the following chart). Just follow the horizontal line until you get to the proper weighting factor, and then follow your result until you intersect with the proper price horizontal line. Put a dot there and label the dot. Repeat this process for your company and all others. You can now see graphically where you are compared to the competition.

Notice from the example that the competitor charges a higher price and also provides a higher weighting factor, which probably justifies their charging a higher price. If you keep your products and services the same and then offer a discount price, you will continue to move down along a vertical line because you are decreasing pricing and keeping the weighting the same. Keep this up, and you will be busy and out of business.

On the other hand, decreasing services and keeping the price the same also eventually rings the death knell for your business because people will eventually stop buying from you. Graphically, you move to the left along a horizontal line when you keep price the same and decrease services, which decreases your weighting.

Where do you need to beef up services? Where do you get the best weighting-factor return for the dollars spent? Offering longer hours of operation or better credit terms increases your weighting factors on two items of high importance, whereas spending money on certification provides a lower weighting-factor return.

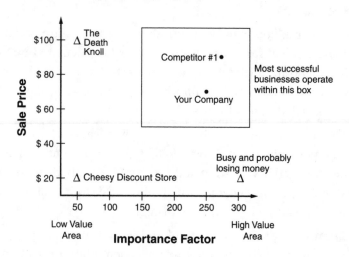

Total Relative Weighting Importance Factor

Hot Tip

The pricing section of Chapter 7 outlines the difference between price and customer-perceived value. If you haven't read that section, you should take a few minutes and read it in the context of comparing yourself to the competition. Customers buy value, not price. Check it out.

Will you make decisions strictly by this weighting analysis and chart? Probably not. Will the results from this analysis provide you with a structured way of analyzing your competition so that you can make informed decisions? Absolutely yes. This is a good reality check and one worth performing on a regular basis, when you're not checking out your competitors.

You should now have a pretty good idea of how you stack up against your competition. You might be less expensive than they are, for instance, but now you realize that you don't offer the extra services that they do. You can deal with this lack of services either by adding services (and potentially raising your prices) or by emphasizing in your marketing program that customers will get a bargain when dealing with your company.

On the other hand, if your price is too low and you have a higher total value, you might want to consider raising the price on your offering.

The Price Wars

Suppose your competition decides to gain customers by dropping their price. This often starts a *price war* where all companies try to keep their customers by matching or lowering their prices even more. This is a dangerous cycle that usually winds up with suppliers hurt, the customer confused and dissatisfied, and substantially lower profit margins all around. The airline and computer industries go through this cycle on a regular basis. It tears the entire industry apart and takes years (if ever) to recover lost finances, and there's really no reason for it.

There is a way to beat this cycle if it happens to your industry, but it takes amazing courage and fast reflexes. Instead of lowering your price, keep the price where it is. Beef up your extra services and sell the increased quality that you can provide for the higher price. Any experienced corporate business person knows you have to make a reasonable profit margin to stay in business. Instead of automatically dropping price as a reflex reaction, try this approach first, but continue to monitor your sales carefully. If you can't keep sales up, then you might just have to join the fray and hope that you survive.

> **That's the Spirit**
>
> Don't ever consider any types of bribes or kickbacks in order to beat your competitors. "Dishonest money brings grief to the whole family, but those who hate bribes will live." (Proverbs 15:27)

> **Business Buzzword**
>
> When all competitors compete based on price and keep undercutting their competitors to get sales, they are engaged in a **price war.** As each company lowers its own price, others drop their prices to compete, resulting in profit margins in the industry as a whole falling to critically low levels.

Are You a Specialty Store or a Superstore?

Are the other folks in your industry large companies with deep pockets and a wide selection of offerings (superstores such as Wal-Mart)? Are they smaller companies that provide a specialized, niche offering that a few people use (specialty stores such as Candles Are Us)? It's important that you understand where you want to fit in the continuum. Note that these terms apply equally well to service or product businesses. You could be a full-service health club or a specialty massage practitioner.

If you're trying to be a superstore but don't have the money to provide the variety and volume of products, you will probably go out of business. The financial demands of making a business of this size work will affect your ability to maintain inventory or personnel expertise levels. Once your "shelves" appear naked or you don't provide a proper service level, customers take their business elsewhere.

If you're a smaller business that tries to cater to everyone's needs, you will probably fail—not because you lack skills or ability, but because your customers will expect more than you can offer. In addition, your smaller quantity of purchases will keep your costs, and prices, higher. The superstore firms will clobber you on price alone.

It is interesting that the superstores are wary of the specialty stores eroding their business in key areas. A specialty store can provide a much higher level of personalized service to customers. The specialty store can also charge a little more for the service because the customer perceives it as having more value. In this way, the specialty store keeps margins high and expenses low. However, you need to know your customers and offer the specialty items they need.

In technical areas, a specialty store may be one that customizes computer equipment or software for the customer while also selling the software. The company makes money on both the software product and the service. The customer wins because she knows that her purchase will be handled in a low-risk, professional manner. Customers will pay for the service, especially if the cheap or large department store route has burned them.

In retail, a specialty store might be one that deals only in candles and related items. The customer might be able to find a cheaper candle in a superstore, but could he find "just the right one"? Probably not, and that is the benefit of a specialty store. People expect to pay more for the added selection and service. Value is what sells; don't shortchange yourself on that count, but don't gouge your customers either.

A typical service-oriented superstore is one of the "big" accounting firms that provide a wide array of accounting and consulting services. The local tax preparation service would be the industry's specialty store because they do taxes, and only taxes, and may or may not charge a premium for the specialization.

Trying to be a superstore when you should be a specialty store is surefire trouble, as is the reverse. If you don't have the broad range of products or services to qualify as a superstore in your industry, stick with serving a small niche as a specialty store. You'll probably make more money by establishing a reputation as a specialist in a particular area, rather than a generalist who tries to do everything.

Market Makers and Followers

Market makers are those companies with the financial backing and marketing know-how to create whole new business opportunities. Some examples of current market makers include larger companies such as Microsoft, AT&T, and General Foods. They have the deep pockets required to pay for the process of educating consumers about a new product or service. The gradual increase in customer awareness required to create new market opportunities is both expensive and time-consuming. Larger corporations can afford to be the leaders in creating whole new markets because they have other business areas that subsidize the new venture, but you don't have to be a leader to succeed in a new market.

Even if you have a product that is unique and innovative, you still might have a difficult time convincing the public to buy it. Be prepared. Generating enough interest in your product (or service) to result in sales might not be worth your effort unless you have an established distribution channel—that is, unless you have a way to get it out quickly to the people who want to buy it.

Getting your product into a distributor's hands might be one of the most difficult challenges you'll face, especially if you're selling a kind of food. Competition for retail "shelf space" at grocery and convenience stores is brutal, and most grocery stores charge the manufacturer for the privilege of being able to sell their products there. Sounds unbelievable, doesn't it? The grocery stores know that they are the key to reaching your potential customers, and they have thousands of products to choose from, so why not ask for a fee to showcase your product?

If you offer a service, distribution is less of an issue because there are fewer ways that you can provide your service to your customers; you either perform the service yourself, such as hairstyling or copywriting, or you have sales representatives making contacts for you, lining up new customers. Website designers faced this "new" service problem a few years ago but have now become a highly sought-after service.

It is always cheaper, and less risky, to piggyback your offering on something that is already accepted and trusted in the market. Instead of creating a new market or introducing a totally new kind of product that no one has ever seen before, let the big folks spend their money doing it. Let them increase understanding and awareness of this new market opportunity. Then you can jump in later with your own product and benefit from all the money they've spent marketing to the public. This is called a *free rider* in MBA-ese, and free is always good.

When you're just starting out, try first to be a market follower. You can become a leader later when you have the big bank account and the market acceptance needed to steer the market ship.

Using Market Segmentation to Your Advantage

Within every market and industry are smaller pockets of opportunity called market niches. Larger companies don't waste their time trying to meet the needs of a small portion of the market, but you might want to. Niches can be very profitable if you have the right offering.

These market niches are often like a vacuum in that once you make your product available, everything you produce will get sucked into the niche, too. You can also easily establish a strong reputation that will make it difficult for larger competitors to compete with. Too cool! Even though niches might have fewer potential customers, they are often easier to sell to.

Cooperation Versus Competition

A Christian business person has a dual challenge to meet. He or she must always conduct business in a fair and ethical manner. He or she will care about employees, the community, and the state of the economy. At the same time, this owner must follow sound business principles to maximize profit for all concerned. There is nothing wrong with successful businesses as long as the wealth is spread to all who work for it.

Another aspect of the challenge is to treat ones' competitors with respect so that, eventually, both can prosper in an environment of cooperation and good will. Actually, it is not uncommon to find that you and your competitors, or even your noncompetitors, have more in common than it initially appears. They might address a particular market niche much more effectively than you and vice versa. Combined, you might offer something that is truly more powerful than each of your individual strengths. You can cooperatively market your offerings. You can share mailing and administrative costs and aid each other in new product development activities.

Now, as you gear up to face your competition, have you considered how you'll use the Internet? That's the topic of the chapter ahead.

Cybermarket: Using the Internet

I once heard Steve Jobs, the founder of Apple Computer, on a radio talk show about the Internet. He commented that one of the most fascinating aspects of the Internet is that a small company can look just as large as IBM. Nobody physically visits the company's building, but rather only sees what an owner puts on the Internet. Do a good job on your company's Internet presentation, and you can play with the big guys.

Is there a technological challenge associated with making this leap into the Internet? Yes. Can you jump these hurdles? The answer once again is yes, and you can do it yourself or hire someone to do it for you. In either event, you must address this important business tool or be left in the electronic dust.

So … are you ready to get started setting up your own website?

Setting Up on the Internet

Several components compose an Internet site. This section presents some of the major terms that you will encounter and shows you how you can use Internet technology in your own business. This section is not designed to make you a technical geek (or expert). It does, however, give you an overview of the language and technology of the Internet so that you can fully appreciate the business opportunities it presents.

To make the connection you will need a computer, modem (or cable-access), Internet connection software, and an agreement with a company that provides a local telephone number or cable hook-up for Internet access. This process used to be pretty complicated and now is about as simple as software installation. Don't be scared off by the technology. Our kids use the Internet. You can, too.

Web Words

Think of the World Wide Web (WWW) as a huge network of interconnected computers. If you draw lines between all of these computers, you have something that looks like a spider web. Picture the WWW as an interconnected, or inter-networked, group of computers.

These computers are connected for all types of Internet-related services. I am going to concentrate on the components that you control, create, or purchase for use by your company on a daily basis.

Your home computer that accesses information from the WWW primarily deals with computers that host, or act as the home computer, for a website. A website is an electronic location on the WWW where a company stores and displays the information that it wants seen by others.

Like an individual's street address, all websites have addresses, known as *domain names*. For example, if you type an address such as *http://www._edpaulson.com* (my web address), your computer looks for the WWW location with a domain name of *edpaulson.com*. (The HTTP tells the computer to transport what it finds there to your computer using the *Hypertext Transfer Protocol (HTTP)*, which means that the underlying text information is translated and displayed using the *Hypertext Markup Language (HTML)*.

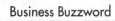 **Business Buzzword**

A **domain name** is a unique name given to your Internet location that is used by people who want to view your Internet site. Most business domain names end with ".com."

Hypertext Markup Language (HTML) is the language used by Internet websites.

Hypertext Transfer Protocol (HTTP) is the mechanism by which HTML information is transferred from one point to another over the Internet.

If all of this seems like a lot of jargon, just think of it this way: Your computer uses the www._edpaulson.com address to find that computer on the Internet. The HTTP tells the two systems how to transfer the information and the HTML allows the underlying information to be displayed as intended by the person who created the received document.

Here is the really cool and magical part: Every computer in the world that uses a *browser* (a software tool used to surf the Internet) can read a file stored in HTML format on a website location. Every computer connected to the Internet has some form of browser associated with it. This means that anyone who has access to the Internet can access your website and perform any number of standardized operations—such as reading site information, placing orders, providing feedback to the site designers, and paying for purchased products.

Finding an Internet Service Provider

All this talk about websites is good, but how do you even get onto the Internet in the first place? Well, you can set up your own Internet access by purchasing a computer, setting up the network connections, spending weeks in training classes, and losing hairs off your head. If you are into that kind of "challenge," then have at it and call me from your asylum room on visiting days.

That's the Spirit

Maintaining impeccable business ethics is a hallmark of the Christian business owner. Let your word be your bond. Be blameless in all your dealings, honest in all the claims you make on your website. This will not only benefit your customers and associates, it will keep you in the center of God's will:

He holds victory in store
for the upright,
he is a shield to those
whose walk is blameless.
(Proverbs 2:7)

An easier way is to rely on an *Internet service provider (ISP)*. Your ISP is the company that connects you to the Internet. This may be done through a dial-up telephone number that is accessed by your computer's modem. However, the trend is moving away from dial-up modems to cable-access. In this case, your ISP provides Internet connection over a TV-cable for much faster speeds while keeping your phone line free for family use (RoadRunner service from AOL-Time Warner is an example.)

There are numerous ISPs, and you probably have local ones that provide specials for your local area. A few of the national ISPs include FlashNet, AT&T WorldNet, and SpryNet.

Other vendors that provide their own private networks along with Internet access include America Online (AOL), CompuServe (CIS), and Microsoft Network (MSN). With these services, you can send mail and messages to other users who are members of the same network, use custom services that are only available to that network's members, access the Internet, and also send and receive electronic mail to other Internet users.

Let the ISP worry about the latest and greatest methods of connecting to the Internet. You just worry about connecting to your ISP, letting your customers know about your e-mail and website addresses (more on that later), and keeping your website up to date.

How do you choose an ISP? This choice really depends on your specific situation, but here are a few rules to get you started:

- Choose a provider that charges a flat connection fee per month, independent of the number of connected hours. (The flat monthly fee is usually in the $15 to $29 range.)

- Make sure that the ISP has 24-hour, 7-days-a-week access.

- Make sure that there is a customer service line that you can call when you need help.

- If you travel and want to retrieve your electronic mail messages while on the road, or even in another country, then make sure that your ISP has local access numbers in the cities that you visit most often. If it does not have these local access numbers, then you inherit the toll telephone charge back to your home city so that you can access the network.

- Make sure that your ISP provides enough hard disk space for you to store your anticipated electronic mail messages and website information if applicable.

- Check to see if the ISP for your electronic mail service also provides website hosting services. You can often get the two features in a single package for a discount rate.

• Get the name of a few customers who already use the ISP's services, and find out how often they receive a busy signal when trying to connect by modem. The answer should be "rarely" or "never," or you should look somewhere else. Or simply choose a company offering cable-access to avoid dial-up problems altogether.

Naming Your Domain

The domain name is the address that people go to when they want to find your company. Your domain name is how Internet people learn to recognize you. For example, Microsoft uses www.microsoft.com, which makes sense and is easy to remember.

When you have your own unique domain name, you must also have a unique IP (Internet Protocol) address. Your ISP will handle all of this for you.

You obtain your IP address from the InterNic (www.internic.net), an organization that manages the Internet. Your Internet service provider handles this registration for you. Just know that you need to find an ISP and a domain that is not taken to set up a domain name and website location.

Hot Tip

When we first tried to find a domain name for my company, Technology and Communications, Inc., we struck out because other companies had taken all the names related to our own. Surprising? Not really, when you consider that a domain name must be unique on the entire Internet. We finally tried course-store.com and found that it was available, so we took it. You can use the WHOIS feature of the www.internic.net site to see if a domain name is available for use.

You can have a domain name that is related to another vendor, such as jones-inc.worldnet.att.net, which means that your website is hosted by AT&T on its WorldNet service. This is the simplest way to establish a website—even though the name looks complicated—but it also has its drawbacks. Suppose that you promote your AT&T-associated website for months, and all your customers are accustomed to visiting this site when they need information or want to place an order. Now also suppose that you decide to change to another network provider, such as MCI or

SPRINT. You will probably have to change your domain name because it is associated with AT&T and you no longer use their services. This means that every time you change Internet website hosting providers, you have to give your customers a new web address. This is not a good idea.

I set up my company's domain name so that it would be separate from any website-hosting provider. I can change providers without having to change my domain name or retrain my customers. This might seem like a small point, but it can be incredibly important if you want to change website providers, so I highly recommend that you set up a domain name that is independent of the underlying provider and tell your customers to use this site.

Once you establish an Internet-based electronic mail account with your ISP, talk with your ISP about registering a non-ISP specific domain name that is hosted by your ISP. In this way, you can minimize your headaches, use the same ISP for both your electronic mail and website hosting, and write one check for both services. I am now contacted through author@edpaulson.com, which I then forward to whatever e-mail system I choose. In this way I can change my e-mail provider without having to retrain my customers.

Browsing the Internet

Assume that you sign up with an ISP. You perform your setup as directed and now you want to access the Internet. Here's where the fun starts. (By the way, make sure that you allocate plenty of time for your first trip onto the Internet because a number of people go on and don't come back for hours on their first visit. It is easy to do, even for nongeeks, so be forewarned.)

Your ISP provided you with a *browser*, which is a software tool used to cruise, surf, or browse your way from one Internet site to another and also send and receive electronic mail. Just as you browse a book by flipping the pages, you can browse the Internet by flipping from one site to another. The major difference is that pages in a book are all in your hand, but the separate websites might be on opposite ends of the globe.

The browser's job is to connect you to various sites, relay the proper commands to translate the HTML code, and then display the HTML information on your computer screen in a way that matches the document creator's intention.

That's the Spirit

I made a covenant with my eyes not to look lustfully at a girl. (Job 31:1)

Along with all the great information the Internet puts at your fingertips, it can put a lot of objectionable material at your disposal as well. It's estimated that about half of all websites are dedicated to selling pornography.

If you are tempted in this area, or if children have access to your computer, take preventive actions. First, make sure your computer(s) are in public view to discourage secretive surfing. Then hook up with an ISP offering "filtered access" to the Internet. These ISPs—such as cleanweb.net or afo.net (American Family Online)—"take out the garbage" at the server level before you even begin browsing.

There are many browser variations, but the two major contenders for your browser space are Netscape Navigator and Microsoft Internet Explorer. Both companies partner with ISPs to get their browsers on your desktop, and each provides all kinds of different financial deals to get you into their technology. Why? Simply because the larger the number of installed browsers, the more marketing and political clout that particular vendor has with the Internet community.

In either case, you win. Both are good products and certainly can serve your needs at this stage of the game, unless you specifically plan to be an ISP or more sophisticated Internet design or consulting firm.

I suggest that you simply use the browser provided by your ISP and be happy that it works. Once your site is up and running, leave well enough alone until you are forced to upgrade to the next generation of browsers, which will happen around every 9 to 18 months.

Business Buzzword

E-mail (electronic mail) is a method of delivering mail between people with access to a message network such as the Internet. It allows you to send a message and even attached files, such as an Excel document, instantly across the room or around the world.

Sending and Receiving E-Mail

E-mail allows you to send messages and files instantly from one e-mail address to another. Your clients can now say, "Why not e-mail it to me, and I'll review it in a few minutes?" This way, you save on postage and you know that your mail is delivered regardless of the weather.

Your ISP usually provides you with an electronic mail address that you can give to clients. You use this account for sending and receiving mail. Mail is a built-in function of most ISP browser/mail signup combinations.

Once again, beware of connecting yourself with a single vendor. If you tell all of your clients to send e-mail to a CompuServe account, for example, and then you change to a standard Internet mail account, you have to retrain your customers to send mail to the new address. For this reason, many companies tie their e-mail accounts to their domain names, which, if kept independent of the provider's name, allows you to move from one ISP provider to another without retraining your customers.

Creating Your Website

Just look at you now—with your new ISP connection, your hot e-mail address, and your own personal website location. Oops! There isn't any information on your website! When people access the Internet through their ISP and connect to your website, they get a blank screen or an exciting message such as "site under construction." Somehow, this leaves something to be desired.

You fix this situation by creating *website content*, which is displayed when someone accesses your site with a browser. Content is actually a bunch of HTML-coded pages that display in a specific way when the browser downloads and translates the information.

HTML code is pretty cryptic for the uninitiated. Early website designers had to live with direct HTML coding to make any kind of attractive site. HTML is still around, but the software world has made it easier for normal people like you and me to create content by developing automated content-creation tools such as Microsoft FrontPage, Corel WebMaster Suite, DeltaPoint QuickSite, Adobe PageMill, ClarisWorks Internet Edition, Cold Fusion, and Netscape Navigator Gold. These tools work similarly to any Windows graphic design utility, but the final output is an HTML file that can be placed on a website for viewing with a browser.

These content creation tools are not for the computer novice, but they are also not so complicated that you need three college degrees and a pocket protector to create an

> **def·i·ni·tion** **Business Buzzword**
>
> Your **website content** is the text and visuals that are displayed on your website. Typical content includes company history, company logo, mail and phone addresses, products and services offered, and sales or marketing contact information.

attractive and functional website. Some people pay to have the initial site created and use it as a training experience for a standard employee.

All of this website technology is pretty impressive. But just wait until I talk about links. A *link* is a section of your HTML page that refers to another Internet location, such as another website. For example, assume that your company sells widgets for the XYZ Widget Company and that your website refers to the BANGO product also produced by XYZ Widget. Your website can include a link to the www.xyzwidget.com website location for additional information about the BANGO product. Your site is referring, or linking, the browser to the other website that you don't control. You are now taking advantage of XYZ Widget's website development effort by automatically sending your users to its site when they click the link. (Oh, by the way, your site may be in New Jersey and the BANGO information may be on a site in Tokyo. It is all automatic to the person viewing the information and clicking the link.)

Business Buzzword

A **link** is a section of a displayed web page. When clicked by the user, the link connects the user to the Internet site associated (or linked) with the clicked selection. Think of the website as a magazine, and a web page as a page in that magazine.

Links can also refer to various locations in your own website, which is common when your site becomes longer than a few pages. In fact, the majority of your links refer to other pages within your own site. Links are easily created, tested, and managed using the technology built into the content-creation software packages mentioned earlier.

Here are a few words of caution regarding website creation strategies:

- Don't forget that the site is a sales tool first and not some place to show "cool" stuff that does not contribute to your sales and advertising goals.

- Snazzy design is important, but not as important as providing the information that your clients want.

- Make your site easy to follow and user friendly.

- Keep the site information current and display the date that you last modified the page contents.

- Keep page download times at 28.8 kbps speeds to under 20 seconds at most, if at all possible. High-quality graphic images are an exception to this rule since the viewer will expect a high-quality graphic to take longer to download.

- Ask around for sites that people like, and model your initial site after what already works.

- Graphics (visual images) download slowly from the Internet, so keep the number and size of graphics on your site to a minimum.

- Make sure that the content-creation software you use does not lock you into a specific browser type that excludes all others. As a result, people might not be able to view or use your site. For example, make sure that the content you create will at least work with both Microsoft Internet Explorer and Netscape Navigator.

- Anything you put on your site can also be viewed by your competition. Don't put it out there unless you want it found.

- Talk to your ISP about ways of obtaining site statistics so that you can determine how many people visited your site, where they went, and other important information.

What if you don't feel up to writing and designing your own website? Thankfully, website design services are popping up all over the place. Some are good, and some just don't get it. Make sure that you work with someone who understands that the site is first a business and sales tool and secondly a cool technology play toy.

Bankruptcy Alert

I have seen some cool, trendy sites that just did not get used. "Why?" you might ask. Simple. It took a lot of large graphic files to make them look flashy, and graphics take forever to download. In addition, they allowed content to suffer in favor of form. Even though the sites were flashy, they weren't very useful. Remember to make your site a useful business service tool for your customers.

For around $1,000, you should be able to get a decent site design that is functional. The monthly hosting of the site by a service provider should run between $15 and $50, depending on the level of advanced services required and the size of the site.

E-commerce is a natural extension of Internet access in that customers can both get information and order at the same time. Adding e-commerce to your site will greatly increase the site development costs and also exposes your company to liability that you should be aware of. When you simply provided information you did not obtain anything of a proprietary nature from your customers. And if someone hacked into your site they really couldn't do too much damage. Once you have credit card information, addresses, names, and other customer-confidential information entered into your site, you may become a hacker target. If successfully hacked, someone could obtain a lot of financial information that, if used illegally, could put your company in a precarious legal position.

Have a long talk with your e-commerce developer and ISP regarding hacking safeguards to make sure that any confidential customer information remains confidential. If you are not comfortable with their responses, you may want to put off your e-commerce venture or find other suppliers.

This section was designed to introduce you to the processes involved in creating your own website. The process is not that difficult, and it can really be a lot of fun. Once your site is set up, you are sure that your customers are receiving your sales and marketing information in the way that you want.

Helping People Find You on the Net

Once you've got a beautiful, informative site, how can you ensure that surfers will find your page among the hundreds of thousands of sites out there? Luckily, *search services* help web readers find the sites related to subjects that interest them.

 Business Buzzword

A **search engine** scans the Internet for new sites and determines how they should be categorized.

A **search service** is a website location where users can search for information on specific topics that may be contained on Internet sites.

The most popular search services are Yahoo!, Lycos, Excite, Altavista, Google, and several others. You can go to one of these sites, type the subject you are interested in (business or parenting or stamps, for example), and you are given a list of links to sites that meet your criteria.

How do the search services collect all those lists? They use *search engines* to scan the Internet for new sites and determine the content of those sites.

You want to make sure that search engines can appropriately categorize your site. You can do this by learning a lot about the hidden metafields that are used by search engines to categorize your site. (A hidden metafield is information that is part of your content but is not visible on your site.) If you do not use metafields properly, you can create a great site and nobody will know that it exists.

Finally, you should know that the search engines will make special arrangements that ensure that your name appears at the top of any search list result. This will cost you something but might be worthy of a discussion. This area of website relationships and cross-marketing is constantly evolving and becoming ever more complicated. Finding an expert in this area is not a bad idea if the Internet is planned to be an integral part of your business plan.

Money, or Not?

At this point, you are fully Internet functional. Can you expect to make money directly off your website and other Internet-related activities? Probably not in the short term. You should think of your Internet activities, such as a website or electronic mail, as the modern-day equivalent of a business card. Have you ever made money directly from your business card? Probably not. Is transacting business easier because of your business card? Absolutely.

Once your clients get trained to use your website for information and mail, you can present them with the electronic commerce features that allow you to process orders online. For instance, when they want to place an order, they might call a 1-800 telephone number or send a fax order form that they obtained from your website. A fulfillment center then processes the order.

Once you are Internet functional, you might still want to advance to another level of efficiency. What if you can make your site adapt its presentation to whomever is accessing it? For example, if certain viewers present a name and password, they get access to special areas of the site. Maybe their standard logon name is the passkey to special chat areas on your site. In short, you can program your site to behave one way with one user and another way with another user.

Are you going to do this programming yourself? Probably not. But the technology is ready when you are. Your computer-automated systems can really start to pay dividends for you. But will you know how to handle all that money? Read on to Chapter 11!

Part 4

Facing Your Financials

I know that you're tempted to skip right over this part because it has that ugly word in it—financial. Yes, I know financial stuff can be boring and confusing if not explained well. But have no fear—this part isn't that bad. More importantly, if you skip it, you can lose a lot of money that your family would have appreciated.

There are many different ways to figure out whether you're succeeding in business, and the most fundamental one is to look at your financial situation. Are you making money with all your hard work? Unless you read this part, you won't know how to answer that question, will you? So stick with me and I'll help you through it. If you have to put the book down every once in a while to take a breather, I'll understand, but make sure you come back! Finally, make sure that you at least skim the international chapter. The information contained in that chapter might open a whole new world for you.

11

Making Sure That You're Making It

As an entrepreneur, you like making money. But do you enjoy keeping track of your funds? Most business owners treat accounting as a necessary evil. However, accounting is how business keeps score, and, just like keeping score in baseball, there are numerous rules and procedures to accurately reflect the results of the actions on the field.

Thankfully, accounting principles and policies can make accounting for your business easier. The most foundational elements to know are such things as: accounting periods, sales costs, types of accounting methods, and financial statements. So, ready to take a deeper look into accounting for your new business?

Accounting 101

The following sections provide some basic accounting concepts so that you can understand what's involved in setting up and maintaining your accounting systems. Time spent planning and developing good procedures can save you countless hours of frustration that may slip into your family time.

Accounting Periods

Accounting periods are periods of time, such as months, quarters, or years. Keeping records by accounting periods allows a company's financial reports to be compared from one time frame to another. It's a good idea to review your company's performance on a regular basis so you can become aware of potential problems, such as running out of cash or lower sales figures, before it's too late.

For starters, you need to determine when your company will evaluate its financial performance. Most companies, small and large, look at their basic financial statements at least quarterly (every three months) to measure their progress toward long-term goals, and most managers review their financial statements on a daily or weekly basis. It's always good to know where your sales are coming from and how your money is being spent.

The next question is, "When does your company's financial year begin and end?" A year in a company's history is a *fiscal year.* Unless there is some reason to do otherwise (as recommended by your accountant), keep your fiscal year the same as the calendar year, from January 1st to December 31st. This means your quarters will end on March 31, June 30, September 30, and December 31.

Sales and Costs

Assume that your client pays you today for work you intend to perform in 60 days. First off, kiss this customer and keep him happy; this type of client is rare, indeed. Second, take a look at whether you should declare that payment as *earned income.* (In other words, can you spend the money today knowing you won't have to give it back, or should you wait?)

> **Business Buzzword**
>
> **Income** is the general term for money received from selling a product or service to a customer. Any money paid to you before the product or service is fully given to the customer is **unearned income.** If the customer can cancel his or her contract and get the money back, you have not truly earned it.
>
> On the other hand, money you have received for work performed or for products provided is known as **earned income.** You've done everything the customer requested, according to some formal or informal agreement, and you can consider the money yours.

In the *accrual* accounting world, when you receive payment from a customer for work that hasn't been completed yet, for accounting purposes, you need to show that payment as *unearned income* until the work is done. When the earning process is complete, the accrual basis of accounting reports that transaction as *income*.

If the customer can cancel his order, then the money really hasn't been earned yet, has it? You are essentially holding the money for him until you complete the work. In short, if you haven't finished earning the money by meeting all the terms of your contract with the customer, you shouldn't consider the revenue from those sales as truly yours.

If you have a noncancelable contract along with a nonrefundable advance, then the money you received is yours. At that point, you can include it as revenue.

If you use the cash basis of accounting, you don't need to know the difference between collections and earned income. In the cash-based accounting world, everything you receive from sales is considered income when it is collected, and you don't make any special accounting entries to show when it is earned.

I usually recognize the sales revenue at the time of invoice generation unless the dollars involved are so large that they can make a material difference to my company's financial well-being.

But here's a fundamental accounting question: When do you actually incur an expense? Is it when you use the product or service, or when you pay for the product or service? The answer is different depending on whether you use the *cash basis* or *accrual basis* of accounting.

That's the Spirit

The devil took [Jesus] to a very high mountain and showed him all the kingdoms of the world and their splendor. "All this I will give you," he said, "if you will bow down and worship me." (Matthew 4:8–9)

Obviously, you're not planning to worship the devil any time soon! However, what are you tempted to "worship" these days, in terms of what receives most of your precious time and energy? Take a moment to reflect upon a crucial question: "In what ways am I letting my relationship to family, friends, and God suffer for the sake of my business pursuits?"

The cash basis of accounting recognizes sales and expenses when money (cash) is actually received or spent. The accrual basis of accounting focuses on the earning process and matches sales revenue to the period when the earning process is completed, not simply when the cash is received. The accrual basis also matches expenses

incurred to generate those sales to the period in which the income is reported. So …
these are two approaches to accounting, and you need to know which one is more
appropriate for your business. Let's look at these methods a little closer.

The Cash Basis Accounting Method

How do you track money owed to you when you're using the cash basis of accounting? Very simply, you complete work for customers and you bill them. In some businesses, you receive payment right away, such as if you are running a restaurant;
customers pay after they eat. You keep track of who owes what by having waiters
and waitresses use order slips. At the end of the night, you total the amount on all
the order slips collected and match them with the amount of money in your cash
register. You then deposit most of that money in your bank account and keep some
in the register to use as change the next day.

If you run almost any other kind of business, however, you probably have to wait
to receive payment. You might bill a customer on the first of the month and have to
wait 30 days until the check arrives. To keep track of who owes what, create a file of
all the invoices sent to customers. As customers pay, you deposit their checks in the
bank and take their invoice copies out of the file. You can always check to see whose
invoice is outstanding by looking in your file. Once more than 30 days has passed, you
want to give the customer a call and find out if there is a problem. (See Chapter 15 for
more on collections.)

The Accrual Accounting Method

Accrual accounting imposes an additional accounting step; now you have to use the
accounting system to track when a customer is billed as well as when the collection
comes in, and you might be making accounting entries at times when no cash has
changed hands.

Furthermore, accrual accounting might report handsome profits while you have
no cash in the bank to pay suppliers—because your customers haven't paid you yet.
When managing any business, large or small, remember that cash is king, and track
your bank balances and expectations about cash flows using the techniques discussed later in this chapter. Many businesses have shared the sad experience of running out of cash before all the bills have been paid; try not to join them!

Accrual accounting might also impose tax complications. No one likes paying taxes on reported income before the cash from those sales has been collected, but that can be the way accrual accounting works. Your accountant or tax advisor can give you suggestions on techniques to minimize this source of pain.

The following table summarizes the advantages and disadvantages of cash basis and accrual basis accounting.

Cash Versus Accrual Accounting

Cash Basis	Accrual Basis
Advantages	
Relatively simple to use.	Provides a conceptually more correct picture of the results of your business operations.
Understandable to anyone who has balanced a checkbook.	Consistent with the way bigger companies report their financial results.
Reports income when you have the cash to pay the taxes.	Accepted by the IRS if your business has inventory.
	Simplifies accounting during change in ownership.
	Makes reporting to outsiders (bankers, potential investors, and so on) more comprehensible because they are used to accrual-basis statements.
Disadvantages	
Can distort the results of operations, possibly leading to bad business decisions.	Can be costly and time consuming.
Not acceptable to the IRS if your business has inventory.	Might not match reported income and cash availability.
Not comparable to the way bigger companies report their financial results.	Requires some thought to understand the accrual accounting concepts.
Complicates accounting during changes in ownership.	
Can make your company's financial condition appear worse than it is if you offer credit terms to your customers.	

Understanding Financial Statements

Understanding financial statements isn't difficult—really! Using financial statements effectively along with a valid sales forecast gives you a preview of good and bad times before they hit, so you can take proactive measures if necessary.

> **def·i·ni·tion** **Business Buzzword**
>
> There are three basic financial statements. The **income statement** reflects all income and expenses for a particular period of time (usually a year). The **balance sheet** shows your total assets and liabilities. The **cash flow analysis** shows exactly how much you received and how much you spent on a monthly basis.

This section introduces you to financial statements and explains their basic purpose. There are three basic financial statements: the *income statement, balance sheet,* and *cash flow analysis.* The income statement shows you the amount of money brought in and spent during a specific accounting period, which is usually a fiscal quarter or year. The balance sheet shows you how much you own and how much you owe at a particular point in time, which is usually calculated at the end of a fiscal quarter and on the last day of the year. The cash flow analysis shows exactly how much you actually received in revenue and how much you spent on a monthly or periodic basis. You really need to watch your cash flow statement carefully. Your cash flow statement keeps you informed about how much money you actually have in your bank account to pay all your bills.

A Chart of Accounts

One of the procedures accountants use to make record-keeping easier and more understandable is summarizing transactions so that similar transactions are grouped together. They do this by using a *chart of accounts,* which lists all the possible categories of transactions and organizes them to make producing financial statements easier. Accounts that summarize the assets and liabilities of the company are grouped together to form the balance sheet. Accounts that summarize the sales and expenses of the company are grouped together to form the income statement. Those statements, taken together, describe the total financial condition and results of operations for the company.

> **def·i·ni·tion** **Business Buzzword**
>
> A **chart of accounts** is a list of all the categories used by a business to organize its financial expenditures and sales.

It is critically important to set up these accounts so they are not only useful for tax purposes but also so you can get the financial management information (reports) you need to make effective financial decisions.

For example, tax accounting only requires that you know the amount of revenue received and the total costs associated with earning that revenue. Management accounting tracks the revenues and costs associated with products or business areas, so management can determine which business activities are profitable, and which are losers. The specifics of setting up these management accounting categories is dependent upon your particular business, but the importance of setting these management accounts up early in the process applies to all businesses.

def·i·ni·tion	**Business Buzzword**

Revenue is the total sales amount received by the company. **Pretax profit** is the amount of money left over after all expenses, except for tax payments, have been deducted. **Cost of sales** expenses are the costs directly linked to the production or sale of a product or service (raw materials, labor, and other expenses). **Operating expenses** are those expenses associated with running your company (salaries, rent, utilities, and so on).

If you are using the accrual basis of accounting, you also need a financial statement that details cash flow activity, which is likely to be different from the activity shown on the income statement. Cash-basis companies might not need as elaborate an analysis to generate a good understanding of their cash flows, but they should still be aware that lags between billing and collection could adversely affect their cash position. Depending on the size of the business and the complexity of the collections, a cash-basis company might need to develop a full-fledged cash flow analysis report, too.

The Income Statement

Your *income statement* (or *profit and loss statement* or *P and L*) tells you whether your business is profitable. The income statement totals the amount of *revenue* and then subtracts the expenses associated with making that revenue. The result is the *pretax profit.*

Income statements show you how much you sold and how much it cost you to create those sales during a particular period of time. Most businesses prepare year-end income statements so they can see how they did during the year. You can also prepare income statements for any period, such as quarterly or year-to-date.

> **That's the Spirit**
>
> I gave you a land on which you did not toil and cities you did not build; and you live in them and eat from vineyards and olive groves that you did not plant. (Joshua 24:13)
>
> The Hebrews of biblical times followed their General Joshua into lands that God had promised to their forefather Abraham. The promises and acquisitions flowed from the grace of God—something that can't be earned or deserved. The same is true in our lives today, especially with regard to our success in business. Ultimately, all that we are and have—including profits—come from God's hands. Have you paused to give thanks today?

Expenses fall into two categories: *cost of sales expenses* and *operating expenses*. Cost of sales expenses (also called the cost of goods sold, or COGS) are those directly related to producing your product or providing your service. These generally include the cost of raw materials, the cost of labor to run the machine that produced the widget you sold, and other expenses required to obtain or create the product or service.

For example, suppose you sold a coffee mug for $5.00 and it cost you $3.00 to purchase it. The cost of sales is $3.00, which is what you paid for the mug. The *gross profit* calculation associated with this single mug's sale is Revenue – Cost of Sales = Gross Profit, or $5.00 – $3.00 = $2.00 Gross Profit. Because the costs of producing your product change depending on how much you manufacture at a time, cost of sales are called *variable expenses*. Just as things usually cost less when you buy them in bulk, producing a product in large quantities works the same way. Generally speaking, the more you produce, the lower the cost per product and the higher the gross profit.

Operating expenses are those expenses associated with running your business. You still have some amount of these expenses regardless of how much you sell in a month. These include your salary, your rent payment, the cost of the electricity in your office, insurance, administrative salaries, commissions, and other similar costs of operating the company. Operating expenses are paid out of the gross profit. Notice that operating expenses include commissions that vary with the sales level, so they are not strictly "fixed" expenses.

Now that I've given you an overview of what the income statement provides for you, take a look at one.

Remember the earlier coverage of accrual and cash basis accounting? Look at the following income statement and notice how the relationship between expenses and revenues is directly linked to profit calculations. Unless the two are synchronized, there is no way to accurately determine if you made money during the time period that you're examining.

The Balance Sheet

Whereas an income statement reflects the flow of money in and out of a company during a specific time frame (as videotape records events over a period of time), the *balance sheet* shows the amount of company assets and liabilities at a particular point in time (a snapshot of how things are at a particular moment). The balance sheet is based on a fundamental equation of accounting: Assets = Liabilities + Owner's Equity.

---

def·i·ni·tion   **Business Buzzword**

Assets are items of value owned by the company, including cash, property, and machinery. The value of an asset is based on its initial purchase price minus any applicable **depreciation** (the decrease in value that occurs as an asset ages).

Liquid assets include cash and anything that can be quickly converted into cash (such as inventory and stock and bonds). **Fixed assets** are those that are difficult to convert quickly, such as buildings or machinery.

The **book value** of an asset is its purchase price less the total amount of depreciation that has already been applied to the asset.

The **market value** of an asset is what someone would pay for the asset, even though it may have been partially or fully depreciated.

Assets are those items of value the company owns, such as cash in the checking account, accounts receivable, equipment, and property. The value of an asset is based on its initial purchase price minus any applicable *depreciation* (the accounting-tracked decrease in value that occurs as an asset ages).

For example, cash is an asset. You obtain the cash either from selling stock, obtaining a loan, or selling your services or products. Cash is money you can spend on the spot. It is called a liquid asset; you can use it immediately to pay off a debt or to purchase items. Other common liquid assets include accounts receivable and inventory. *Liquid assets* are part of current assets and represent those assets that you expect to be converted into cash within a year.

A typical income statement.

A Simplified Income Statement
Jackson Surveying—Income Statement
Period Ending December 31, 20XX

Income Statement

Item	Dollar Amount	Description of Its Income Statement Function
Sales	$250,000	All revenues
Cost of Sales (variable costs)	$95,000	Variable costs associated with the revenues
Gross Profit (Gross Margin)	$155,000	Sales - Cost of Sales
Operating (Fixed) Expenses:		All nonvariable expenses:
Salaries	$65,000	Usually administrative and executive salaries
Rent	$18,000	What you pay to keep your doors open
Marketing and Sales	$55,000	What it costs you to sell your offering
Total Other Expenses	$138,000	Total of All Other Expenses
Pre-Tax Profit	$17,000	Gross Profit - Total Other Expenses
Federal/State Taxes	$5,950	Taxes due on the Pre-Tax Profit
Net Income	$11,050	Pre-Tax Profit - Federal and State Taxes

Fixed assets have a longer life and are more difficult to convert into cash quickly. Typical fixed assets include buildings, machinery, and land. The net book value of an asset is based on its initial purchase price less any depreciation. Different fixed assets have different depreciation terms, or depreciable lives. Check with an accountant to determine the proper depreciable life of a given item.

Liabilities are amounts that you owe. Typical liabilities include accounts payable, which reflects amounts owed to suppliers, loans, credit cards, taxes, and other people or organizations to whom you owe money. Short-term liabilities, which are paid back within 12 months, are also called current liabilities. Long-term liabilities include the portions of mortgages and equipment loans that are not due in the next year.

Owner's equity is what is left over when the liabilities are subtracted from the assets. Take what you have, subtract what you owe, and you are left with owner's equity. This is the number that you want to maximize because it

def·i·ni·tion **Business Buzzword**

Liabilities are amounts that you owe, including loans, credit cards, and taxes. **Short-term liabilities** (those due within 12 months) are also called **accounts payable.**

can reflect the book value of your company. The initial investment of your company stock and retained earnings are added together to calculate owner's equity.

Business Buzzword

Owner's equity is what is left when you subtract your liabilities from your assets.

Net income is money left over after all company expenses have been paid out of revenues.

The amount of *net income* (see the sample income statement earlier in this chapter) determined at the end of the year is added to an equity account named retained earnings. You add the current year's net income to the prior year's *retained earnings* to calculate the company's retained earnings at the end of the period in question. Ideally, retained earnings become cash used by the company to promote further growth.

The following table is an example of how to organize your accounts in preparation for making your balance sheet.

Typical Balance Sheet Accounts

Assets	Description
Cash	Bank accounts, petty cash, investments.
Accounts Receivable	What other companies owe you on a credit basis, to be paid within 30 days.
Inventory	Raw materials, finished goods, product being built, retail merchandise, training manuals, and so on.
Fixed Assets	Land, buildings, machinery, office equipment, depreciation expense.

Liabilities	Description
Short-Term (Current) Liabilities	Must be paid in less than 12 months. Includes accounts payable to suppliers, unpaid wages, taxes, credit card debt, short-term loans, and long-term notes with less than 12 months left on their term.
Long-Term Liabilities	Due over a period that is longer than 12 months. Includes mortgages, equipment loans, bank loans, and other long-term financial obligations.
Equity	Assets – Liabilities = Equity
Capital Stock	Owned by shareholders. Includes common stock and preferred stock.
Retained Earnings	Current and cumulative year's net profits or losses as accumulated from prior- and current-year income statements.

So here you are with accounts and numbers. Now look at the following figure to see how to put them together to create a balance sheet.

This typical balance sheet shows the format for organizing all your balance sheet accounts.

A Simplified Balance Statement Jackson Surveying—Balance Sheet Period Ending December 31, 20XX	
Current Assets	
Cash in Bank	$15,000
Accounts Receivable	$25,000
Inventory	$18,000
Other Current Assets	$7,000
Total Current Assets	$65,000
Fixed Assets	
Land and Building	$250,000
Machinery	$75,000
Office Equipment	$35,000
Accumulated Depreciation	($25,000)
Total Fixed Assets	$335,000
Total Assets	**$400,000**
Current Liabilities	
Credit Cards	$3,000
Wages Payable	$9,500
Taxes Payable	$3,000
Line of Credit	$5,500
Accounts Payable	$4,500
Total Current Liabilities	$25,500
Long-Term Liabilities	
Mortgage Loan	$185,000
Machinery Loan	$55,000
Equipment Loan	$30,000
Total Long-Term Liabilities	$270,000
Total Liabilities	**$295,500**
Owner's Equity	
Common Stock	$45,000
Retained Earnings	$59,500
Total Owner's Equity	$104,500
Total Liabilities and Equity	**$400,000**

Owner's equity, your company's net worth, is calculated by subtracting the liabilities from the assets. This means that as your assets (what you own) increase and your liabilities (what you owe) decrease, your equity increases. This makes logical sense, and the balance sheet puts it into a form where it can be precisely calculated. Realize, however, that your owner's equity usually does not reflect your company's market value. Setting the market value for an ongoing company is usually a complicated matter and heavily industry-dependent.

Although your balance sheet might not change drastically from week to week, it's a good idea to regularly review whether you are taking on more debt or increasing the equity of the company. Most financial software packages can easily provide you with a balance sheet and income statement whenever you want to look at it.

Cash Flow Analysis

A *cash flow analysis* can be your most important financial statement because it tells you whether you have enough cash to pay your bills. Although tracking your assets and liabilities is important over the long term, when you're just starting out, the key challenge is keeping the money coming in.

A cash flow analysis, or cash flow statement, looks a lot like an income statement (see the following figure). The major difference is that your income statement focuses on earnings from operations, whereas the cash flow analysis also reflects investments, borrowings, repayments of loans, and other balance sheet changes. Cash flow from operations might also be significantly different from reported earnings, especially if you are using the accrual basis of accounting. Remember also that your income statement might be based on accrual accounting methods that prepare the cash flow statement based on actual cash in and out flows.

The reason you need both an income statement and a cash flow analysis is that you might have a really good month of sales followed by a really bad month of sales. So bad, in fact, that you have to get a loan to cover your expenses. By watching your cash flow analysis, you can see in advance when you will start to run out of cash during that month. However, because an income statement based on an accrual basis of accounting records when obligations are made, not when the cash is either spent or received, the good months and bad months often even themselves out. You wouldn't know by looking at your income statement that August almost put you out of business due to lack of available cash, but your monthly cash flow analysis would alert you to potential problems before they become real problems. You should now see that you must use all three financial statements to get an accurate picture of your company's financial condition.

It is also a good idea to become good friends with your receivable aging report. This is the report that tells you who still owes you money and how far past due they are with their payments. If you offer net 30-day terms, and you see most of your clients paying in 45 to 60 days, then you are providing them with additional credit for the extra 15 to 30 days. In essence, you are taking out a loan to cover for their delayed payment. If that is okay with you, then you are more generous than most small business owners I know are. Get your collections in order, and you might find your need for cash decrease accordingly. See Chapter 15 for actions you can take if they don't pay.

	January	February	March	April	May	June
Revenues						
Product Sales	$1,200	$1,620	$2,187	$2,952	$3,986	$5,381
Services	$300	$405	$547	$738	$996	$1,345
Net Revenues	**$1,500**	**$2,025**	**$2,734**	**$3,691**	**$4,982**	**$6,726**
Cost of Sales						
Product Cost	$300	$405	$547	$738	$996	$1,345
Services Cost	$45	$61	$82	$111	$149	$202
Total Cost of Sales	**$345**	**$466**	**$629**	**$849**	**$1,146**	**$1,547**
Gross Margin	**$1,155**	**$1,559**	**$2,105**	**$2,842**	**$3,836**	**$5,179**
Overhead Expenses						
Salaries	$3,500	$3,500	$3,500	$3,500	$3,500	$3,500
Payroll Taxes and Benefits	$700	$700	$700	$700	$700	$700
Advertising and Promotion	$300	$300	$300	$300	$300	$300
Depreciation	$150	$150	$150	$150	$150	$150
Supplies and Postage	$100	$100	$100	$100	$100	$100
Professional Fees	$175	$175	$175	$175	$175	$175
Printing	$200	$200	$200	$200	$200	$200
Telephone	$250	$250	$250	$250	$250	$250
Equipment Rental and Repair	$50	$50	$50	$50	$50	$50
Travel	$650	$650	$650	$650	$650	$650
Miscellaneous	$225	$225	$225	$225	$225	$225
Office Space	$900	$900	$900	$900	$900	$900
Total Overhead Expenses	**$7,200**	**$7,200**	**$7,200**	**$7,200**	**$7,200**	**$7,200**
Net Income (Loss) Before Tax	**($6,045)**	**($5,641)**	**($5,095)**	**($4,358)**	**($3,364)**	**($2,021)**
Provisions for Income Tax						
Federal Income Tax	$ -	$ -	$ -	$ -	$ -	$ -	$
State Income Tax	$ -	$ -	$ -	$ -	$ -	$ -	$
Total Tax Provisions	$ -	$ -	$ -	$ -	$ -	$ -	$
Net Income (loss)	**($6,045)**	**($5,641)**	**($5,095)**	**($4,358)**	**($3,364)**	**($2,021)**

Note: Tax deductions not included to simplify analysis.

July	August	September	October	November	December	2000
$6,995	$9,094	$11,822	$15,368	$19,979	$25,972	$106,556
$1,749	$2,273	$2,955	$3,842	$4,995	$6,493	$26,639
$8,744	**$11,367**	**$14,777**	**$19,210**	**$24,973**	**$32,465**	**$133,195**
$1,749	$2,273	$2,955	$3,842	$4,995	$6,493	$26,639
$262	$341	$443	$576	$749	$974	$3,996
$2,011	**$2,614**	**$3,399**	**$4,418**	**$5,744**	**$7,467**	**$30,635**
$6,733	**$8,753**	**$11,378**	**$14,792**	**$19,229**	**$24,998**	**$102,560**
$3,500	$3,500	$3,500	$3,500	$3,500	$3,500	$42,000
$700	$700	$700	$700	$700	$700	$8,400
$300	$300	$300	$300	$300	$300	$3,600
$150	$150	$150	$150	$150	$150	$1,800
$100	$100	$100	$100	$100	$100	$1,200
$175	$175	$175	$175	$175	$175	$2,100
$200	$200	$200	$200	$200	$200	$2,400
$250	$250	$250	$250	$250	$250	$3,000
$50	$50	$50	$50	$50	$50	$600
$650	$650	$650	$650	$650	$650	$7,800
$225	$225	$225	$225	$225	$225	$2,700
$900	$900	$900	$900	$900	$900	$10,800
$7,200	**$7,200**	**$7,200**	**$7,200**	**$7,200**	**$7,200**	**$86,400**
($467)	**$1,553**	**$4,178**	**$7,592**	**$12,029**	**$17,798**	**$16,160**
$ -	$ -	$ -	$ -	$ -	$ -	$0
$ -	$ -	$ -	$ -	$ -	$ -	$0
$ -	$ -	$ -	$ -	$ -	$ -	$0
($467)	**$1,553**	**$4,178**	**$7,592**	**$12,029**	**$17,798**	**$16,160**

A typical cash flow analysis.

Using Financial Statements

You now have tons of information neatly arranged in little columns. So what? How do you use it to your financial and management benefit? Try the following suggestions on for size:

- Use last year's cash flow analysis as a guide to estimating what your sales and expenses will be this year, month by month. Use it as a goal-setting tool to help improve your company's financial situation month by month.

- Use your income statement to estimate year-end totals for sales and expenses so you can compare where you are today to where you expect to be by the end of the year. Are you ahead of where you thought you would be sales-wise?

- Create a projected balance sheet for the coming year. Estimate what your balance sheet will look like once you pay off debts during the year or after you buy equipment.

To CPA or Not to CPA

Face it: You probably don't want to be an accountant or bookkeeper. Although you want to stay closely involved with monitoring your financial statements, you can certainly hire a tax accountant or bookkeeper to help in those areas. Tax returns are becoming more complex, requiring a dedicated effort to take the best advantage of legal deductions. An accountant, even a CPA (certified public accountant), generally pays for herself in this area.

That's the Spirit

I can delegate a lot of my responsibilities at work, but I cannot delegate my hopes for my family. The primary values, attitudes, skills, and competencies that my children will grow up with will be learned (or not learned) in my home. —Tim Hansel

In general, if you don't know the financially accepted practices for your industry or business, consider consulting a professional who has the necessary industry experience to help you set up efficient systems. Once good accounting systems are established, keeping the records becomes a clerical task that can be delegated to an adequately trained employee or performed by an outsider if you aren't interested in keeping the books yourself.

But suppose you're keeping track of your business's money—but there's just not enough of it? That's when it's time to head to the bank (and on to Chapter 12).

Chapter 12

Banking on Your Business

"These guys have absolutely no vision," said Bill. "This is a great idea, and our whole family is ready to work day and night to make it work. All I need is $25,000. That's nothing to a bank their size, but NO-O-O! They want all of this supporting documentation before they will even consider the loan. Why do I bother with banks in the first place?"

Answer: Because you're going to need them. And, thankfully, banks exist to serve customers. But as the old joke says, "The only way you can get a loan is to prove you don't need it." Consequently, many start-up companies have difficulty getting a loan from a bank—even if they have the best idea in the world. This is where your personal credit becomes very important (more about this later).

The point is, you have to deal with banks anyway, loan or not, for your business checking account, payroll tax deposits, credit card processing, and other administrative details. It's a good idea to start now to develop a good relationship with your bank—and with the loan officers at your branch. One of these days your business will be well established and a banker who understands your company can be a great resource in supporting your profitable growth.

So start now, long before you ask for money, to lay the groundwork that will convince your banker that you are a solid customer and a good business risk. After you establish a track record in business, how do you deal with a bank? The following sections boil down the lessons it took me several years and a lot of rejection to learn. I hope these lessons make it easier for you.

The Loan Officer Is Your Friend

Would you give money for a risky venture to someone you barely know or someone you have known for a while and trust? The answer to these questions is simple, and my point is probably already made. Meet the loan officer responsible for your account when you first open the account—before you need money. Keep him updated on your progress and help him become more familiar with your company. You'll find that bringing him into the loop early will make him an ally when you need to ask for a loan. Don't wait until you're desperate for money to bring him up to speed on your activities.

> **Hot Tip**
>
> It's a good idea to get to know several loan officers at your branch, so that if your main contact leaves, you don't have to start from scratch getting to know someone else. These days, people don't stay at one job very long, so it's likely that by the time you're ready to apply for a loan, your original loan officer will be working somewhere else. It is also a good idea to get to know your loan officer's boss. Positive strokes to a boss even works for bankers.

Make sure that this first meeting goes well—no matter what! The initial impression on the loan officer will stay. Look and act like the president of your own company, like someone who deserves as much money as you want! This meeting doesn't have to be lengthy, but you must leave a positive impression so the loan officer will remember you when you need to borrow money.

Don't underestimate the value that this loan officer brings to your business. As with any bureaucracy, it is really good to know someone inside who can steer you through the maze and support your cause when needed.

Banks Will Give You Money Only When You Don't Need It

Banks make money by lending it to individuals and businesses. The loan officer's obligation to the bank is to make loans to the businesses that are most likely to pay them back.

The lending policies of nationally regulated banks are monitored by the state's Office of the Comptroller of Currency, or OCC. (You can recognize a national bank by the word "national" or letters "NA" in its name.) The loan officer of a national bank must walk the line between pursuing the best business opportunity for the bank and complying with regulatory agencies such as the OCC. Private banks, on the other hand, have more discretion about their lending policies.

From a bank's perspective, lending money to a small business provides risks and advantages that are different from those associated with a large company. Take a look at some of these risks and advantages.

The smaller business loans have a higher risk associated with them because the business is usually newer and might have fewer assets to be used as collateral. This increases the interest rate the small business must pay, which increases the revenue banks receive. Small businesses are also attractive as loan customers because funds from a loan can usually be covered by money from company checking and savings accounts at the bank. Because small businesses are likely to keep their money in one bank, banks are becoming more willing to lend them money.

Note that when you request a loan for an amount greater than the loan officer's lending authority (which can be as little as $15,000 or as much as $100,000, depending on the bank), the loan officer must get approval from her supervisor or from a loan committee that makes decisions regarding larger loans.

Larger companies have large lending needs that require extra attention from the bank (401(k) plans, lock box, and so on). These lending services generate fee income for the bank, but the loans are priced at a lower interest rate because the larger customers are in a better negotiating position. However, larger businesses rarely have all their money in one or two accounts; it's invested in several other places.

To get them to provide you and your company with money, you must sell them on your company, your ideas, and on you, or this money may go to other, less risky ventures. Be prepared to present a case to your banker on why you should get the loan.

That's the Spirit

At the end of every seven years you must cancel debts. This is how it is to be done: Every creditor shall cancel the loan he has made to his fellow Israelite. He shall not require payment from his fellow Israelite or brother, because the LORD's time for canceling debts has been proclaimed. (Deuteronomy 15:1–3)

Moses stated the principle of the "Sabbatic Year" here in Deuteronomy 15. It was an amazing ongoing practice within the Israelite community. Yet it makes sense. The people served a God of grace and mercy. Therefore, they were to be gracious toward one another, as well.

Hot Tip

Banks often use tax returns as the basis for determining a business's and individual's financial (and consequently loan) status. Keep both your company and personal returns in order to improve your loan chances with the bank.

In addition, it is generally safer for a bank to invest money in several ways, rather than all in one basket. Several small business loans spread the risk over several businesses so that even if one business owner starts to have trouble repaying his loan, the whole bank is not threatened.

The primary reason banks have conservative lending policies is that loan defaults are expensive. They can only provide loans that are acceptable risks in the eyes of their depositors and the regulatory agencies to which they report. They are not in the business of providing high-risk, high-profit, potential venture capital loans.

As a small business owner, you must create a personal and business track record in advance that will qualify your company for a loan when you need it. Here's what you can do:

- Keep your personal and business financial situation healthy by using standard accounting practices and watching your cash flow.

- Try to get a small line of credit early on to get your credit established with the bank. A business line of credit is usually increased when you pay it off on a regular basis.

Calling your loan officer and saying, "I need the money tomorrow" is a red flag that something is out of control with the company and its management. A panic situation raises questions about your managerial ability. Plan ahead to make sure that you can get a bank to lend you money when you really do need it.

You can also expect to personally guarantee any loans given to your company by a bank. Every bank that I have ever worked with has wanted the same thing, and the first time you sign the papers giving the bank the right to go after your personal stuff should the business loan go into default, you can feel your skin crawl a little. It just comes with the territory and you should not take it personally. On the other hand, more than one business owner has worked those extra hours with the image of his banker sitting in the other room monitoring loan payment status.

That's the Spirit

Give everyone what you owe him … Let no debt remain outstanding, except the continuing debt to love one another, for he who loves his fellowman has fulfilled the law. (Romans 13:7–8)

A good credit history has always been important, and the early Christians knew it. Though borrowing for various business needs will likely be necessary, we can work to keep overall debt at a minimum—except for the special kind of "continuing debt" the apostle Paul mentioned above.

I know of a bank in Illinois that waives this personal guarantee ritual when the company officers and owners each individually own less than 20 percent of the company.

Bank Loans That You Can Get

Now you understand the world of finance from the bankers' perspective. How does this translate into your ability to get money when you need it? Here are some loan options for you to consider.

An *unsecured line of credit* can be given on a personal basis to the company officers. This is essentially a personal loan to officers (based on the personal credit history of the individuals), who then loan it to the company. The bank does not give this loan directly to the company because the company has not proven it can pay the loan back. The officers arrange reasonable repayment terms with the company.

A *secured line of credit* is the next best option. In this scenario, the bank loans the company money to purchase an asset, such as new equipment or a new building. The asset is then used to secure the loan until the company pays it back, just like a house secures a mortgage, which is simply another kind of loan. In this case, the company typically must provide at least 20 percent of the purchase amount. If the loan can't be repaid, the assets are sold to recover the bank's investment.

You might also be able to get *short-term loans* (under a year) by using receivables or inventory as your collateral. This type of loan is really a line of credit with special provisions. You provide a summary to the bank showing that your company has a certain level of liquid assets—accounts receivables from customers, inventory, or CDs—that can be used as security on the loan. The bank will only loan 70 to 80 percent of the value of the assets, which is recalculated each month. The danger is that if your assets decline from one month to the next, you might have to shell out some additional money.

That is the strict letter of the relationship. Now, here is what usually happens in reality. You talk to your banker and show a historical record of receivables, inventory, and receivables aging. From the amounts and aging, you and your banker agree on a reasonable amount of liquid asset value and the bank opens a line of credit for that amount. The 70 to 80 percent rule still applies, and my experience has been that this keeping of the loan no more than the agreed-upon 80 percent value is handled on the honor system. My banker only asked for my receivables value at the one-year anniversary but reserved the right to investigate them monthly if desired. Your banker will probably only exercise this right if she believes that the note or the company is in jeopardy.

For example, assume that you secured your line of credit last month with $50,000 in receivables, giving you $35,000 in credit (70 percent of $50,000). If your receivables drop to $40,000 the next month, your collateral is worth only $28,000 (70 percent of $40,000). The $7,000 difference between the $35,000 and the $28,000 value of your assets must be paid to the bank immediately to meet the terms of the original loan agreement. This can be a tough check to write if you haven't planned for it.

> **Hot Tip**
>
> The value of assets is usually discounted when used as security for a loan. As my banker says, "We are in the business of lending money, not selling items to recover debt."
>
> Notes, or loans, secured by larger assets such as major equipment and property are considered long-term and can have a 36- to 60-month repayment period.

> **Bankruptcy Alert**
>
> When calculating the value of your inventory, bankers use 50 percent of the retail price as the value. They don't consider the inventory worth the full price you paid for it because the bank must sell it for less if you go out of business.

> ### That's the Spirit
>
> If a man runs after money, he's money-mad; if he keeps it, he's a capitalist; if he spends it, he's a playboy; if he doesn't try to get it, he lacks ambition. If he gets it without working for it, he's a parasite; and if he accumulates it after a lifetime of hard work, people call him a fool who never got anything out of life. —Vic Oliver

Sell Your Banker on Your Company

People naturally avoid risk, and bankers make risk avoidance an art form. Your bank wants to be sure you've thought through all aspects of your business and believe it can work. If you don't believe in it, why should they? Can you imagine giving $50,000 to someone who is wishy-washy about where he or she plans to go, how they'll get there, when they'll arrive, and how they'll pay you back? Therefore, your business plan is your opportunity to explain what you want to do and how you intend to succeed.

The bank is going to expect something from you before it gives credit. First, you must do your homework and prepare a comprehensive business plan with realistic sales and expense projections. Next, you must provide personal financial statements to give the bank an idea of your own financial situation, separate from the company. Any person with 20 percent or more ownership in the venture is required to personally guarantee the debt, meaning that they agree to repay it if the company defaults. Period. Later you will have more negotiating room, but early on, this is the norm.

Your challenge is to convince your bank that you are credit worthy. As a new business owner, your personal credit history along with a well thought out business plan are the best tools you can use.

Banks will evaluate you based on the five Cs of lending:

- **Character.** What are you like? Confident? Ethical? Self-assured? This is treated as a very important consideration when first starting out. Make the initial meetings count!
- **Capacity or cash flow.** Can you repay the debt? Do you have the cash flow to support the monthly, or periodic, payments required?
- **Collateral.** What can the bank take if the loan defaults? Make it clear that you don't intend to default but that the bank is covered should the worst happen.

- **Condition.** What is the general economic condition of the area and what is the intended use for the money?

- **Capital.** What is the company's net worth or equity?

Banks make their money by lending money, and they are always looking for solid loan prospects. If you have a clean financial report, both personal and business, and a company with a solid, proven financial record, you can get money from your bank. Notice that you must perform to a certain level before your bank will consider lending you money, and only for minimum risk opportunities. You would treat anyone with money as a friend, and that should apply to your banker also.

Commercial Checking Accounts: A Different Animal

Balance your commercial checking account just as you do your personal checkbook—but do it more often! Your company writes checks and makes deposits as you do in your personal checking account, but the rules are slightly different. You can shop around and find a better deal on fees and transaction costs on business checking accounts, but make sure the rules and requirements fit your needs. Don't overlook the important factors of convenience and security; after all, you hope to be taking a lot of money to the bank, so make sure the bank you select is accessible and safe.

Keep the following in mind when you set up a commercial checking account for your company:

- You are charged for your commercial account based on the number of transactions and the average account balance.

- You can expect to pay around $.10 for each check you deposit, along with a transaction fee for the deposit. At some banks, the rate billed for each check varies according to whether it is local, in state, or out of state.

- You are also billed for each check you write.

- You receive a statement from the bank that outlines the charges billed to your checking account for those transactions. This statement is in addition to the basic checking statement listing all the checks and deposits that have cleared. The formal term for this is an *analysis statement*.

Business Buzzword

An **analysis statement** is a statement from your bank that outlines the various bank charges and credits incurred with respect to your business account.

An **earning credit** is a credit offered by the bank in the place of earning interest because federal law does not allow you to earn interest on a business checking account.

- Banks charge transaction fees for each deposit you make and check you write, but they also give you an *earning credit* on the money in your account, which you can use to pay those transaction fees. By keeping enough in your account to offset transaction fees, you save some money.

You should shop around to get the best checking account for your company, based on whether you expect to have a lot of transactions or just a few and whether you can maintain the minimum balance to avoid additional charges.

Hot Tip

When nobody else will help, the Small Business Administration (SBA) comes to the rescue. Maybe. It used to be difficult to get an SBA loan, but the SBA has changed and might be able to help if the loan amount is under $100,000.

There are several different SBA loan types, and they change on a regular basis. Contact your local SBA office and sit through one of their introductory talks. You'll learn how to work with a bank to obtain a loan.

Big Banks, Small Banks

Which is better—a small bank with easy access to the lending managers or a big bank with deeper pockets and higher approval levels? The answer: It depends.

All banks have lending guidelines, but the internal policies are more flexible with a small bank. The officers are more likely to bend the rules in a small bank than in a big one. With a small bank, you get to know the officers better and quicker, but the loan amount that can be approved might be smaller. This means that you should check out the bank's philosophy of operation and verify that they actually do what their marketing literature says they do. Ask for a few references of companies in your size range and then call these references and ask them questions.

Start with the banks where you already have a relationship. If the big banks give you grief, go to a smaller one. You might look like a large fish in a small pond, so beware that the pond might not be deep enough as you grow.

Average small business loan amounts are in the $25,000 to $50,000 range, which is well within the reach of any bank. Be aware that because it takes just as much paperwork to process a $25,000 loan as a $250,000 loan, most banks prefer to process the larger amount, where they earn more interest on the loan.

Now that you're a great banking customer, there are a few more things to know about your cash, for instance: "floating," factoring, equity funding, and considering the stock exchange. These are some of the topics just ahead in Chapter 13.

Cash Is King In Your Business

How good can it get? Here you are with a 300 percent increase in sales over the last six months. Your family members at home are flying high, and you just can't seem to do anything wrong. As a matter of fact, the projects coming your way are larger than you ever thought you would have, and it looks like you'll get them all! Your initial dreams have come true, and you're on the verge of becoming unbearable to everyone around you.

Don't worry. Life is about to humble you, unless you have taken the proper steps to deal with the growth. Without solid planning, even a rapid growth spurt can hurt cash flow. And keeping the cash flowing into your business is key to growth and expansion (not to mention paying your bills in a timely manner). This chapter will help you develop strategies for keeping the money flowing into your business so that you don't run into the same trouble Laurie's company did.

When You're Out of Money, You're Out of Business (Usually)

Try to keep an employee around when you cannot pay him, and you will understand that cash is the business equivalent of air. Lose your employees, the good ones, and you have substantially hurt your business. Once they're gone, they're usually gone for good.

Take a look at your vendors, too. How long will they keep providing you with the materials you need if you cannot pay your bills? About as long as a snowball would last in a west Texas desert. Once again, you cannot blame them for putting a stop to your credit line.

Now, what about you? What happens if you cannot pay yourself? How long will you keep the business alive and pay your employees when you are not being paid? A few months, maybe, but when it becomes a way of life, you will be seriously tempted to pull the plug and "get a real job," not because you don't love what you do, but simply because that's what an organism does when its air supply is taken away.

That's the Spirit

Look! The wages you failed to pay the workmen who mowed your fields are crying out against you. The cries of the harvesters have reached the ears of the Lord Almighty. You have lived on earth in luxury and self-indulgence. You have fattened yourselves in the day of slaughter. (James 5:4–5)

A cash problem hurts on many levels. James lays out the harsh spiritual implications. But even on the most practical level, lack of cash might cause your usually professional employees to become disgruntled, might cause the quality of your product to decline, and might lead to your own loss of enthusiasm. Beware!

Another result is that your customers will be affected, and they probably won't like it. Their opinion of your company might drop as employees become snippier over the phone or in person. Unfortunately, customers don't really care why the quality has declined; they just recognize that it has, and they might decide to take their business elsewhere if it continues.

All this because you forgot that cash is king in your business! (Of course, the Lord Almighty is King of the Universe; you can keep that in mind, too.) Anyway ... income is great, nothing wrong with it. Equipment is wonderful. Receivables are heartwarming. Inventory gives you something to count on boring weekends and at the end of the year. But cash is what makes it all work on a daily basis.

How Success Can Kill Your Business

Have you ever met someone who told you that he was so successful, he went out of business? If not, you should look for such a person and buy him dinner. Just as you don't need to go through a windshield to learn that seatbelts are a good thing, you don't need to go out of business to learn the dangers of rapid growth.

Picture this scenario: You used to provide $10,000 per month in services and all your customers paid cash on delivery or by credit card. When you completed the sale, you got the cash. Everyone was happy. Then customers began asking for credit terms. After all, your competitor offered them credit, and they have consistently used your company instead. It wasn't such a big deal, and they were stable. Why not offer them credit? So you did.

Take a look at what happened when you agreed to accept credit terms instead of cash. You took the cash you would have received this month and told the customer that they could pay you next month, at the earliest. However, you still need to pay your employees and vendors at the end of this month. Where is that money going to come from? Unless your company has a lot of cash on hand (and wouldn't we all like that situation?), it will have to come from you. When the customer pays, you will simply pay yourself back and all is fine. Sort of ….

Now let's be really successful and bump your monthly sales to $30,000. Wonderful! Who is going to provide the cash needed to cover the month-end bills? You? Do you have the $30,000 on hand to lend the company? Even if you do have the cash at $30,000, you might not when monthly sales hit $50,000 or $100,000.

Bankruptcy Alert

Don't put all your eggs in one basket. As dangerous as it is to grow your company quickly, it's even more risky for that growth to be the result of a relationship with just a few customers. Keep trying to expand and diversify your customer base while managing your growth.

My point is this: Someday you will no longer be able to personally provide this kind of cash advance to the company. Uh-oh! There go your employees and all those wonderful vendor relationships. When they leave, they place everything that made you successful in jeopardy. In short, the whopping success that you enjoyed has just put you precariously close to being out of business—if you don't take steps to avoid a cash crunch.

I'm not trying to talk you out of making your business as wildly successful as you can imagine. I'm just trying to convince you to open your eyes to the fact that success can destroy all that you have built if you don't also deal with its potential risks.

Factoring, Credit Terms, Loans, and "Float"

Here you are, all dressed up to go to go out with your spouse ... and no cash to pay for the cab. Now what do you do? You go to someone and borrow money against your next paycheck or income tax refund. Well, the same thing can be done with a business, and it's called *factoring*. With factoring, a company gives you a percentage of what customers owe you, sort of like a short-term loan.

You can also improve your cash situation by providing your customers with an incentive for paying their bills early (or even on time) and extending payments to your own vendors with whom you have credit. This improves your cash position by improving the *float* between when you receive money and when you must pay your bills.

> **def·i·ni·tion Business Buzzword**
>
> **Factoring** is the process of receiving money now for payments your customers are expected to make to you in the next few weeks.

Finally, you can get a short-term loan that is secured by your receivables from a bank or other funding source. This technique is less expensive than factoring and provides greater stability, along with other benefits.

Factoring Receivables

If you need cash now to cover business expenses, there are companies out there who will provide you with cash for your receivables in exchange for a fee. Here's how factoring, or discounting, of receivable notes works:

1. You close the deal and the customer agrees to pay you for your product or service.

2. The company that plans to factor your receivables issues an invoice to the customer (usually on your letterhead), which the customer is to pay.

> **def·i·ni·tion Business Buzzword**
>
> **Float** refers to the time frame in which you receive money that is owed to someone else and when you actually give him or her the money.

3. The factoring company immediately gives you cash worth between 80 and 95 percent of the receivable value.

4. The factoring company then gives back a portion of the fee (usually up to 10 percent of the initial 5 to 20 percent discount) if the customer repays within the specified time frame.

For example, assume that a client contracts from you $10,000 worth of your product or service. You can realistically expect to receive that money within 45 to 60 days, which can put you in a bind depending on your company's cash situation. You could factor the note using the previously outlined procedure and have the numbers work out as follows:

1. You close the deal for $10,000.

2. The factoring company issues an invoice to your customer for $10,000 and indicates the terms in which the payment should be made to the factoring company.

3. The factoring company writes you a check for between $8,000 and $9,500.

4. If the customer pays within the allowed 30 days, then the factoring company writes you another check for around 10 percent (or $1,000) when payment is received. (The longer it takes for your customer to pay the factor, the less of a rebate you get back.)

Assuming that you receive an 85 percent factoring rate with a 10 percent rebate for payment received within 30 days, you see $8,500 immediately and $1,000 within 30 days. You give up 5 percent, or $500, to get your money up front instead of later and for pushing the collections issue over to the factoring company. Collection becomes their problem, not yours.

If you are in a cash crunch, factoring can save your hide. However, here are the down sides, and they are not trivial. If you factor on a regular basis at 5 percent per month, then you are paying 5 percent × 12 = 60 percent annual interest on your money. Wow! That's big bucks for the convenience of having your cash earlier instead of later. On the other hand, if you need it, you need it.

You can minimize the sour taste that factoring percentages can create by performing your own factoring services. If you have substantial personal resources and you own a corporation, you can use your own money to replace the need for factoring. You can buy the receivables from your corporation with your personal funds and provide the same terms as a factoring company. At least, the interest is going into your favorite account (yours!) instead of some other company's. You will, however, need to declare the interest income on your personal tax return. After all, it is income that you earned as a private individual even if the money did come from your own corporation.

Unfortunately, you can only factor up to the limit allowed by your personal resources. You then must look for other options.

Using Credit Terms to Enhance Your Cash Position

Timing is the secret to success, and that is particularly true when working with money. The time that money is in your hands, or in someone else's, either makes you money or costs you money. You must make every possible effort to turn your sales into cash as quickly as possible, paying as little as possible to get your money faster, such as by factoring or offering fast-payment discounts.

You have an excellent opportunity to improve your cash flow by simply changing the way you pay your bills and collect receivables from your clients. If you must pay in 30 days and your clients must pay in 60 days, you have a problem. On the other hand, if they pay in 10 days and you pay in 45 days, you are in excellent shape. You accomplish this by simply offering your customers a discount (such as 2 percent of what they owe you) for payment within 10 days. Many companies will jump at the chance to save the 2 percent, and it's certainly cheaper for you to offer this discount than to pay a factoring service 5 to 15 percent for the same result!

That's the Spirit

Ultimately, the way we handle our money indicates our spiritual maturity. No matter how much we have, we are called to find our security in the Lord. The poor widow is a good example of keeping a loose grip on our bank accounts:

[Jesus] watched the crowd putting their money into the temple treasury. Many rich people threw in large amounts. But a poor widow came and put in two very small copper coins, worth only a fraction of a penny.

Calling his disciples to him, Jesus said, "I tell you the truth, this poor widow has put more into the treasury than all the others. They all gave out of their wealth; but she, out of her poverty, put in everything—all she had to live on." (Mark 12:41–44)

Think about it. Plot out on a piece of paper the timing of payments made and received. Assume that a $10,000 sale is made today. Mark on a calendar when you expect to provide the products or services, when you plan to receive the payment made under your credit terms, and when you have to pay your vendors and employees. Notice that the arrows for money going out and money coming in have a delay between them that usually doesn't work in your favor. You must pay the suppliers before you receive payment. Now mark where payment would be received with a 2 percent per 10-day incentive. Isn't life easier when the cash is in your hands, instead of in your customer's account?

Buying on Credit

Your grandmother may have always told you to stay debt-free because a person in debt is a person in trouble. Well, that might be true for certain people, but credit is the lifeblood of a growing company. Credit in itself is not bad. It is how you use this credit that matters.

Try this technique for increasing your cash situation. Instead of paying $25,000 in cash for that bunch of computer equipment you intend to buy, why not go to your bank and have them give you a loan secured by the equipment? The bank will probably want 20 percent ($5,000) down and the rest financed over 24 to 36 months at the going interest rate. Notice that your monthly expenses go up, but you have $20,000 cash in your bank account to handle unexpected cash shortfalls.

How much debt is too much? This is often determined by ratio analysis, which is discussed in Chapter 11. Keeping the applicable ratios under the danger levels for your industry should allow you to use credit to your benefit and increase your cash situation. By the way, you can also use ratio analysis to monitor when you have too much or too little cash on hand.

Even your grandmother would agree that paying your bills while keeping some cash on hand is a healthy state of financial being and relieves day to day financial stress on your family.

Taking Out a Loan

You can imagine that every business has exactly the same problems in turning its receivables into cash. It should not surprise you that people, even banks, provide loans designed to cover exactly this short-term timing situation. It is essentially a line of credit secured by the receivables, and you are expected to pay it down as quickly as possible. (See Chapter 12 for information on this type of loan.) The interest rate is around 9 to 13 percent annually, instead of 60 percent, and you establish a credit history with your bank. That always pays off in the long run because the bank can become an integral partner as your success requires higher and higher borrowing levels.

Equity Funding

One reason to incorporate (see Chapter 6) is to be able to sell stock for funding purposes. Notice that a stock sale makes the shareholders owners of the corporation and you do not need to repay their stock investment. They are taking a risk with their investment and get a say in the company operation in exchange. Taking out a loan still keeps the company 100 percent under your ownership and control, but you have to repay the debt. These shareholders now own a portion of the company. This is called *equity financing* or *equity funding*.

---

def·i·ni·tion | **Business Buzzword**

When someone gives you money in return for owning a portion of your company, they are providing **equity financing** or **equity funding**. You are giving up equity in the business in return for capital. You don't pay back equity financing. Investors get their money back by selling their shares to someone else. The other kind of financing is **debt financing**, in which you get a loan that you must pay back later.

Equity funding is obtained through three basic means: selling shares of stock to private investors, selling shares of stock to professional investors such as venture capitalists, and "going public," which involves selling shares to the general public on one of the stock exchanges. You will initially deal with the first two financing options and, if you are successful, eventually have the opportunity to go public.

Pick Your Investors Well

Selling shares of stock looks pretty good on the surface: You sell a portion of the company in exchange for some cash. All you give up is a little ownership in the company to get the cash you need. What is the down side? As usual, it comes down to whom you choose as your investors.

The more sophisticated the investor, the better an ally she will make down the road. A professional investor knows the pitfalls associated with running a business and can guide you through potential minefields. However, professional investors also tend to be demanding and relatively heartless when you do not perform as expected. From their perspective, not living up to your plan indicates a lack of business control. A professional investor will take you to task if needed because she has a vested interest in your success.

Your Uncle Billy, on the other hand, might not need monthly reports from you on your progress and might purchase your company's stock on his faith in your ability alone. This makes getting your initial funding easier but might hurt you down the road. Suppose that the company has a rough quarter, for reasons that are out of your control, such as flood or war. Billy might not understand why that dividend check you promised didn't arrive. He might not understand why you need more money due to the unforeseen circumstances. In fact, Billy might not have deep enough pockets to fund the next round of investing.

Be forewarned that many family conflicts have erupted over investments made in businesses that ultimately went under. Do you really want to be responsible for risking your Uncle Billy's retirement fund?

That's the Spirit

Money is "circulation." It needs to flow. When you are frightened, selfish, or when you hoard everything for yourself, you literally stop the circulation. ... The way to get the flow going again is to start giving. Be generous. Pay others well, tip your waitress that extra dollar. Support several charities. Give back. Watch what happens! Things start popping up out of nowhere. The same dynamic is true if you want to fill your life with love or anything else worthwhile. Giving and receiving are two sides of the same coin. —Richard Carlson

Professional investors also bring a wide array of business expertise and contacts to the table. This broadens the business resources available to you as the founder while also opening potential new marketing opportunities. In short, if you can get a trustworthy professional on your side, that is a better route than Uncle Billy.

In fact, the optimal investor might be another company with services or products that complement your offering. This other company might buy a certain percentage of your company's shares to provide a legal link between their organization and yours. This not only provides you with cash but also allows you to partner with them on a tighter basis when approaching the marketplace.

That's the Spirit

As Jesus said to his disciples, " Give as freely as you have received." (Matthew 10:8)

Some companies specialize in marrying one company's offerings with another company's in such a way that everyone wins. Naturally, they get a portion of the deal as payment for their matchmaking services, but without them, you might not have found the proper business mate.

Never knowingly involve someone in your business that you do not trust. You will be busy enough worrying about expanding your business; you do not need someone questioning your every move and undermining what you do. Work harder, cut expenses, and adjust your cash float before getting involved with an investor who might be a potential headache.

Ultimately, it is your job to increase the value of the shareholders' investments. You can do this by improving the company's sales while decreasing the cost of making those sales. In short, your job is to make the company more profitable from one year to the next. If the profit the investors see is not substantially greater than what they could get from other investments such as the stock market or bonds, then why should they invest in you? Your job is to give them a better return on their investment than they could have with traditional methods.

The Stock Exchange

The likelihood of selling stock in a successful public offering is slim to none in the first few years of operation. The reason? You have no track record for an investor to evaluate. In general, you should not consider making a public offering until your company has seen at least four to eight quarters of profitable operation, with profits growing in each quarter.

The first time you sell shares to the public is called an *initial public offering* (IPO) and an excellent means for new companies to raise large amounts of capital for expansion.

A company needs $5 to $10 million in sales to make an IPO worthwhile because the $250,000 to $500,000 cost to handle the offering makes it almost impossible for smaller companies. Those expenses include legal and filing fees, public accounting fees, document printing (not a trivial item), and underwriter fees.

def·i·ni·tion

Business Buzzword

The first time you sell shares of your stock to the public is an **initial public offering (IPO)**. An **underwriter** is a company that handles all the paperwork and filings associated with marketing your stock.

The *underwriter* is critical to the success of the offering and receives a hefty fee for that assistance (around 9 to 12 percent of the offering). Start looking for an underwriter today if you plan to go public in the next few years. An underwriter will advise you when and how to go public so you get the most money for your stock sale. Ask other companies that had successful IPOs who they recommend.

The basic procedure for an ideal public offering is …

- Have at least four profitable quarters with sales of at least $5 million a year.
- Find an underwriter who sees your company vision and believes in what you have to offer.
- The underwriter prepares an investment *prospectus* (a formal legal document detailing the pros and cons of investing in your company) and SEC registration statement, while coordinating accounting and legal activities.
- The underwriter then handles the marketing and sale of the stock. He gets 1 to 2 percent of the initial offering amount and another 7 to 10 percent of the total value of the actual stock offering.
- Hope that the stock market is in an upbeat mood on the day that your IPO issues.

Business Buzzword

A **prospectus** is a formal legal document detailing the pros and cons of investing in a company. An underwriter prepares it.

As the business owner of a public company, you must do the following:

- File quarterly and annual reports with the SEC, along with annual certified financial audits.
- Create quarterly *proxy statements* (forms through which shareholders can vote on important issues) for new shareholders and annual financial reports.
- Announce and hold shareholder meetings.
- Prepare and issue special statements whenever a major, or "material," change such as new company ownership, directorship, or operation changes occurs.
- Send out dividend statements, checks, and tax reports.
- Complete special paperwork for the stock exchanges themselves.

In short, going public requires a lot of additional paperwork and staff. Consider these costs before deciding to go public.

The four basic public exchanges used in North America are the New York Stock Exchange (NYSE), the American Stock Exchange (AMEX), the NASDAQ, and the Canadian Stock Exchange. The New York Stock Exchange is usually for more established companies; the American Stock Exchange is another alternative for medium to large companies. The NASDAQ is where most new companies find a stock-trading home. The Canadian Stock Exchange is becoming a viable alternative funding avenue for firms based in the United States. Stocks are often priced at low investment amounts (under $1.00), and the restrictions are less stringent than those of NYSE, AMEX, or NASDAQ. Your underwriter is your guide into this world.

That covers the basics of cash flow in a nutshell. But the wonderful world of credit still beckons. How will you respond? (Read on.)

Taking Charge:
Credit Card Sales

Phil was pumped up! Sales were going through the roof and things appeared to be financially on track. Why did his accountant want to talk with him? What could possibly be wrong? His trusty accountant, Raymond, was smiling but also shaking his head.

"Phil, how would you feel about having another $1,000 in your pocket this month without lifting a finger?" asked Raymond. He knew Phil well enough to already know the answer.

"Sure, and what's your cut for bringing this opportunity to me?" asked Phil.

"Not a nickel. Do you remember those two large training contracts you signed last month? The one for $17,000 and the other for $15,000? Well, guess what? The clients decided to charge the sales to their American Express card, and American Express charged you 4.5 percent for processing those charges! These clients both have great credit records and probably would have jumped on the 2 percent discount we offer for payment within 10 days. In short, you gave up at least 2.5 percent of the sale price because your salespeople wanted to get credit for the sale before the end of the quarter!"

"Hmmm," Phil thought. "2.5 percent of $32,000 is around $800, and 4.5 percent of $32,000 is worth close to $1,500. The sales reps just cost me enough to pay for a family vacation to Hawaii!"

Credit cards are becoming the new form of legal tender. I know people who carry credit cards, a checkbook, and an ATM card, but little or no cash. It is important to consider whether offering your clients the opportunity to pay using a credit card, instead of cash or a check, is a good thing. This chapter shows you how to make that decision.

How Do Credit Cards Work?

If you plan to go into a retail business, you have no choice. You must offer credit cards as a payment option or you risk losing sales. Period. However, if you'll be selling consulting services costing tens of thousands of dollars, a credit card is probably not the best way to get paid. Instead, request a completed credit application and a company check.

That's the Spirit

As you think about credit, take a moment to consider the basis of your relationship to God. The Bible, over and over again, makes it clear that you are a beneficiary of God's free credit (Jesus paid for your forgiveness). Here is how the prophet Isaiah proclaimed the heavenly "credit terms":

Come, all you who are thirsty, come to the waters; and you who have no money, come, buy and eat! Come, buy wine and milk without money and without cost.

Why spend money on what is not bread, and your labor on what does not satisfy? (Isaiah 55:1–2)

A person obtains a credit card from a bank, which provides a line of credit to the person whose name is on the card. The credit card is issued as a Visa, MasterCard, Discover, or some other brand name. (American Express produces its own card, which requires payment in full each month, and provides its own credit processing operations, which I'll discuss in more detail later.)

You, as a business owner, set up your own account so that you can have credit card sales deposited in this account. You are issued a *merchant number* by your credit card processing company that helps them identify exactly who you are and where your money should be deposited.

> **Business Buzzword**
>
> A **merchant number** is a number given to your company that is used to identify which account should be credited when a customer makes a purchase. It also verifies that you're allowed to accept credit cards in payment.

The line of credit is generally *unsecured,* meaning the bank has nothing that it can take and sell to repay the person's debt if the person defaults on payments. The only recourse is to cancel the card and bother him until he pays. Fortunately for you, the business owner, you get paid whether your customer pays his or her bill or not. That's what you pay the credit card companies for.

When a person purchases something from you and pays using a credit card, he is using his line of credit from the bank. The bank is essentially agreeing to pay the person's obligation to your company and takes the responsibility for obtaining payment from the person whose name appears on the card. In short, the bank is giving the person a loan that he uses to buy a product or service from you. In return for taking responsibility for collecting payment from the cardholder, the bank charges you a fee. Of course, you still get paid even if the credit card company doesn't.

You can generally think of a buyer who uses a credit card as someone with a line of credit from a bank. The company whose name appears on the card, such as Citibank or Chase, handles the cardholder credit application and marketing of the card. You process a customer's purchase using the credit card and signed receipt. In return, the bank deposits the amount of the purchase (minus the fees) into your bank account. The company that processes and clears your company's credit card transactions, debiting the charged amount from the proper credit card and then crediting your bank account, is called the *card processing company.* Such a company can be an independent business just like yours, and thus not affiliated with the credit card issuer. On the other hand, some banks now have their own credit card processing units.

PaymenTech (1-800-866-9113) is one credit card processing company you might want to contact.

> **Business Buzzword**
>
> An **unsecured line** of credit is a line of credit that is not backed by some form of collateral.

> **Business Buzzword**
>
> A **card processing company** is one that processes and clears your company's credit card transactions.

The Costs of Credit

Sounds pretty simple, doesn't it? Run the card through the credit card machine, punch in the purchase amount, and press Enter. You've just gotten paid. Too cool! Too easy! What's the catch?

The catch is that there's a cost to this great service. Take a look at who gets a piece of that simple transaction.

For the purposes of this discussion, I assume you are processing the transaction electronically as opposed to manually. With a manual system, you have to call and request authorization by voice, rather than let the credit card machine dial automatically by modem. The processing company also typically charges a higher fee for manual processing. Electronically is truly the way to go unless you only process a few credit transactions per month.

Terminal Fees

First is the cost of the equipment used for processing the cards. It is sometimes called a swipe machine because you can either type in the numbers on the keypad or swipe the card through the slot on the top of the unit. It comes from a *credit card transaction processing company*, a company that is often a bank or a bank's sales representative who acts as a liaison between your company and the credit card processing network. The machine is essentially a small computer terminal that connects you directly to your credit card processing company.

The credit card processing company typically charges you an application fee ($65–$100) and a programming and installation fee ($35–$50). For these fees, you can accept payment by Visa, MasterCard, and probably Diner's Club and Carte Blanche, but not American Express or Discover.

> **def·i·ni·tion** **Business Buzzword**
>
> A credit card trans-action processing company acts as a liaison between your company and the credit card processing network.

American Express has its own processing network called the Electronic Draft Capture (EDC) network. This is AmEx's way of processing customer purchases made using its card. Once American Express receives and completes your request, you must contact your terminal provider (the folks who are renting you the credit card processing machine) and make sure that they program your machine to process American Express transactions.

Bankruptcy Alert

Trying to avoid hassles by not going electronic will probably cost you money. Everyone is better protected with electronic processing because you lessen the chances of mistakes and omissions, and you should probably just take the electronic plunge from the start or expect to pay higher discount and transaction fees.

American Express charges you a fee for the privilege of being set up on its network, usually $65 to $100. It also sends you a box full of supplies, including an imprinting machine (the box you use to imprint a person's name and number onto a sales slip) and sales and credit receipts. Of the organizations I worked with in setting up my accounts, American Express was by far the easiest to work with.

Of course, nowadays, credit card companies provide all-in-one units that automatically print out a computerized receipt after the card is swiped; no imprinting is done anymore except on manual systems.

But wait, there's more! The Discover Card also has its own network and requires the same actions. Call Discover at 1-800-347-2000 to start the process and get the electronic terminal.

Should you simply buy your own terminal instead of renting one? Good question, and the answer depends on your volume, monthly rental fee, and current cash situation. Rent for a few months and see how it goes. If after six months you start to resent the monthly charges, you should either go back to a hand processing system (in which you manually call each charge for verification) or buy your own electronic terminal. Typical costs for such terminals are $250 to $300.

Here you are with your credit card terminal and some receipts, ready to sell your product or service using credit cards. You thought the analysis was over, but it is really just beginning. In addition to the setup charges and terminal costs, the credit card companies also want a percentage of the transaction amount and often a per-transaction fee as their compensation for guaranteeing the charge. Read on to find out how much you have to pay for this privilege.

Hot Tip

American Express has been, and probably still is, the preferred credit card for business-related expenses. American Express claims that more than 70 percent of Fortune 500 companies use its card and that many companies require that all business expenses be placed on the American Express Corporate Card. Be aware, however, that American Express frequently charges higher fees than the other credit card companies.

Monthly Fees

First, you pay a monthly fee for the electronic terminal ($25–$40) that is automatically deducted from your bank account by the service company. You are also going to pay a monthly service fee ($5–$10) for the reporting of your account activity during the month. This is also automatically taken from your company checking account.

The credit card company then charges your company a percentage of the transaction amount for each purchase. This fee varies between service providers, credit card companies, the type of transaction involved, the size and frequency of the transaction, and whether the transaction is processed electronically or manually. The bank charges you a transaction fee for each deposit made to your account. The following table shows typical discount and transaction fees for the various credit card types.

Typical Discount and Transaction Fees

Credit Card Type	Discount Rate (Percentage of Purchase Amount)	Transaction Fee (Cost to Deposit in Bank Account)
Visa	1.8–3.0%	20 cents
MasterCard	1.8–3.0%	20 cents
American Express	4.0–4.5%	Varies
Discover	1.8–3.0%	20 cents

Keep in mind that home-based businesses may be charged higher fees by the processing companies—often starting at 3 percent.

Here is what you get for the fee and how the process works when you have an electronic system:

1. You run the card through the credit card machine (called swiping the card). The terminal reads the card number and card type off the black magnetic strip on the back of the card.

2. The credit card terminal requests the transaction amount and expiration date of the card. You type both when requested and tell it to process the transaction.

3. The terminal dials the card processing company and sends the information to the computer, which then confirms the card isn't stolen and the cardholder has enough money available on the card to process the charge.

4. If everything is okay, the computer responds with an approval code that you write on the sales receipt. If your machine is connected directly to a printer, the receipt prints automatically when the transaction is approved, just as you see in most restaurants and high-volume retail stores these days.

5. The credit card processing company deducts the proper percentage from the purchase amount and deposits the rest in your business checking account. You essentially get the money right away instead of waiting for 30 days and taking the risk the customer won't pay. Make sure that your bookkeeping system is set up to track these charges.

Hot Tip

Find a company that provides access to Visa, MasterCard, Discover, and American Express as a single service. If your company doesn't want to do this, at least find out how to set up your machine so that it processes all the different credit cards.

6. Most banks also charge businesses a transaction fee for each deposit you make, so you are also charged for credit card deposits.

7. The processing company sends you a summary statement every month that outlines all transaction dates, sale amounts, credits applied (product returns), discount rates applied, and net deposits. This statement is handy for reconciling your bank deposits, invoices, and receivables when you have customers paying by different methods. Your bookkeeper definitely needs this statement, so don't throw it away.

Covering Your Legal Bases

We are always happy to sell our products or services and receive payment, but what happens if the client later contests the charge and refuses to pay? What if the person using the card isn't supposed to be using it? You could be stuck with a huge bad debt that takes a large number of healthy sales to correct. The following table lists a few things you can do to minimize the chance of those situations occurring.

Credit Card Sales Protection Procedures

When Someone Charges Something in Person	Actions and Reasons
Check the expiration date to make sure it is still valid.	Look at the Valid From and Good and Through dates on the card and check that it is embossed, not printed.
Look for a hologram or other security mark.	These emblems are difficult to duplicate. If you can't find one, you might be holding a fake card.
Disclose the terms of the sale and get a signature, if possible.	The more that's in writing and signed by the customer, the harder it is for him to contest the charge. Make sure terms and conditions are easily spelled out on the receipt.
Run the card through an imprint machine, fill out the sales draft completely, and get a signature.	Take the customer's card and run it through an imprint machine using the proper sales receipt. Make sure it is legible and completed with all pertinent information included. Verify that the signature on the card matches that provided by the customer on the sales form.
Get an authorization number for each transaction.	Run the card, amount, and expiration date through the electronic terminal to receive a sales authorization from the service company. Write the authorization number on the sales draft.

The preceding information is taken from the December 1992 issue of the Agency Inc. Newsletter, Volume 3, Number 12. This publication is dedicated to servicing the SABRE-related travel agencies and is available for subscription by calling Source Publications at 918-491-9088.

If you plan to take orders over the telephone without seeing the customer and getting his signature, you can still take a few steps to better protect yourself. Because the chances of getting burned over the phone or by mail are much higher than in person, the credit card companies will probably charge you a higher discount rate for this type of transaction.

When processing a telephone transaction, follow these steps:

1. Get all credit card information and repeat all numbers, dates, and names.

2. Verify that the person making the purchase is the person to whom the card was issued.

3. Always get an authorization number and write it on the sales receipt.

4. Verify the person's billing address before he hangs up.

5. Get him to come by to pick up the merchandise. Have him sign the sales form at that time.

That's the Spirit

When you lie down, you will not be afraid;
when you lie down, your sleep will be sweet.
Have no fear of sudden disaster
or of the ruin that overtakes the wicked,
for the LORD will be your confidence.
(Proverbs 3:24–26)

If you are conducting e-commerce, remember that the Internet is open to everyone. Your website is like an open invitation to break in when viewed by a hacker. Don't stay awake at night worrying about this; however, you must consider the legal and financial responsibilities associated with taking customer payments by credit card over the Internet.

If you are processing a credit card sale by phone, if at all possible, fax the customer a copy of the invoice including all credit card information. Request that he sign the invoice and return it to you by fax for a rough "signature on file" agreement. A signature on file agreement means the customer agrees to pay you for all future charges against that credit card by the same customer. A formal signature on a file card includes the agreement duration of effectiveness, the names and sample signatures of all persons authorized to charge against this credit card, an imprint of the credit card, credit card expiration date, termination stipulations, and change-related conditions.

What to Do if a Charge Is Contested

Unfortunately, even if you have a credit card payment approved, you can still run into problems. There is a lot of credit card fraud floating around these days, and certain people take advantage of situations if given the chance. Your established customers are not usually the problem. New customers, or those you will never see again, can leave you with a bad bill or a contested charge that can cost you a lot of money.

Taking the steps outlined here might seem like a hassle, but you will have a fighting chance with the credit card company if the charge is ever contested or disputed by the customer. If the customer signed the sales draft, saw the terms and conditions, and clearly knew what was being purchased and the proper amount, you have an excellent case in your favor. The more of the transaction that was handled in writing, the better the chance you have of keeping the money. Caution and procedures make the solution to this possible trouble area. Define credit terms, stick with them, and fight for your money when the time comes.

Sometimes individuals "forget" that they authorized a charge to your business and they challenge the payment. Then the card processor automatically removes the money from your bank account. I contacted one customer who genuinely forgot a purchase that had been delivered to her winter residence. Even when I produced her written agreement that the charge was valid, and I filed all the correct paperwork with my merchant bank, the customer's card company has yet to pay me back after nine months of waiting. Seller, beware!

> **That's the Spirit**
>
> As a Christian, you want to find a balance between forgiving "seven times seventy" and yet holding customers accountable under the law. Do watch out for unscrupulous offenders who will use your Christian faith to manipulate your responses when credit card fraud is obvious. As the Scripture teaches, Christians are to be "shrewd as snakes and as innocent as doves." (Matthew 10:16)

> **Bankruptcy Alert**
>
> Beware of how discount and transaction fees affect your profits. Accepting American Express for a $10,000 charge from a solid account customer, for example, puts $450 to $500 in American Express's pocket instead of yours. In that case, you might be better off persuading the customer to pay by other means. Using American Express instead of net 30-day payment terms with solid credit customers can cost you thousands in unnecessary credit protection expenses.

Responding immediately to any inquiries from your credit card companies is essential to maintaining your merchant status. For many retailers, losing merchant status would be disastrous. Don't test the system. Answer their questions, provide any information requested, and enjoy the additional sales you're earning because you are able to accept credit cards.

Of course, you do need to fully prepare yourself for the customers who might refuse to pay. How do you handle those situations? Find out in Chapter 15.

Chapter 5

Collections: When Customers Don't Pay

It is an unfortunate fact of business life that some people do not pay their bills on time. That's why billing customers for products and services you've sold is only part of the process of getting paid. You must plan from the start to have an effective credit and collections policy, and stick to it.

Not handling credit and collection properly can put you out of business, even though your sales exceed expectations. Staying on top of payment due dates is also critical to ensure you're paid promptly. This chapter will teach you strategies for collecting from customers, as well as tips for dealing with customers who don't pay as promised.

Avoidance Is the Best Remedy

Just as avoiding saturated fats is a great way to minimize the likelihood of a heart attack from clogged arteries, avoiding non-paying clients is the best way to avoid business problems from depleted cash reserves. Here are some things you can do:

- Maintain close contact to be sure customers are happy. Don't just deliver goods and send out the invoice. Follow up with a phone call. Once your customer is happy, your chances of being paid rise significantly.

That's the Spirit

Nonpayment of debt is classified in the Bible as a form of sin. Paul says in his letter to the Romans: "Pay all your debts, except the debt of love for others. You can never finish paying that." (Romans 13:8)

Bankruptcy Alert

If your business is growing quickly, your expenses are also growing quickly, giving you even more reasons to pay closer attention to your collections. If you aren't receiving customer payments in a timely fashion, you may soon be bankrupt.

- Implement credit policies from the beginning. Do not make exceptions to the policy without good reason to back it up.

- Avoid giving credit to new customers without first having them complete a credit report.

- Set up credit approval arrangements with finance companies for easy purchase of high-ticket items on credit. Once approved, the consumer receives a loan and you receive money from the finance company. Everyone wins.

- With service contracts, stage payments based on job completion levels. In this way, you have gradual payment for services provided and also have checkpoint milestones where you can gauge the customer's satisfaction level.

- Follow-up after you've sent out the invoice. Be friendly but firm as soon as the payment is due. Always give customers the benefit of the doubt if they have a history of purchases from you and have paid promptly in the past. But do ask for a date when you can expect payment, and follow up on that date.

By being friendly with customers—but getting across the point that payment is expected—you increase the chances of keeping that customer, rather than losing him over some angry words. However, if you've spoken with a customer two or three times and a promised payment has still not arrived, it's time to get more assertive.

You do not want to provide a service or sell a product to a customer only to find out that the customer cannot pay. If you run the financial numbers, you will find you must sell three or more of what you originally sold to recover the profits you would have received from the deadbeat order. However, you can never really make up for a customer sale that never gets paid and turns into a bad debt expense.

For example, at a 50 percent profit margin, a $20 sale costs $10 to produce; you make a $10 profit on the sale. When that client does not pay, you lose not only the profit but also the initial cost of the product, or $20. To recover that $20, you must sell two more items that make you $10 each in profit to recover the initially lost $20 sale, and at this point, you still haven't made any money. Add to this cost the collection fees, court costs, employee expenses, and interest expense on the loan you took out to cover the delinquency, and you can easily see that nonpaying clients are an expensive problem you need to avoid. The moral of the story is that no matter how hard you work, you can't make up for lost profits or cost of goods sold.

Some people treat the first deadbeat sale as a sunk cost (that is, money already spent that can't be recovered) and only look at recovering the $10 cost to produce the product as what they need to break even. I prefer to consider the cost of the entire lost opportunity, which makes me more respectful of the value of good customers and more leery of offering credit to companies or people I don't know.

Products Versus Services

Dig into a few of the legal issues before you start offering products or services to your customers. All product sales transactions are covered by the Uniform Commercial Code (UCC), which are laws developed in the 1940s to ensure uniform sale transaction laws across the country. Although UCC rules are complicated, I will try to simplify them for you here.

A thorough understanding of contract law is critical to understanding business because you are really selling an agreement, or contract, to perform a service or sell a product. In its simplest form, the customers agree to buy what you agree to sell, with all of the mutually agreed upon contingencies attached. The contract usually only comes into play when something has gone wrong and the parties involved cannot work out their differences among themselves.

The UCC only covers the sale of products ("goods" in UCC terms) and does not cover the sale of services. According to the Statute of Frauds section of the UCC, if you are selling goods with a sale price of $500 or more, then you must have a written contract before you can go after someone for a breach of contract. Under $500, a verbal agreement is enforceable, but it is still a good idea to get it in writing. If a client is serious, he will sign an agreement that outlines what is to be provided. If you think about it, the agreement protects both sides and helps prevent the possibility of a misunderstanding.

To have an enforceable agreement or contract, you must at least have

1. The seller and buyer specifics, such as name, address, and phone number.

2. The specifics regarding the products in question, such as quantity, price, and description.

3. Specific delivery and payment terms.

This might sound like a lot, but if you think about it, you couldn't really provide the product unless you knew this information anyway. Most importantly, both parties must sign the agreement.

If you plan to provide services, then you should have some type of written agreement between the client and you that outlines the services to be provided, the amount of up-front expense involved, the total amount of the service contract, when services are to be performed, and when payment is expected. Once again, if a customer hedges on signing a simple agreement with this basic information, then he will probably hassle you when it comes time to pay.

Getting some type of nonrefundable deposit up front (somewhere between 25 and 50 percent) is also a good idea as an indication of the client's seriousness and might help minimize the possibility of his changing his mind after you have already started the project. It is also a good idea to have clear, objective completion milestones that trigger partial payments.

For example, assume that you are an architect designing a house for a client. You might request 25 percent payment upon signing of the agreement, 25 percent upon completion of the first artist renderings, 25 percent upon completion of the final drawings, and the final 25 percent upon acceptance of the plans by the local building authorities. Notice that each of these steps provides the customer with a clear picture of the overall project, you get paid for the work done to date, and you built in quality checks to make sure that everyone is happy. Happy customers pay. Unhappy customers gripe, complain, take up time and energy, and often don't pay.

Cash First—Credit Later

Possession is nine tenths of the law, and this is particularly true when it comes to cash. Whoever has the cash is in the catbird seat, and more cash is almost always better than a lot of receivables from customers who can choose to pay at their discretion.

There are various ways to receive cash instead of dealing with credit of any kind. Cash comes in its standard green form (which is almost never used in nonretail businesses), personal or company check, bank draft, cashier's check, or letter of credit (which is typically used when dealing with international shipments).

Hot Tip

If you are burnt by a bad check, start a list that shows the bad checks received and from whom. Some companies post the bad checks for public display. This is not necessarily legal, but peer pressure is often a strong motivator.

Bank drafts and cashier's checks are like cash because the issuing financial institution took money from the customer or an account before issuing the draft or check. There is a warm fuzzy feeling that you get deep in your pocketbook when you get a check that you know will go into default only if the issuing bank goes out of business.

When accepting a personal check, make sure the person giving you the check signs it and that the signatures match, and get two forms of identification, such as a driver's license (for identity) and a major credit card (which indicates acceptable credit). Make sure it is not postdated or written in two different colors of ink.

When shipping products, you can request COD, usually provided by United Parcel Service (UPS), which means that the customer must write a check to the delivering driver before the product is left. There is a COD processing fee for the service. UPS then sends you the customer's check for you to cash.

Letters of credit are used frequently for international transactions. The customer's bank issues the letter of credit, which ensures that the funds in question are available for transfer once the company receives the desired products or services it ordered. The funds are then transferred from the issuing bank to your bank, and everyone is happy. (See Chapter 16 for additional information on international credit.)

That's the Spirit

It is better not to vow than to make a vow and not fulfill it. Do not let your mouth lead you into sin. ... Much dreaming and many words are meaningless. (Ecclesiastes 5:5–7) High-ticket credit sales agreements should always be in writing. If a customer is afraid to commit to a sale in writing, what makes you think that he won't hedge on paying you later?

Selling products or services using credit terms (such as net 30 days) is at the bottom of the credit ladder when dealing with consumers. Most larger commercial transactions are handled on a credit basis, meaning the customer has a specified time frame within which he can pay, which is usually 30 days. After 30 days, the account is considered delinquent, and collection procedures are started. (See "Know Your Rights When It Comes to Collections" later in this chapter for more about collecting from delinquent accounts.) Attaching a late payment penalty and interest for late payment helps keep commercial accounts current, although in some states, it might affect your collection position should the company become insolvent and declare bankruptcy. Check this out in your state before making this decision.

You probably need to offer credit terms to your standard customers, just as you want credit terms from your regular vendors. It is just a part of doing business that most people accept as a standard requirement. Here are some suggestions for handling credit transactions:

- Set an amount above which you require a credit application and credit background check before extending the credit.

  Sample credit applications are available at most office supply stores. Make sure that you ask for at least three credit references as part of the application, and then call the references to verify the prospective customer's credit standing.

- Do the background check before you issue the credit or risk being disappointed later. Customers understand your need to protect yourself.

  Some of the bigger credit information agencies include EquiFax Credit Information Services and Trans Union Credit. A credit report costs a few dollars but can save thousands if it keeps you from making a poor credit extension decision.

- Offer customers early payment benefits, such as a 2 percent discount for payment within 10 days of invoice receipt. I know of one business that always takes advantage of these 2 percent terms; the owner claims that they save a lot of money doing that.

  For example, if you pay $20,000 each month to vendors and each offers the 2 percent early payment discount option, you can save $.02 \times \$20,000 = \$400$ monthly, which could be the monthly payment for another piece of equipment.

- Separate the sales process from the credit decision. If the salesperson is paid commission on sales revenue and not on paid accounts, then there is an incentive for the salesperson to provide a liberal credit policy because it makes it easier to sell. She gets her commission and you get a possible bad debt. Avoid this conflict of interest by separating the credit and sales decisions, unless you plan to do both yourself.

- Make sure that you run a credit check on your larger companies, and perform your credit checks every 12 months or so because company situations change. You are always looking to verify the "three Cs" of credit: character, collateral, and cash. If you know that company to be one of integrity, they pass the character test. Collateral and cash tell you about the company's current ability to pay the debt it is incurring. You can often verify the cash situation by calling their bank and verifying that they have enough cash to cover the credit they are requesting.

Collection Letters

Okay, you've decided that offering credit to your customers is a good thing. What can you do to best ensure they pay as agreed? There are four steps to take:

1. Make sure your clients understand the credit policy when they initiate the transaction. This means being clear about when payment is due, what the interest rate is for late payments, and whether there are any additional fees or penalties for late payments. Do not hide the specifics because this only contributes to later misunderstandings. They can either accept the terms or negotiate new ones.

2. Give an incentive to pay early. Offer a small discount (2 to 5 percent) for payment within 10 days. This gets the cash into your hands more quickly and provides them with a financial incentive to pay earlier instead of later.

3. Call 3 to 5 days before the 30-day point (or whatever due date you've set) to verify billing information and to remind them the payment is due in a few days. It is also a good idea to ask if there will be any problems with payment.

4. Once the account goes past the payment due date, it is time to begin the collection process. Your customer has broken his agreement and should be handled as a delinquent account. If you are prompt with the follow-up, he will probably pay more promptly in the future to avoid the embarrassment.

A standard accounting report, called an *accounts receivable aging report*, shows you the customers who currently have credit, the total amount they owe you, and the number of days the account is past due. Most computerized accounting packages can easily provide an aging report that you can use as your trigger for focusing on trouble accounts. Run the aging report at least every two weeks, and make sure the collection follow-up is prompt, consistent, and professional, yet firm. Collecting outstanding debts is an interesting balancing act as you keep your customers on track with their payments without offending them.

Bad-Debt Ratio: Counting on the Nonpayers

Each industry has its own standard *bad-debt ratio* (the ratio of the uncollectable funds divided by total sales, expressed as a percent). This information is generally provided by Standard Industrial Code (SIC) or North American Industry Classification System (NAICS) and is available from Dun and Bradstreet or through the *Almanac of Business and Industrial Financial Ratios* (Prentice Hall).

In general, your bad-debt ratio should be under 1 percent of your sales, but certain industries might see bad debts as high as 2.5 percent. Mail-order businesses can have bad-debt ratios that are much higher than businesses that deal with customers directly. Companies with high bad-debt ratios must take this into account each year or they will face a rude awakening when the bills come due and they are out of cash.

You need to create a policy that dictates when an account is treated as a bad debt. Talk with your accountant to determine when this should happen. No matter what your situation, develop a tracking ratio that allows you to monitor changes in the situation closely.

In-house personnel can handle everything outlined so far. However, there may come a point where you need the assistance of a collection agency (more on this to come).

 That's the Spirit

Neil Orchard writes in *Illustrations for Preaching and Teaching* (Baker Books):

I was talking with a farmer about his soybean and corn crops. Rain had been abundant, and the results were evident. So his comment surprised me: "My crops are especially vulnerable. Even a short drought could have a devastating effect."

"Why?" I asked.

He explained that while we see the frequent rains as a benefit, during that time the plants are not required to push roots deeper in search of water. The roots remain near the surface. A drought would find the plants unprepared and quickly kill them.

Some Christians receive abundant "rains" of worship, fellowship, and teaching. Yet when stress enters their lives, many suddenly abandon God or think him unfaithful. Their roots have never pushed much below the surface. Only roots grown deep into God (Colossians 2:6–7) help us endure times of drought in our lives. So hang in there even if some customers aren't paying you.

Know Your Rights When It Comes to Collections

Suppose you come to the conclusion that a person is clearly not going to pay you. This should not happen very often, but when it does, you need to decide if pursuing this customer is worth the time and effort. Make every effort to resolve the disputed amount before pushing things into court. Once the legal gavel falls, the conversation becomes stilted and often nonproductive. Get all agreements in writing to build your case if you ever have to take legal actions.

Small claims court is provided for resolving smaller dollar disputes in the $500 to $5,000 range, depending on the state you're in. Small claims court is designed for non-lawyer types, and the rules are a lot less strict than seen on Perry Mason. Larger dollar disputes are handled in other courts and usually require the assistance of an attorney.

You will need two trips, minimum, to file a small claim: one to file the claim and the other to appear in court. You have to file in the county where the events occurred or where the nonpayer is resident. If you are suing a company, you need to file suit in the county in which the company is doing business. Unfortunately, it is much easier to win a judgment in small claims court than it is to collect the money. The judgment in your favor is a necessary first step and might be ego gratifying, but receiving the payment is your goal.

Just because you won doesn't mean that you will be paid! It is your responsibility to collect the money involved, not the court's. Your basic collection options are:

Hot Tip

A collection agency charges a fee for their services, usually between 25 and 33 percent of the amount they collect for you. Higher fees might be charged for specialty accounts that require more involvement by the agency.

- Wage garnishment, where the employer is instructed to remove a specific amount of money from the customer's paycheck.

- Nonwage garnishments, where the money involved is deducted from a company bank account.

- Property attachments, in which physical property is confiscated to pay the debt.

- Attaching the bank account, which means the company has to pay you first before paying any other bills. This might work if you are suing a business and know the company's bank account number.

Of course, none of these are options unless and until you have a judgment in your hands.

You can also file a lien against property owned by the nonpaying party. This lien is recorded at the courthouse and secures the debt with the prescribed property. The property cannot be sold until all liens are removed.

Numerous books on the market deal with the detailed intricacies of collections in general and the small claims process in particular. The best medicine for bad debts is to avoid them, if at all possible, using some of the techniques covered earlier in this chapter.

And when all else fails, and you still want to pursue a nonpaying customer, then you might consider a collection agency. Whether the agency is national or local in coverage depends on your specific situation. Both kinds of agencies are listed in the Yellow Pages of your phone book. No matter where you find the agency, get a few references from their existing clients before you let them represent your company to your clients (even if they are nonpaying clients).

The Tax Man Never Rests

Beware of the tax man when assessing the impact of bad debts. If you are using an accrual basis of accounting, then you are taxed on the outstanding receivables until they are declared as bad debts. This is because the receivable was recorded as income when the work or sale was completed. Consequently, you could be paying taxes on bad debts. Unfortunately, you have the burden of proving the debt is uncollectable, or bad, should the IRS call you on the expense deduction. Discuss your bad debts with your accountant before taking the deduction.

If you are on a cash basis of accounting, then the tax man only appears when the cash is received. Because you only record a sale as income when you actually get paid, there is no such thing as "bad debt" from the IRS's perspective. Of course, you want to pursue the money that's owed to you, but you only pay taxes on the sale when you actually receive the money.

Now, assuming your credit policies are working just fine, and business is thriving in your own country, suppose you want to open up markets internationally. Chapter 16 will show you how to proceed.

Chapter 16

Doing Business Internationally

History and literature are full of stories of entrepreneurs who weathered the high seas and foreign cultures to create business empires for themselves. These stories make international business sound like the last bastion of "wild west" entrepreneurship. In fact, international business is nowhere near as perilous as the stories might have you believe.

Is doing business internationally more complicated than simply selling domestically in your home country? Yes. Are the risks associated with international business higher? Yes. Are there opportunities that exist on the international market that just do not exist in your country? Yes. Can you turn those opportunities into financial rewards for you, your company, and your family? Absolutely, but you need to be smart about how you take advantage of them. This chapter shows you how.

However, this chapter is not designed to teach you how to create an international business. That topic is far too complicated to cover adequately in a single chapter, and Appendix B lists several books that provide an excellent starting point. My intent is to explain the realities of international business transactions so that when you start getting marketing interest or orders from international customers, you are prepared with enough information to transact the business in a credible way.

International Business and the Internet

Believe it or not, if you have an Internet presence, you could find yourself in the international sales business, whether intended or not. (See Chapter 10.) Remember that when dealing with the Internet, a person in Tokyo is just as close to you as a person in Chicago. Assuming that the Tokyo person can read your site, which is possible because English is rapidly becoming a primary international business language, that person might want to order what you advertise on your site.

> **That's the Spirit**
>
> Though your purpose is profit, never lose sight of the fact that you are in business to serve others. "They serve God well, who serve his creatures." —Caroline Sheridan Norton

> **Bankruptcy Alert**
>
> Faxing is great in that it transcends all time zone barriers, but beware the cost of sending faxes internationally because these costs can mount quickly. Using the Internet and e-mail for international communication is much cheaper.

How do you get the product to them? How do make sure that you get paid? How do you collect if they default on payment? How do you plan to service your product if it has trouble? By the way, there are many English-speaking countries around the world such as Australia, New Zealand, South Africa, England, Canada, and others. You have the same collection, delivery, and service problems with them as you would with the prospective Japanese customer.

In short, as soon as you present a site on the Internet, you open yourself to international orders. Is this good? I believe orders in most any denomination are good, as long as the customer gets what he expected when he ordered and you get paid as you expected. Read the rest of this chapter to familiarize yourself with the basics of taking an international order, shipping the product, and receiving payment. Take the risk out of doing business with that enormous international community by setting a few procedures based on these simple rules.

Taking and Processing Orders

I remember when my company got its first international order request. First we were excited, but as we walked through the many details associated with filling the request, we started to panic.

Use your international customer as a resource with respect to determining the best way to ship from your country to theirs. Ask them about the methods that have worked best for them, use their advice, and then protect your financial interests. In this way you can save a lot of legwork, get your customer the products and delivery schedule they want, and minimize your financial exposure. Communication is always important, but it is particularly important when dealing across cultures, even when both parties share a common Christian faith!

Giving Product Information

For starters, look at the information request itself. Remember that the person at the other end of the request might not speak English as a primary language, and you should make this process as simple for her as possible.

If you received a request for information by a posted letter, fax, or e-mail message, responding with a lot of words is generally not a sound approach. Responding with product number, prices, and pictures is better. Keep your message short, polite, and clear, and you stand a better chance of your response being well received.

Finally, you may want to investigate the use of a translation service that will actually convert your literature from English into your selected foreign language. There are even some computer programs that claim to do a solid translation job. You might try one of the programs and then give the translator both the original copy and computer-generated translation for a critique. It might save time on the first translation and may save money on future ones.

Shipping and Handling

Both you and your customer should understand that products take a longer period of time to ship. When you ship internationally within shorter periods of time, the costs increase substantially.

Your customer is responsible for paying the shipping and insurance costs associated with the order. Let her tell you how the order should be processed so that it passes through her country's customs service with the least amount of headache and unnecessary expense.

If you incur the shipping charges because your customer bills them against your account, then make sure that you have a guaranteed method of payment with either a letter of credit or credit card (as discussed later in this chapter). If possible, use one of their designated shipping accounts so that you can avoid as much of the risk associated with international shipping as possible.

Let's face it: Boats sink. Planes crash. Countries go to war and economies falter. You don't want to be in a position where you ship $15,000 worth of products to a country that just began a civil war and find out that you cannot get paid.

Pricing and Exchange Rates

When you establish prices, you do so using your home economy denominations, such as U.S. dollars. Designate this by including "USD" after all prices or by stating on the invoice that all amounts are in U.S. dollars. In this way, your customer inherits the *exchange rate liability* because you are paid in your home country currency.

If you keep up with international exchange rate trends, it is possible to make money off the exchange rate variations between countries by quoting prices in the currency of your customer's country or by specifying an exchange rate that is used for the transaction. (Assume that there are no exchange fees to simplify the discussion.) There is money to be made here, but it will take diligence on your part. And I suggest that you get your international business up and running before you worry about optimizing exchange rate financial opportunities.

For example, assume that your product sells for $10 USD, and the Euro is trading for 1.79 per dollar. This means that a person buying your product must pay you 17.9 Euros (1.79 × 10) to buy the product. You then convert that 17.9 into $10 US (17.9/1.79 = 10). Simple so far. Yes? This example is simple because it assumes that the exchange rate does not change between the time that you agree on a price and the time that you receive the payment and convert it into your home country's currency. Now, look at the same example and see what happens when the exchange rate fluctuates.

For the day in question, you quote a price of 17.9 Euros. Assume that the exchange rate on the day that you convert the Euro payment into USD is 1.60. When you convert your 17.9 into dollars, you now receive 17.9/1.6 = 11.19, or 1.19 more than the price in US dollars. Why? Simply because the international exchange rate changed enough, and in your favor, to allow you to squeak an extra $1.19 out of the transaction.

> **def·i·ni·tion** **Business Buzzword**
>
> **Exchange rate** is the number of one country's currency in exchange for one of yours. For example, you can exchange a certain number of U.S. dollars for a certain number of Euros.
>
> **Exchange rate liability** is the negative impact of a fluctuation in the exchange rate from the time that you make a purchase agreement to the time the money actually changes hands.

Could the exchange rate have just as easily gone the other way and cost you money instead? Absolutely. Prove it to yourself by using an exchange rate of 1.85 Euro per USD and show that this type of fluctuation would have cost you money.

That's the Spirit

Many factors might influence your decision *not* to do business internationally. You may need to secure your local markets first. You may not have the time, capital, or other resources to handle expansion. However, there's one reason that should never keep you from reaching out to internationals: pure prejudice.

Do not oppress an alien; you yourselves know how it feels to be aliens, because you were aliens in Egypt. (Exodus 23:9)

He giveth to all life, and breath, and all things; and hath made of one blood all nations of men. (Acts 17:25–26, KJV)

There is neither Jew nor Greek, slave nor free, male nor female, for you are all one in Christ Jesus. (Galatians 3:28)

Making Sure That You Get Paid

Collecting from nonpaying customers in your home country is bad enough. Now try collecting from a person who lives 10,000 miles away. Not a chance! Extending credit for international shipments is very risky business indeed, and should only be considered once you have an excellent working relationship with the client and you understand the legal safeguards on both sides for the specific country in question.

When getting paid, cash is always king, but few people are going to send cash internationally in exchange for goods unless your company is well known to them and they perceive that the transaction has minimum risk. You can start out with your terms being "Shipment upon receipt of payment in full in USD as a cashier's check for products and shipping" and see how this is received. If it works, great. If not, then try some of the other approaches.

Credit cards are another excellent way of ensuring that you get paid for internationally shipped products. The credit card transaction is basically the same throughout the world, and most people are familiar with the process of paying for something over the phone with a credit card.

Bankruptcy Alert

Don't assume that the laws of your customer's home country match those of yours. Even in the U.S., laws vary between states. Assuming a law to be true is simply setting yourself up for a disappointment at best, and a disaster at worst. Check with a specialist on your target country or make sure that you are financially covered before committing yourself. You can find a specialist through your country's embassy that is based in the target country or by trying SCORE for referrals.

For smaller dollar amounts and working with smaller companies, I have found this to be the best approach. You perform a standard credit card verification, just as you do with a domestic shipment (see Chapter 14). In this case, however, make absolutely sure that you get a fax of the order signed by the cardholder with his or her printed name and date next to it before shipping your products. You don't want an international order going into dispute. As the dollar amounts and companies become larger, you must use other payment methods.

Some clients may offer to send a set of financial statements from which you can provide credit. This is risky business in that there is no guarantee that their financial statements were created using the same GAAP guidelines used in the United States. In short, you may not really understand what you are reading and the statements could be more fiction than fact.

The most common form of international financial transaction for sale of products or services is a *documentary letter of credit* (L/C). With this type of payment, your bank deals with your customer's bank and both banks act as intermediaries to ensure that the transaction happens as agreed. This provides protection to both of you. The following steps outline a standard *irrevocable L/C* transaction between your customer (suppose she's in India) and your company in the United States.

1. You and the customer agree upon the terms of the sale. Typical items agreed upon during this stage are price, quantity, time frame, shipping dates and method, payment terms, revocability of the L/C (discussed later), the banks involved on both the buyer and seller sides, whether partial shipments are allowed, when the letter is opened and when it expires, and how the letter is to be transmitted between the parties. Notice that the banks are not involved in any of these terms; you and your customer must work them out.

def·i·ni·tion **Business Buzzword**

> An **irrevocable L/C** is one in which the customer who issued the L/C cannot change the L/C terms.
>
> A **confirmed L/C** obligates your bank to make payment on the L/C to you upon presentation of the proper paperwork. This means that your customer's bank is extending the customer enough credit to cover the purchase.
>
> A **documentary L/C** is a financial arrangement set up between your bank and your international customer's bank. The banks act as third parties that verify receipt of product and transfer the funds.

2. The customer goes to her bank, in India, and establishes the L/C.

3. The customer's bank opens an irrevocable L/C naming your company as the recipient, which includes all the terms and conditions that you and your customer agreed upon.

4. The customer's bank sends the L/C to your bank, requesting confirmation of its receipt.

5. Your bank then faxes to you a copy of the L/C along with a confirmation letter.

6. You review the L/C and confirmation letter for proper terms and conditions. At this time, it is a good idea to verify with your freight forwarder that it can meet the delivery deadlines specified. If not, then you should contact the customer to change the L/C terms to reflect the proper dates. The banks then re-issue the documentation.

Hot Tip

Be a good steward of your business resources. It is not uncommon to request payment in advance for a percentage of a large order. This is a good-faith gesture on the customer's part and it provides you with some protection later if the customer is slow to pay. (By the way, this rule holds equally true for domestic orders.)

7. You arrange with your freight forwarder to ship the product as indicated in the L/C.

8. When the forwarder has the products ready for shipment, they prepare all the needed documentation including the *bill of lading*, which lists products included in this shipment.

9. The freight forwarder sends a copy of the paperwork, including the bill of lading, to your company.

10. You present the documentation to your bank, indicating that the shipment is on its way.

11. Your bank usually airmails the documentation to your customer's bank, which then reviews the paperwork and sends it to your customer.

12. Your customer uses the paperwork to claim the goods when they arrive in India.

13. Your bank then honors the L/C payment terms and deposits the proper amount in your account. The timing of this deposit is based on the terms agreed upon at the beginning of the procedure.

Notice that the documentation is critical to proper execution of an L/C transaction. If the documentation is not executed properly, and consistently, it is very likely that your product shipment and payment receipt will be held up for a long time.

Here are some things to check when executing an L/C:

- Make sure that you have an irrevocable statement that states that the L/C is confirmed by the designated bank.

- Verify the spelling of the name and address of both the customer and your company. It must be consistent across the board.

- Make sure that the L/C amount is enough to cover not only the product involved, but also the shipping, insurance, and other fees associated with the shipment.

- Beware of shipping or other documentation dated outside of the date range defined on the L/C.

- Watch for extraneous markings on the invoice that are different from those found on other documentation.

- Make sure you allow for breakage or loss during shipment, called *shrinkage*. To accommodate this situation, include the term "approximately" or "about" before the L/C amount. This provides a 10 percent variance allowance.

- Watch for inconsistent pricing, quantities, product descriptions, or other terms of sale.

Is this starting to look like a lot of paperwork? It can be, but that's better than not getting paid. Notice that this bank-to-bank handshake confirmation provides protection for both the seller and the buyer.

Are you going to handle all of this paperwork yourself? Probably not in the early days. Instead, you want to work with a *freight forwarder* who can walk you through the paperwork maze. A freight forwarder is a company that manages the shipping of products from your country to others.

Find a forwarder who works with your target countries by looking in the Yellow Pages under "Freight Forwarding". Try this procedure for selecting a freight forwarder: Pick a typical shipping scenario regarding country, products, and so on that applies to your company and have several forwarders bid on the cost of their services for handling this shipment for you. Compare the services and costs and then make the decision that is right for you.

That's the Spirit

Almighty God, who hast so linked our lives one with another that all we do affects, for good or ill, all other lives: So guide us in the work we do, that we may do it not for self alone, but for the common good; and, as we seek a proper return for our own labor, make us mindful of the rightful aspirations of other workers, and arouse our concern for those who are out of work; through Jesus Christ our Lord, who liveth and reigneth with thee and the Holy Spirit, one God, for ever and ever. —The Book of Common Prayer

There are various types of L/Cs; talk with your banker to determine the one that is right for your particular situation. The first few times you go through this letter of credit process, you might wonder why you ever got involved, but once you see the checks appearing in your bank account, you will wonder why you waited so long.

Going International—All the Way

Assume that you have been bitten by the international bug and want to make that a primary focus of your business. I admire your fortitude and sense of adventure, but I want to caution you on the complexity of your intended venture.

It is difficult enough to run a successful business within your own country. Those difficulties increase exponentially (that is, a lot!) when you decide to cross cultural, language, economic, and geographic boundaries. Unless you have a specific country, market niche, and maybe even a product in mind for your international venture, then I suggest you test it at home first before moving overseas.

Opening up foreign markets takes time and money. Most small businesses have limited amounts of both. To address this situation, they look for established outlets in their target countries and allow these outlets to sell and distribute their products for them. You get ready market exposure, and the distributor gets products that might otherwise be unavailable. Once you find the right outlet in your target country, follow their advice on how to present the product for best acceptance.

Pick your countries carefully or you can find yourself spread all over the globe and not making money anywhere, including at home. Most people I know choose countries where they once lived or where they have relatives. Speaking the local language is also a plus that is hard to over-emphasize.

Also, don't underestimate the overall complexity of selling a product or service internationally. You must comply with legal and governmental regulations, or you can incur the wrath of your government, the target country's government, or both. Check with your country's consulate office in the target country for advice on how to break into the local market. They often employ people who are dedicated to fostering economic relationships between the two countries. These people can save you hours of struggle and introduce you to people who can provide the services you need.

Can it be great if it works? You bet. Can it be overwhelming as it ramps up? Yes again. I suggest that you take your international orders when they come and follow the letter of credit procedures outlined in this chapter. As your experience in other countries increases, you will find the natural migration path for taking your company and offerings international. Now, with all those world-wide orders flowing in, do you need to add some help? Time to move into Chapter 17!

Part 5

Growing Your Business

You probably hope to create a business that grows quickly. Every entrepreneur does. As you start to succeed, you may find yourself asking a pretty strange question: "What am I going to do if I get too many orders for my product today?" Trust me, this is a good problem, but a very real one. Eventually, you will probably find that you need to hire employees to keep the business going and growing.

The majority of businesses in the United States are one-person shops with no employees. If you hire someone, you're bigger than most businesses—so congratulate yourself when you get to that point.

In this part, you'll learn how to find employees, calculate how much you need to take out of their paychecks in taxes, and use other automated systems to make your life much easier. The production chapter forces you to consider all the little details you must think about if you plan to build your dream widget. Then when you become really, really successful, the last chapter of the book will help you keep your feet on the ground.

Help Wanted: Adding Employees

So your business is growing, and you need help. Great! Adding employees represents a great leap forward for your business; there is so much demand for your product or service that you need to expand your staff. Yet managing other people brings with it a number of issues that you don't have to deal with when you work alone. In this chapter, I'll show you how to manage and lead your employees—successfully.

When You're Successful, You'll Need Help

If you follow all the great advice I'm giving you, you will probably become so successful that you just won't be able to do it alone. At that point, you need to add employees to your organization. It might be only a clerical person who handles billing and answers the telephone or a complete staff of people who handle all those new projects you just brought in as a result of your incredible marketing skills.

In either case, you need to address the new challenges associated with running an organization that now has staff members. There are lots of ways to find employees, but before I jump into how to find the right employees, how to manage them, and all that detailed stuff, let me briefly present a few bigger issues for you to consider:

1. Make sure that you actually need an employee for functional reasons, not simply because you want someone around the office for business companionship.

2. Realize that employees cost money and must pay for themselves either today or in the near future.

3. Remember that you become the last employee to be paid if the company has cash flow problems.

4. Expand your business operations to include employees; they'll take up space, use telephones, and make decisions.

5. Become familiar with the challenges of encouraging and leading employees. A training course is probably a good idea.

6. Be aware of the large effect one person can have on your business, your customers, and your earnings.

7. If you are in a service business, make sure that your employees reflect the image you have worked hard to establish. Each new employee must maintain the same level of dedication to customer satisfaction.

8. Don't forget that employees can always (and probably eventually will) find another job.

9. Don't ignore the numerous legal issues related to having employees. Check into them!

Bankruptcy Alert

If the company only makes money when you are there, then a vacation becomes much more costly than the trip itself. You're really paying for: the actual vacation expenses, lost company revenues as a result of not being at work, and the time needed to get back up to speed once you return to the office and find you are very behind in your work. The solution? Set up your pricing so that the times you work cover the times that you are off.

Don't ever forget that you started this business. It is yours, not your employees'. Try to let go of the daily decisions so that they can carve a place for themselves in the operation of the business, or you will wind up with morale problems down the road. Remember, however: You sign the checks, co-sign all company debts, and ultimately make the big decisions. They might also need to be reminded of this as you give them increasing responsibilities and they naturally take more initiative. How you do this is a matter of style; don't be too heavy-handed because an over-bearing boss can easily drive away a good employee. It is an interesting balancing act to promote employee initiative while also making sure that the employee doesn't get you into financial trouble.

Once employees take on more responsibility for the company's activities, you might wonder how you ever did everything yourself. There isn't a more satisfying business experience than to find a series of orders, invoices, projects, and bank deposits that your employees created without your involvement. To call in from a well-deserved vacation and find thousands of dollars worth of revenues and profits coming into the company while you are gone is the essence of small business success.

That's the Spirit

Entrust to reliable men who will also be qualified to teach others. (2 Timothy 2:2)

The concept of hiring up is critical to your success. Essentially, hiring up means you hire and work with people that are more qualified than you. That's right, better than you.

It won't come as a surprise to very many of you that the factor that prevents people from subscribing to this philosophy is fear. The fear that "I can be replaced" or "someone might be better than me." —Richard Carlson

Your business needs to be able to create revenue without your involvement or it will never grow beyond your own abilities. That can only happen when employees get involved and have the freedom to act on their own, within certain guidelines you set.

Keep an eye on your strategic goals (check out Chapter 3). Do you want the company to become bigger than you or simply support you and your family? If you want to keep it small, then you might never need another employee, other than an occasional relative or temporary helper to handle clerical stuff. If you want to grow so the company works on a relatively independent basis, then you need employees. Accept that as a reality and plan for it in advance. That way, you can be on the lookout for the right person and snatch her up when the timing is right.

Business Buzzword

An **independent contractor** is a temporary worker hired on a per-project basis.

Good Help Isn't Hard to Find

Start out the hiring process by first getting a clear picture of what you want this person to do. In essence, create a job description. Then picture the personality type you want in that job. Ask other business owners about personnel that they have worked with that might be right for your job opening. Place ads in the paper and prepare yourself for hours, or days, of reading resumés and interviewing applicants.

Business Buzzword

Work-study programs at many universities provide an excellent way to test-drive a new employee, without exposing yourself to

Depending on your personnel needs, there are a few avenues you can take when you begin seriously looking for employees. First, you can try out potential employees through a part-time employment arrangement before making a full-time hiring commitment. You can also hire candidates for a specific project, as *independent contractors*, and see how they work out. Finally, temporary help agencies can serve as excellent sources of candidates who have already been screened for your particular job opening.

Temporary Agencies

Temporary agencies provide a wide array of personnel talents, from clerical (secretarial or typist) to industrial (heavy lifting or construction) to professional (CPAs or consultants). Turn to a temporary employment agency if you need someone on relatively little notice or for a short period of time. These people are also great for seasonal work, such as during the holiday rush, or for periodic work, such as end-of-month inventory taking.

There is rarely any long-term commitment for a specific temporary person, so when you decide to stop using him, make a phone call and he is gone. You can bring in temporary help almost on a moment's notice and use his services only for the amount of time you need them, but you do pay a price for this convenience.

That's the Spirit

The power and authority of your service will correspond to your dedication to a hidden life of prayer. —Anonymous

Expect to pay at least $12 per hour for a worker through a temporary agency with minimal computer and clerical skills. The price goes up from there and varies based on geography. (You tell the agency the skill set you need and they give you an hourly rate that they charge for that person.) You do not pay that person's payroll taxes, medical, or other benefits, and she is never an employee of your business; she is employed by the temporary agency.

Independent Contractors

Independent contractors come in all shapes and sizes. As with temporary agencies, you hire a contractor for a particular job and you let her go when you are done. Contractors expect to be let go at some point, so the parting is rarely accompanied by hard feelings. Typically, the length of a project is specified in a contract when a contractor is brought in, so there are no surprises about what happens when the work is done. (She leaves unless you want to hire her to work on a different project.)

Generally, these folks have an area of expertise such as accounting, computer graphics training, or specific business skills you know your company needs. You must qualify a contractor on your own and decide whether that person is the best for your specific project. The working relationship is between your company and the contractor directly, but she works as a consultant to your firm, not as an employee. You have no ongoing obligations to the contractor.

One of the major differences between working with a contract employee and a temporary employee is that your company directly hires the contractor to do a specific task. A temporary employee is actually an employee of the temporary agency, and this agency "rents" her to you for a fee. With independent contractors, you spell out up front exactly how long they are asked to work, on what project, to do what specific types of activities, and at what cost. It is also a good idea to spell out the risks that you expect the contractor to assume, such as liability insurance and all associated payroll taxes.

Hot Tip

It is incredible how complicated it becomes to determine whether a person is an independent contractor or an employee. The IRS has a set of criteria that they consider when defining an employee's status. Use these criteria to substantiate your claim that a person is a contractor instead of an employee. Check out the IRS website for more information (www.irs.ustreas.gov). Also, you might call the IRS office in your city and request its Publication 937 on independent contractors to determine whether you have employees or contractors, or call 1-800-TAX-FORM.

Temporary employees, on the other hand, really don't have any part in setting the terms of their work with you; their employer discusses those with you and then provides the individual best suited to help you out. In many cases, temporary employment contracts are open-ended so you can end them whenever you want. With an independent contractor, you work out the specific end date of the project up front.

Expect to pay more for the contractor than a temp. One reason is that the contractor is operating as a business owner, too, and must cover all his business costs with each project. Typical price ranges for writing services start at $15 to $20 per hour, document layout and design contractor fees range between $20 to $45 per hour, and professional services such as attorneys range from $65 to $150 per hour. The beauty of working with a contractor is that the person comes in with well-developed skills that are immediately applied to your situation with little or no training needed. You get the desired results quickly and efficiently.

When hiring an independent contractor, remember that the IRS has specific criteria that determine whether a person is a contractor or an employee. If you hire someone as an independent contractor but the IRS decides later that she was really an employee of your company, you might be liable for past payroll taxes, Social Security payments, and penalties. Be clear up front about how the IRS would characterize your relationship before taking chances with an independent contractor.

Take Your Employee for a Test Drive

Because everyone is always on his best behavior during job interviews, it is very difficult to determine whether a person is a good fit for your company in that setting. You need to observe the job candidate in other situations before deciding whether to hire him.

In other words, just as you can date for a while before deciding to get married, you can test potential job candidates before making a long-term commitment. There are several intermediate steps you can try before taking the plunge.

Part-time employment is a great "try-and-buy" approach where you get to test the water with the prospective employee. Use the employee 20 to 30 hours per week, and see how you work together. If it works, you have someone who comes on full-time with a lot of background and who would otherwise need training at full-time rates. If it doesn't work, you can count your blessings and let him go.

Similarly, you can "try before you buy" with temporary employees. Why not leave the hassles of advertising for employees, interviewing them, and qualifying them to temporary employment agencies who specialize in that kind of thing? All you have to do is tell them what kinds of skills you need; they send over their best candidates for you to check out. After you select a temp and work with her for a while, you can decide whether to try a new employee when her initial contract is up, or you can hire her permanently, which generally means simply paying the temp agency a small fee for all its work.

Checking out college and high school students through co-op programs where the student works for you a set number of hours per week for a semester or during a summer vacation is another option for testing potential full-time employees. After working with a student for several months, you can decide whether to offer her a full-time job when she graduates.

At a minimum, you should establish a 90-day probationary period that every new employee must endure. A probationary period is a time for both you and your new employee to decide whether this is the best job for him. Before the 90 days is up, you must let this person go or he automatically becomes a full-fledged employee, which means he is now entitled to any of the benefits you give your other employees. In other words, on day 91, this person automatically becomes an employee.

There's no reason to rush right into hiring full-time employees if you feel more comfortable taking it slowly. Try some of these approaches to checking your potential employees before making a big commitment to them, even when you're hiring a family member.

More Employees, More Restrictions

All companies are not created equal. Depending on the state where you are doing business and how many employees you have, you will be affected by different rules and regulations. One way to deal with these various state and federal government regulations is to develop a company policy manual, or employee manual, for everyone's reference.

A few personnel issues apply to all companies, regardless of the number of employees. You should clearly spell out the number of company holidays provided to employees each year and the amount of vacation and sick time a person is eligible to take during the year. If you have other company policies that employees need to know, state them in the policy manual.

Drafting your own handbook is cheaper than having an attorney write it, but a legal review is essential to make sure you haven't made significant errors.

State and federal laws kick in at different company-size levels:

- If you have fewer than four employees (depending upon the state), you are the master of your domain and can hire, fire, and reward pretty much as you see fit.

- If you have fewer than 15 employees, you still have a lot of personal discretion on how you work with your employees. For example, race and sex discrimination laws do not apply to businesses of fewer than 15 employees, except as defined by specific states. However, some state employment laws do kick in, based on the state in which you do business.

- If you have between 15 and 49 employees, you have to worry about a wide array of federal laws that address discrimination and other important personnel-related issues.

- If you have 50 or more employees, you need the same level of policy manual as IBM or General Motors. It must include policies on family and medical leave, harassment, drug-related issues, discrimination, and virtually any other workplace-related issue such as smoking.

Bankruptcy Alert

Beware the "policies in a can" approach, which uses a standard software package or standard forms to define your personnel manual. They are probably overkill for your small organization and could open you to unnecessary exposure to legal action.

My recommendation regarding your personnel policy is this: Until you need a comprehensive manual as outlined in the previous paragraphs, simply include those items that you absolutely want and intend to absolutely enforce. A few of these might be no drinking on the job, no smoking in the workplace, excessive tardiness or absenteeism as grounds for dismissal, no sexual harassment, no discrimination in the workplace, and other rules that you know will be enforced.

Medical Insurance

Determining the right medical insurance plan for you and your employees is a potentially confusing and time-consuming process. For starters, you generally must have at least two employees (you and one other) before you qualify for most group

That's the Spirit

Why would a loving God put his children to work as soon as he created them? Because he knew human labor was a blessing. He knew it would provide them challenges, excitement, adventure, and rewards that nothing else would. He knew that creatures made in his image needed to devote their time to meaningful tasks. —Bill Hybels

plans. The coverage may apply to local incidents, but not cover incidents that occur out of town. Does the plan allow you to choose your doctor or must you use doctors who are members of the plan you choose? The world of medical insurance is interesting and complicated. I suggest that you ask a few other business owners how they worked out their medical insurance situation; you might save yourself a lot of legwork.

Do your homework and don't jump at the first plan you see, or you might find yourself changing plans on a regular basis. After all, you also want to avoid causing your family members unnecessary frustration when they need medical attention.

Solicitation and Competition

How could these former employees do this? You spent three years building up that account, and they stole it away within 90 days of leaving your company. Their overhead isn't as high as yours so they undercut your price by 30 percent. What could you have done to prevent this? A *noncompete clause* might have been one way to go. A noncompete clause is an agreement that your employees sign, saying that they won't steal your business ideas or methods and go to work for a competitor or become competitors by starting their own firm.

Business Buzzword

A **noncompete clause** is an agreement that your employees or suppliers sign, saying that they won't steal your business ideas or methods and go to work for a competitor or become competitors by starting their own firm.

Although noncompete clauses are treated differently from state to state, you should definitely look into them as one way to protect yourself and your company from ex-employees stealing your ideas and opening a business across town. When an employee signs a noncompete agreement, he essentially agrees not to compete with you in a specific geographic area (such as in a particular city or region of the country) for a specified period of time (such as one to two years) by performing the same function for another company as he did for you.

The theory says that your director of sales couldn't quit and go work for your competitor right away in a sales-related position. The reality of an employee non-compete is that it cannot keep a person from making a living in his chosen field. In other words, you really cannot keep a person from taking a job as a sales manager or design engineer with a competing firm.

You can, on the other hand, keep that person from using any privileged, confidential, or proprietary system information in his new job because this information is proprietary to your company. A salesman can still sell; he just can't use your customer list. An engineer can design; she just can't use design procedures that are proprietary to your company.

Enforcing an employee noncompete that keeps a person from being able to earn a living in their selected field is a difficult, and usually fruitless, endeavor. You are better served making sure that people know that contact lists obtained at your company stay at your company and are not to be removed when the person leaves.

Hot Tip

Check with an attorney who specializes in employment law to find out whether your state supports noncompete agreements. If it does, work with an attorney to write an agreement that protects you rather than do it on your own.

Business Buzzword

A **nonsolicitation clause** is an agreement that your employees sign, saying that if they leave your company they will not pursue your existing customers for business that is related to your company.

Company confidential documents, which you should make sure are marked as such, cannot be removed from the company premises.

You cannot keep someone from making a living in his hometown. However, the courts will uphold a company's rights to retain its customers without worrying about a former employee stealing those customers away. This is called a *nonsolicitation clause*, which says that the employee agrees to not pursue your existing customers for business that is related to your company. This agreement lasts for a specific period of time, usually one to two years. Former employees are restricted from using the customer contacts acquired while working with your company to aid another company, including their own.

The best way for you to cover yourself in this situation is to have the employee sign a noncompete agreement as part of his employment. This is particularly true for an employee who has regular customer contact. It makes you seem a little paranoid, but it might also save thousands of dollars of business from walking out your front door. When a customer starts to wave cash in front of a former employee, her loyalty to you will be severely tested. Without the noncompete agreement, you might end up with a personal disappointment and a financial loss without legal recourse.

Interviewing Techniques

Start any job search with a clear definition of what you want in the ideal person for the job. Create a job description that includes areas of knowledge the person must have to perform the job. Education and former experience must be clearly defined; develop objective criteria by which candidates can be screened. The more clearly you know what job you want them to perform and the kind of expertise you need, the more likely you are to find the right person to fill the open position.

Be specific in your requirements if you want to minimize the amount of training this employee will require. For example, "must know Word for Windows styles operation" is specific where "computer operation required" is general. If you are willing to train the employee, then you can make the requirements more general which broadens the candidate field.

In reality, and in the eyes of the law, you are trying to find the right person for the job, regardless of race, gender, marital status, or other criteria. The suggested interview procedures help ensure that you find the information you need without jeopardizing your company in the process.

That's the Spirit

Always seek to hire the most competent and ethical employees you can—whether they're full-time, temporary, or outside consultants. "Do you see any truly competent workers? They will serve kings rather than ordinary people." (Proverbs 22:29)

Never bring up the following topics while conducting the interview:

- Marital status
- Veteran status
- Race
- Religion
- Nationality
- Children
- The interviewee's age
- Gender and sexual orientation

You need to know answers to many of these questions after the person is hired because emergency and medical information might pertain to children and spouses, but do not include them as part of the interview. In addition, make sure that you provide no verbal agreements about the length of employment or reasons for future possible dismissal. The person being hired might later construe these as commitments. These verbal commitments might be used against you later if problems arise with this person's performance that cause you to let him go.

Here are several do's and don'ts as taken from *The Personnel Policy Handbook for Growing Companies:*

- Give the applicant a copy of the job description and ask if there are problems performing any of the stated functions.
- Make written notes about the interviewee and how this person meets the criteria outlined in the job description.
- Get the applicant to discuss recent, prior work situations.
- Outline the positive and negative sides of your company.
- Explain the company policy on smoking and such.
- Tell the applicant all the great things about the company.
- Don't ask the applicant about his or her personal situation, such as marital status, parental status, religion, sexual orientation, race, or disabilities.
- Don't make notes on the application or resumé about irrelevant information that could be construed as discriminatory such as hair color, weight, height, and clothing.
- Don't tell the applicant that you are looking for people with limited experience.
- Don't tell some applicants the positive parts of the job while telling others the negative aspects. Be consistent in how you describe the position.
- Don't ask about childcare arrangements.
- Don't lie about or cover up any bad news about the company.

Present the most positive aspects of the company in the most consistent manner. Your final intent is to find the best person to fill the job opening—period. If you mislead them about company-related problems, you can find an employee making a substantial career change under false pretense, which can only lead to management troubles and a possible lawsuit.

Instead you want employees who will happily do the work of your company. And you'll be happy to pay them to do it, right? But will you know how to handle the payroll taxes? That's the topic just ahead …

Chapter 18

The Tax Files: Payroll Taxes

Your business won't grow without employees, but adding employees means adding responsibilities, including the need to manage payroll tax deposits. More than one company has gone under due to improper management of payroll taxes and figuring this maze out for yourself can be costly and legally compromising. This chapter introduces the payroll process and outlines the IRS guidelines for making tax deposits. Learn this well and save yourself money and grief.

Payroll Taxes: Learn How to Deal with Them

Unless you intend to be a sole practitioner all your life, you will have employees at some point, and with employees come payroll taxes. No one I know thinks payroll taxes are fun or interesting, but as a business owner, you need to have a basic grasp of the legal requirements. Otherwise, you can get tangled up in bureaucratic red tape and headaches that make asking for a loan sound pleasant by comparison. You don't have to be a rocket scientist to calculate payroll taxes, but you do have to pay attention to the details. As the Scriptures say, "Whoever can be trusted with very little can also be trusted with much." (Luke 16:10)

Here's one of my favorite business secrets: Just because you have employees doesn't mean that you have to do the accounting for your payroll. That's what staff (and service bureaus and accounting software) is for! Read on for an introduction to the regimented, deadline-filled world of payroll tax accounting—so that at least you can find out what you'll be delegating to someone else.

That's the Spirit

The Pharisies asked Jesus if it was right to pay taxes to Caesar. But Jesus, knowing their evil intent, said, "You hypocrites, why are you trying to trap me? Show me the coin used for paying the tax." They brought him a denarius, and he asked them, "Whose portrait is this? And whose inscription?"

"Caesar's," they replied.

Then he said to them, "Give to Caesar what is Caesar's, and to God what is God's." (Matthew 22:18–21)

Payroll Tax Overview

Ever talk to someone from the IRS? The first thing you need to know is that all taxing jurisdictions (federal, state, and local) have their own requirements and filing deadlines that they take seriously. If you file all the right forms on time, you most likely won't have many problems.

That leads to the next question: How do you figure out which forms to file and when to file them? The three basic types of payroll taxes are income taxes (which you withhold from wages), Social Security and Medicare (you pay half, the employee pays half), and unemployment (you pay it all).

- States and some cities have income taxes, as does the federal government, so you need to consult both the federal guidelines and relevant state and local guidelines to determine how much to withhold and when to pay it over to the taxing authority.

- Social Security and Medicare are easier to figure out because they are federal taxes and subject only to the federal rules.

- Unemployment is subject to both state and federal rules, with potentially complex interactions between the rules requiring even more detailed record keeping.

To find the federal rules, contact the Internal Revenue Service (IRS), which has a package of tax rules and guidelines for businesses, including Publication 937, *Employer's Tax Guide.* It's not the most fascinating reading in the world, I'll admit, but it's something you need to know about if you have employees and handle your own payroll tax accounting. The website has a wealth of information, including the forms and instructions, and is located at www.irs.ustreas.gov.

For the state rules that apply to you, contact your state Department of Revenue (for income tax withholding information), Department of Labor (for unemployment tax information), or Secretary of State (in case you can't find the right bureau to answer your question). Look in the blue pages (governmental section) of your phone book under "Federal Government" or "State Government" to find out where to get the information.

Your employees will give you information about their tax status, number of dependents, and withholding allowances on a federal Form W-4, and you can use that information to look up the right withholding amount in the tax tables or apply the right percentages for your state's formula. Some states have their own version of the Form W-4, which might contain different information from the federal form. In fact, some states don't have any personal state income tax at all. You must check the rules for your particular state and proceed accordingly.

However, just because you figure it out once, don't think you're done for the year. If your employee's pay rate, marital status, dependent status, or address changes, the withholding amounts may also change, and you also have to be aware of the relevant ceilings for Social Security taxes and unemployment taxes. Providing detailed, repetitive calculations is what payroll tax reporting is all about, along with weekly, monthly, quarterly, and annual reporting requirements. If you like this sort of stuff, great! I, on the other hand, use a software package to keep me out of trouble.

def·i·ni·tion | Business Buzzword

Your **employer identification number (EIN)** is a number given to any company that has employees, whether it is a corporation or a sole proprietorship. If you have employees, you must have an EIN to ensure that all your tax payments are credited to the correct account, which is indicated by your unique EIN.

You've filled out the forms and followed the instructions; now you just drop them in the mail and relax, right? Wrong! Federal taxes and some state taxes are subject to depository requirements, and you can't just mail a check with your return. In essence, you deposit the taxes at your local bank using either a payroll tax coupon with your *employer identification number (EIN)* on it or paying electronically. The depository schedule might not be the same as the reporting schedule (this depends on a whole bunch of factors), so read the regulations carefully.

Breakdown of Payroll Tax Payments

Tax Type	Employee Portion	Company Portion	Total	Threshold
Federal Income Tax	As determined from the W-4 form	None	15%, 28%, 31%, 36%, or 39%, depending on salary level	Depends on filing status
State Income Tax	As determined from the W-4 form	None	Determined on a state-by-state basis	Depends on filing status
Social Security	6.2%	6.2%	12.4%	$65,400
Medicare	1.45%	1.45%	2.9%	Unlimited

Employee Tax Type	Company Portion	Portion	Total	Threshold
Federal Unemployment	0%	6.2%	6.2% less the state percent	$7,000 payment
State Unemployment	0%	Depends on the state	Depends on the state	Depends on the state

It is one thing to be late on a payment to a creditor. It is another to be late on payroll deposit payments to the IRS because you are essentially playing with the employee income deductions. It is the IRS's money that you are administering for them. The IRS will eat you alive in late payment fees and interest if you delay, so make sure that you read the next section and file on time.

That's the Spirit

Zacchaeus was a Jew who was a tax-collector for the Romans. In typical fashion, he grossly cheated his fellow citizens for his personal gain. But when Jesus pursued him he gave half of his wealth to the poor and repaid four times those he overcharged. (Luke 19:1–10) Only Jesus could have changed the heart of an "IRS" person like Zaccaeus in such a way!

Filing and Paying Payroll Taxes

You now need to report the deductions to the IRS and make a bank deposit or electronic deposit to ensure that the IRS gets the money you've so carefully deducted from everyone's paycheck.

Tax Deposits and IRS Form 941, Employer's Quarterly Federal Tax Return

Make your payroll tax deposit with a company check at your local bank along with the Federal Tax Deposit Coupon that tells the IRS which company is making its deposit. The coupon should have the deposit amount filled in, along with the box associated with the quarter to which the deposit is to be applied and the type of tax based on the particular IRS form number (941, First Quarter). The bank will give you a standard deposit receipt in return.

You deposit the federal payroll taxes on either a monthly or semiweekly basis, depending on the size of your payroll. If your total tax deposits exceeded $50,000 in the prior four quarters, then you probably have to deposit semiweekly. If not, you can deposit on a monthly basis on or before the 15th of the month. The IRS will let you know, but you are ultimately responsible even if the notice was not received. It is a good idea to keep tabs on the amount of tax you pay. In general, you deposit taxes on a monthly basis for your first year.

The IRS has modernized and set up the Electronic Federal Tax Payment System (EFTPS). The plan basically dictates that employers who must make deposits semiweekly must make those deposits electronically. As might be expected from the government, they had problems with the implementation and extended the deadline for compliance to July 1, 1998. Once again, the IRS will notify you if you must comply with the electronic filing requirements, but you probably shouldn't trust them on this one either. You must complete and return to the IRS an enrollment form at least ten weeks before you plan to make your first electronic deposit.

Make sure that you get your payment into the bank before the end of the banking day. There is a time difference between the end of the banking day and the time the bank closes. Be sure you know when the banking day ends. For example, the banking day might end at 2:00 P.M. even though the bank closes at 4:00 P.M. The deposit must be in the bank by 2:00 P.M. in this situation.

Hot Tip

Depository banks don't have to accept checks on other banks for payroll tax deposits, so when you are choosing your business bank, make sure that it can accept payroll tax deposits.

If no wage payments are made in a month, no deposits are needed. If the 15th falls on a holiday or weekend, you can deposit on the following business day and still be on time.

Semiweekly depositors must stay on top of things. If you pay your employees on a Wednesday, Thursday, or Friday, then your tax deposit must be made by Wednesday of the following week. If payday falls on Saturday, Sunday, Monday, or Tuesday, then deposits are due at the bank on Friday of that week. There is a special three-day rule that adds a day to the deposit deadline for each day that a holiday falls between the payday and deposit date.

You report all the deductions you've taken from the payroll to the IRS for a given calendar quarter on IRS Form 941, Employer's Quarterly Federal Tax Return. This is for payroll tax information only. The form must be in the mail, and postmarked, by the last day of the month following each quarter. For example, for the first quarter (January through March), you must complete and mail the 941 form by the last day of April.

The following table summarizes the payroll filing procedures for you.

Payroll Deductions Made	When Payroll Checks Are Written
Federal bank deposits required	Either semiweekly or monthly, depending on deposit levels. Deposits are made with IRS coupon form 8109 or electronically
Payroll deduction form 941 completed and postmarked	On a quarterly basis on the last day of the month following each quarter
State unemployment reporting and payment	Usually quarterly, but the last day of the month following each quarter
Federal unemployment reporting and payment	Annually, using IRS form 940 deposit coupon form 8109

Payroll tax calculations, deposits, and reporting are initially confusing and become a routine part of operation in a short period of time. Ignore them, and you will pay stiff penalties, so step up to the table and do it right from the start.

State and Federal Unemployment Taxes

This part gets easier. After you've been accruing unemployment payments with each payroll period, your state will make you complete a reporting form and deposit the required funds on a quarterly basis by the last day of the month following each quarter. The federal reporting is done on the IRS form 940, which you must complete annually by the end of January of the year following the reporting period and mail along with a check for the proper amount.

The state tells you what rate you must pay for unemployment, based on past unemployment benefits paid to past employees. This unemployment rate indicates their assessment of the amount of risk your company poses to the unemployment fund. If a number of your employees leave your company and file for unemployment compensation, you see your unemployment tax rate increase. Tax rates reflect expected costs for your industry but are adjusted based on your specific experience. If no one leaves your company and files for unemployment, after a few years your rates might even decrease.

Rules to Live (and Save Taxes) By

Here are a few rules that can save you from making big mistakes:

1. Report your payroll taxes—yes, all of them on all of the nice little forms—when the reports are due. That's right—on time!

2. Make sure that your deposits are accurate and on time. Only an act of God can save you from IRS penalties and fines if they are levied against you or your company.

3. Use a payroll software package such as QuickBooks, which includes a payroll module to ease the payroll process. Get to know the payroll features to save yourself a ton of time and uncertainty.

4. Find someone who understands the payroll tax calculation and reporting process. Have them show you their completed forms and walk you through the process when you first start issuing payroll checks.

5. Stay on top of things, and always include the additional payroll tax expenses when considering an employee raise. Perhaps you should offer your employee

additional benefits instead of a raise because a raise has the additional payroll taxes attached, and certain types of benefits do not incur the incremental taxes.

The payroll tax reporting and deposit procedures will eventually become second nature to you, but it is definitely confusing when you first start out. Get the right advice early in the process and follow it. The late fees are tough to swallow.

As a final note, don't fiddle with these taxes. If you look at where the money comes from, you can see that you are holding your employees' money until deposited. If you are delinquent in making these deposits for any length of time at all, it might be viewed as theft and you can get yourself into serious legal trouble that you really don't want. Don't take chances with payroll tax liabilities. If your company goes under, you still owe these taxes, so pay these guys before you pay everyone else.

Using a Payroll Accounting Service

You always have the option of giving this task to someone else. Your accountant will generally do payroll tracking for you as part of a standard service offering. Outside payroll services specialize in nothing but payroll accounting. You might ask your fellow business owners about how they handle their own payrolls. After all, the payroll tax process is an important concern for all business owners regardless of size and age; experience is a good guide in this area.

That's the Spirit

Who of you by worrying can add a single hour to his life? … Therefore do not worry about tomorrow, for tomorrow will worry about itself. Each day has enough trouble of its own. (Matthew 6:27, 34)

Worry is always a temptation for the business owner. Trying to keep up with taxes alone can create a ton of concern. How do you handle your worries? Why not try eliminating three "worry areas" from your list: (1) things that are going to happen anyway; (2) things that have already happened, and (3) things that might happen but couldn't be prevented anyway.

Chapter 19

Working at Home
or Away

"How's it going in your office at home?" Mary called to ask.

"Great! Instead of getting up at 6:00 A.M. to drag myself downtown by 8:30, now I can leave my bedroom at 8:29 and be at work 30 seconds early," Jim explained.

"Sounds wonderful. What do you do with all your free time now?" Mary asked.

"I work! One of the drawbacks of having an office in the basement is that it's just too easy to keep working long after all the downtown workers have left for home. And, while I see more of my children than I used to, they can be a distraction, especially when I'm on the phone."

"So, are you ready to come back to work with the big boys?"

"Not on your life!" came the reply. "I can handle the distractions, and running my own business from a convenient location is one of the most rewarding things I've ever done. Why, some days, the only reason I leave my home office is to make a deposit at the bank."

Who hasn't sat in rush-hour traffic and fantasized about working from home? What? Give up soot, smog, rude drivers, and several hours of my day to work from a spare room at home? Why do that? Simple: It sounds great. And it can be if you have the discipline to make it work.

Home Office: Pros and Cons

Take a look at some of the good and not-so-good points associated with a home-based business in the following table.

The Pros and Cons of a Home Office

Advantages	Discussion
A 30-second commute from the kitchen to the spare bedroom	You save 1–2 hours per day in time commuting, which provides more time for business. You can also work at night, after others have gone to sleep.
Save money	You already pay the rent or mortgage. Save the money you would spend on office space and put it back into your business.
Tax advantages	You should be able to deduct expenses associated with the office section of your house, which otherwise are not deductible. You might actually make money off the deal. (More on this later in the chapter.)
Family benefits	You are closer to the family, which allows for meals at home. You might be able to rope family members into helping, on occasion.
Risk-free trial run	You can test the water regarding your business idea without incurring a lot of outside financial costs and obligations. If your idea takes off, you can always move to a regular office.
Disadvantages	**Discussion**
Motivational liability	You can get sidetracked into personal stuff such as cleaning the kitchen. Personal phone calls can take up a lot of your day when people know you are at home. After all, "you're not at work" in their mind. You're at home. You need to set them straight on this one.
No commute	On the days when you don't want to work, the commute helps to separate your home life from business. When you work at home, you might spend that extra hour on the couch that otherwise would have been productive.
Lack of peer contact	You are relatively isolated in your home office, whereas a regular office provides contact with other business owners. They are not only colleagues, but also sources of leads, business, and guidance.

Starting your business from home is a relatively painless way to begin either a service business (such as consulting, accounting, massage, and so on) or a small product-oriented business such as mail order or light manufacturing. You are already paying for the house and utilities. It makes sense to use these prepaid expenses to your best benefit, but be cautious of the potential pitfalls associated with running a business out of your home.

> **That's the Spirit**
>
> You shouldn't let your business overtake home life, or vice-versa. Work together to support all the goals of the family. "Home: where each lives for the other and all live for God."
> —Anonymous

This section deals with the financial and personal aspects of working from your home. You'll also find a section on determining the right time for moving out and whether you should lease, rent, or buy your office space.

Watch Your Overhead

As we said when I was in the Army: Uncle Sam can't make you do anything. He can only make you really sorry that you didn't! Working out of your home is financially attractive in the early days, but you need to follow the proper steps to ensure that the IRS allows your desired business and personal deductions.

It is tempting, and reasonable, to assume that expenses associated with the business section of your house are tax deductible as a business expense. They might be, but you have to be careful how you present it on your taxes and back up the claim with paperwork.

As the judge says, "He who has the most paperwork wins!" Documentation of expenses is critical in making your case for home-office business deductions to the IRS.

Here is the key: The business section of your house must be used "regularly and exclusively" for business purposes. This means that your home office must be your principal place of business operation, such as where you actually do your work for clients. You must regularly meet with clients, patients, and suppliers in your home office as a part of your business operation. These meetings must occur in your home office and not in other locations within the house.

You must really use your home office as an office, not as a shortcut for some desirable tax deductions. The IRS is getting tighter on these restrictions instead of looser, and you must take the proper steps up front to back up your case for a home-office deduction.

The percentage of your home expenses that is allocated to your office is calculated on either a square-footage or number-of-rooms basis. For example, assume that you have a five-room house of 1,500 square feet. One room comprises one-fifth of your house if all rooms are about the same size. Take one-fifth of all housing expenses and allocate them to the business as expenses. You just saved money on your personal bills but gave up one-fifth of your house to the business in the process.

You can also use the square-footage approach if the one room is much larger than the others are. For example, assume that the room is 500 square feet of the 1,500 square foot house, or one-third. You can still take the one-third deduction, but you should make the case that this particular room was the best candidate for the office and is exclusively used for that purpose.

> **Bankruptcy Alert**
>
> Local zoning, building, or landlord ordinances might keep you from starting a business in your home. If your business requires customer parking, increases street traffic, or causes wear and tear on your property, you might find it difficult to start a home-based business. Check with the city and your landlord for approval before investing too much money and time into working out of your home.

Beware of your home computer. It is not both a home and business toy when speaking with the IRS, no matter how you really use it. By the way, you probably need to keep detailed track of usage hours or you might find yourself pushing Uncle Sam uphill, which is a tough one. If you plan to use it for business, then use it for business. (You really don't want your kids playing with important business files, anyway.) Keep yourself, your clients, and your family out of this minefield and keep your business and personal computers separate.

See IRS publication 587 for details on home-office deductions. There are also numerous tax guides available at most bookstores that provide detailed information on setting up your home office from a tax standpoint. The laws are changing on this hot area every year, and getting timely information is your best way to avoid trouble.

Don't Get Distracted

I mentioned this earlier, but it's worth saying again: When you work at home, you are tempted to start a little later, quit a little earlier, and maybe hang around at the swimming pool instead of making that business phone call. It's tough to leave the backyard on a beautiful summer day and walk into an office full of paperwork and stuff to do. However, if you don't walk into that office and start working, you will not keep that beautiful backyard for very long. It takes a lot of discipline to work at home and keep yourself on a work schedule. Your family also has to support you or you're already set up for failure.

That's the Spirit

How long will you lie there, you sluggard?
When will you get up from your sleep?
A little sleep, a little slumber,
a little folding of the hands to rest—
and poverty will come on you like a bandit
and scarcity like an armed man.
(Proverbs 6:9–11)

I find that if I impose client deadlines on myself, I can make myself work on those days that I feel distracted—or just want to sleep in till noon. Just as a deadline set by a boss in a normal company can prompt you to work beyond your normal hours, so can a deadline commitment to your current boss—the client.

It is tough to discuss a complicated $10,000 project with a client when little Jennifer walks into the room wearing a pint of chocolate ice cream on her face. How do you help with her needs while closing this client on the project? Get the picture? Work together with everybody in the family to put yourself and your family on a schedule and stick with it. Don't take personal calls at home during certain announced hours. You probably wouldn't take them at your company office, so why take them at home?

Hot Tip

The IRS is forever updating and modifying its guidelines for taking the home-office deduction. If this is a tax move you are considering making this year, check out the most up-to-date information on the IRS's website. Request a copy of their form on taking the home-office deduction at www.irs.ustreas.gov/prod/formspubs/index.html.

Business is business, no matter where you transact it. Otherwise, it's a hobby. You wouldn't have made it this far in the book if you only wanted a new hobby. Stick to business, even if it occurs in the second bedroom of your house. One essential piece of equipment for the home office is a door! Make sure you can close your door to shut out the distractions of home and family life.

Make Your Office a Home

Now, here is the good news. If it really is a business office, then you should spend the money to make it work. Get a comfortable chair. Get the desk and table combinations you need to be productive. Spend the money needed for telephone and computer equipment. You might even want to pop the cash for a stereo just for the office. You'll be spending a lot of time in your office, so make it work for you. By the way, these all become business deductions because they are related to the business. Make your office into a home within your home to ensure that you want to go there and are productive once you arrive.

When Is It Time to Move Out?

You have been working diligently in your office for a while now, and things appear to be stabilizing. Clients expect you to remain in business and start providing you with repeat business. The delivery people know that your business exists and are accustomed to delivering business-related packages to your residence. Things appear to be going along well. Why would you consider moving out of the house and into a new location? Simple; to either make your life easier or to make more money—or both.

Typical indicators that it's time to consider a move include some of the following:

- When the office gets too small for the equipment and number of people you need to run your business.

- When the level of business activity at the house gets so high that it disrupts the daily family routine.

- When your clients begin to wonder about your commitment because you don't have a "real" office.

- When your clients appear uncomfortable coming to your home for business meetings, and you start feeling uncomfortable having them walk through your house to get to the office.

- When you can't get temporary help because the agency won't let its people work in a private residence due to insurance reasons.

In short, you should move out when you have made it and when the problems associated with the business become operational and not financial.

> **That's the Spirit**
>
> "Home is where life makes up its mind. It is there with fellow family members that we hammer out our convictions on the anvil of relationships. It is there we cultivate the valuable things in life like attitudes, memories, beliefs, and most of all, character."
> —Charles Swindoll

Location, Location, Location

Locating your new, "real" office is a lot of fun, but it's time-consuming. Just like buying a house for your family, you are setting up an important part of your lifestyle. A long commute means you are away from home more, but this might place you closer to your clients and prospects. A more expensive space might present the desired image and bring in more money but with a higher up-front cost on your part. Consider all these factors when moving to an office that is not in your home.

Try these nine questions on for size when looking at a new location:

1. If you provide a service, does it make sense to be centrally located near your clients and prospects? Probably. Is the potentially longer commute worth it on your part?

2. Are you moving to please yourself or to improve business operations? Either is fine, but understand your motivations.

3. Will you make up the commute time by being more productive while in the office, as compared to working out of your home? You might spend extra time with the commute but find that your day ends earlier because you are more productive while at work without distractions from home.

4. Is there a competitor in the area of your new office? If so, does this hurt you or help you? Sometimes, people want to "shop around" and look for locations where competing companies are easily accessible. This applies to retail and many professional services. Will this competitor cause you to lose existing clients or make it difficult to gain new ones? If so, should you move far enough away from the established competitor so that you have a geographic advantage in your new location?

5. If you have a manufacturing type of business, does the new location make much difference to the operation? Probably not, because you ship to your clients and you can do that from just about anywhere. Once again, move to improve business operations, not to stroke your ego due to your newfound success.

6. Is moving going to cost you customers? People do not like change unless it benefits them. How will this change benefit, or cost, you or your existing clients?

7. How much more business do you have to create from the new location to justify the additional expense? (Not sales revenue, but actual profits after all marginal costs are taken out.) Is this number reasonable, and can you achieve it within the needed time frame?

8. What if you don't move? What would happen? Is there an external reason forcing the move that takes the "if" completely out of your hands and turns it into a where, when, and how?

9. Can you locate your permanent office in an area that allows you to keep the same phone number? This way, you wouldn't have to ask all your clients to call you at a new number.

I'm sorry that I can't give you standard answers to these and the myriad other questions that no doubt will arise. The answers are heavily dependent on your particular situation, but here are a few rules that might help to narrow the field of confusion:

- Manufacturing business locations are most often chosen based on shipping, receiving, parking, space, and other operationally oriented criteria. If you primarily ship, mail, or work over the phone, it really doesn't matter where you locate your office as long as it supports the daily operation.

- Service businesses that require the clients to come to you are heavily location-dependent. Why would clients go out of their way to come to your place when your competition is just down the road from their office? Get geographically close to your clients, and they will come.

- A nicer location might present a better image but might not necessarily generate more revenue. Don't confuse appearance with profits; they are not always equal. (Read the opposite argument next.)

- Basing your service business in a well-recognized location or building might increase name recognition with your clients. You are associated with this respected office location, which should reflect well on you and increase trust. Trust is a necessary ingredient for any successful service business. Does the new location instill that trust without placing your company in financial jeopardy?

- Retail requires high-visibility frontage. Period. If your customers can't find you, they will not buy. They might not even know that you exist. Traffic is needed and encouraged in a high-visibility location such as a mall, craft and service fairs, downtown areas, and busy streets. F. W. Woolworth learned this with his first store and ended up closing after only a few months. After that, he never underestimated the value of location, location, and location.

> **That's the Spirit**
>
> If you're working from home, you may feel that you have your family obligations fully covered. But it's a matter of what your are focusing on. Is there time for focusing on your family members when the work is done for the day? Can you balance working with paying attention to your spouse and children? As Karen Scalf Linamen said in *Working Women, Workable Lives:* "Our families can survive with less of what we do. They just can't get by with less of what we give them out of *who we are.* Maybe we can't 'do it all.' But we can still give our families our hearts."

Look at what your existing and potentially new competition is doing. Ask your customers about their reactions to your possible move. Get as much information as possible before taking the plunge. It would be a shame to take an operation that is working well from your home with its associated low overhead and place it in jeopardy due to an unnecessary office move.

Here is just a quick reminder to consider things such as lighted and adequate parking for your clients. Our training center's female clients like to use the covered, lighted parking area at night. Make sure that the building is in compliance with the Americans with Disabilities Act (ADA), which requires providing easy access for disabled persons. Check for wheelchair ramps, doorways that are wide enough to accommodate a wheelchair, and restrooms that are designed for wheelchair access. Signs should be posted in Braille for those who are visually impaired.

Ask your potential clients about the things that are important to them; I never expected that restroom design would be as important to our female clients as it turned out to be. I worked with the building management to get our women's restrooms upgraded before those on other floors or the men's. It paid off, and we got higher evaluation marks for our improved facilities and more business from our female clients. Your clients know best what they are looking for. If you provide it, they will come.

Lease, Rent, or Buy?

Should you lease, rent, or buy? This one is simple. Which one works out to be the financially most attractive? Leasing ties you into the same location for a longer period of time but provides you with lease-rate stability. Renting provides you with the monthly option of moving elsewhere, but your rent can fluctuate at any time, and the landlord has the option of asking you to vacate. Buying provides tremendous stability but with a large financial commitment on your part.

I suggest that you consider this progression for a service business:

1. Start out at home until your business warrants moving out.

2. Look into renting space in an executive suite of offices. Here you get the clerical support needed to operate without incurring a huge financial commitment. You can also generate contacts with other suite members. Another option is to explore business incubators, which provide the same level of service as executive office suites, but often with more camaraderie and coaching.

3. Lease your own space when the restrictions of the executive suite begin to cost you time, money, or both.

4. Buy your own building when you have a successful track record under your belt. Many companies use the SBA for funding of this type of business-related building purchase.

If you have a manufacturing business, try this approach:

1. Work out of your house for as long as possible. You might be able to do this by using third-party contract manufacturing houses for the actual production-related activities while using your home for office-related functions.

2. See if you can partner with another company that already exists. Use their surplus capacity as an interim step.

3. Lease your own space when you're confident about future business, such as when you have ongoing contracts or automatic stocking-level agreements.

4. Buy when you are ready. Once again, look to the SBA for help in financing the purchase of a building.

As you expand, you should also keep up with the latest time-and-cost-saving methods of automating your business. That's what you'll explore next, in the chapter ahead.

Chapter 20

Get Automated

Computers and other pieces of equipment are an essential part of business life. The sooner you include them in the operation of your business, the easier it will be to grow and make money. In many cases, equipment and technology can make it easier or faster to accomplish routine tasks, making it possible for you to get more done—and, eventually, spend more time with your family.

You can find a software package to automate most routine office tasks such as word processing, making payroll and tax deductions, keeping spreadsheets, maintaining customer contact information, and more.

Setting up similar systems by hand requires a lot of paper, printed spreadsheets and charts, bound reference material, a calculator or adding machine, note cards, and a lot of pens and pencils. The down side is that all your manual record keeping is not as accurate as a computerized, automated system.

And think of the weeks (yes, weeks!) you would have spent setting up these operations on your own. They are instantly eliminated for a small investment. In other words, do it right and automate from the beginning.

Typical Automation Strategies

Everyone has his or her own opinions about automation, computer systems, and software. Because it's always useful to hear others' opinions on important subjects, here are my recommendations for automating your business. It might turn out later that my suggestions are not perfect for your particular situation, but they should work well enough to get you started:

1. Automate the routine areas of your business operation that don't require any creativity. Consider these tasks: generating invoices, sending mass mailings to clients, generating proposals, pricing calculations, tracking customers, sorting employee performance evaluations, and handling payroll, tax-related clerical tasks, accounting, and bookkeeping.

2. Ask other business owners how they handle these areas for themselves. Guess what? They have the same problem. Why not learn from their experience?

3. To handle tasks such as invoicing, bookkeeping, financial report generation, payroll check generation, and tax reporting, look at accounting and payroll packages such as QuickBooks that are compatible with the other software packages you put on your computer.

4. Pick a *suite* of computer software packages that all work with each other to provide word processing, spreadsheet, database, and presentation capabilities. A suite package combines several different software packages in one, rather than having you buy them separately, which typically costs much more. The most popular suite product sold today is Microsoft Office, which includes Word for Windows (word processing), Excel (spreadsheet), Access (database), and PowerPoint (presentation graphics).

5. Take a training class on the software packages. Every day you spend in class will probably save you two to five days of working on your own. Trust me on this one; I see it all the time. The only exception applies to people who already know the packages in question; they stand a chance of making them work without a class.

> **def·i·ni·tion** **Business Buzzword**
>
> A **suite** of software packages all work together to provide word processing, spreadsheet, database, and presentation capabilities. An example of a suite is Microsoft Office.

> **That's the Spirit**
>
> Six days you shall labor, but on the seventh day you shall rest; even during the plowing season and harvest you must rest. (Exodus 34:21)
>
> Sometimes it is hard to admit that overwork is a sin, but it is. Overwork is destructive of the temple of the Holy Spirit. It dims the vision, sharpens the temper, kills creativity, and deadens spiritual sensitivity. —M. Helene Pollock

6. Organize the various working files you create on the computer into meaningful directories, and use meaningful filenames to identify them, just as you organize information in a filing cabinet. If you are not the person who creates and maintains this information, make sure you understand the filing system your assistant creates on the computer. Avoid embarrassing situations because your right-hand person has called in sick or decided to quit without notice.

7. Make a backup of that data on a daily basis, if possible. Computer hard disk drives can fail, so look into backup programs that handle this for you automatically. They're not expensive and will help safeguard all your valuable files.

8. Keep it simple. You don't necessarily want to become a computer geek, spending hours and hours on your computer. You simply want to get your invoices and letters out as easily as possible. Create form letters, standard invoices, and credit letters. Try not to customize everything, and you'll save a lot of time with standard letters and packages.

9. Keep away from the leading (or bleeding) edge of technology unless you specifically have the expertise to know what you are getting yourself into. A simple technology snafu can cost you tons of time, money, and aggravation. Let someone else work out the technical bugs.

10. Always invest in printers or copy machines that create high-quality results. The printed page is what your customers see and provides the impression you leave.

Get Connected: Computers and Phones

Marketing and sales will make or break your business. Sales efforts involve keeping customer information, answering telephones, and responding to the mail. The more people you contact in a professional, timely manner, the more likely you are to increase your sale—and the closer you are to retiring early. Computers and telephones are part of doing business, and you should take steps to use them to their full capacity.

Obviously, you need a computer. Over 75 percent of the computers in use today are Intel-based, IBM PC-compatible types such as IBM, Compaq, Dell, Gateway, and others.

Another kind of computer is the Apple brand, which is particularly popular among people who work in graphic arts, layout, design, and multi-media. Fortunately, most software programs are getting better at recognizing the various programs that are out there, so it's rare that you will be unable to convert a file from Windows to Macintosh or vice versa. You do, however, need to ensure that the disk structures themselves can be properly read or you won't even get to the data conversion stage.

If you don't have the money to invest in a new computer right now, then maybe you should consider leasing. You pay a regular monthly fee for the use of a computer for a particular period of time, and at the end, you give the computer back or buy it for a small fee. Computer leases work a lot like car leases.

I know of several companies that no longer purchase any of their computers and lease everything. Their rationale is simply that computers become obsolete too quickly. These companies feel that they are better off leasing so that they can simply turn in the old for the new every few years.

Hot Tip

IBM or Macintosh? My suggested method for dealing with the Apple/PC clone decision issue is this: Try both a Macintosh and a Windows computer for a couple of days each to see which is easier for you to use and understand. Then, after trying both kinds, decide which one you want to own long term. (Also: consider what kinds of computers your biggest clients use.)

Your basic system should come with the fastest possible processor you can afford, along with the largest hard drive and the maximum amount of RAM that a rational human being can justify. You will also likely need a laser printer for monochrome documents and some type of color printer (probably inkjet) so that you can make that desired positive impression when preparing sales literature. Also include a tape backup system and easy-to-use backup software. You surely don't want a disk crash to also take your data, and your company, with it.

Make sure that the monitor, keyboard, and mouse are comfortable to use. Spend the money on a comfortable chair and desk. You will spend a lot of time using this beast. You might as well save the wear-and-tear on your body from the beginning and get the right stuff to make the boss comfortable.

Reach Out and Touch Someone by Phone

As for telephones, you can use your personal line for business calls, but you'll quickly discover that this approach is inconvenient for your customers, your family, and your business. Naturally, your local telephone company charges you for the privilege of adding a telephone line, so economics plays a part in how many separate phone lines you can afford.

It makes sense to set up a separate business phone line right away. For one thing, customers will more easily find you in the Yellow Pages or through directory assistance. If you're operating from a home office, you have the option of installing another personal line, but don't. The reason is that no one will be able to get your business phone number from the phone book or directory assistance if you use a personal line. You lose business opportunities while only saving a few dollars each month.

That's the Spirit

A child left to himself disgraces his mother. (Proverbs 29:15)

Don't doubt it: You *must* have a business line installed so you can separate your business and personal life. Yes, you love your children, but it is imperative that youngsters not speak with customers. You appear unprofessional if your young children answer calls or can be heard screaming in the background. Therefore, have a plan in place for the times when you are on the phone.

You will find that one- and two-line phones are common and inexpensive. Make the first line your primary telephone line that is listed in the phone book and have it roll over to the second line when the first is busy. This means that calls to the first line ring on line one if the line is free but ring on line two if line one is busy with a call. You might also want to consider installing a separate phone line to handle your fax and computer modem connection. You will need to send and receive faxes at all hours, and you save yourself hassles by simply dedicating a separate line to fax transmissions.

When you need more than two incoming lines and are still operating from a home office, you may need special wiring, which means you'll have to shell out some money. The capabilities are greater, but the added expense can be substantial if you are not careful.

Voice mail is so common these days, it's almost become a mandatory business tool. There will always be a continuing debate about whether a live person answering the phone is better than electronic voice mail, but there are advantages to each. You need to decide what works for you based on your workload and number of phone calls.

I lean toward the electronic approach because the messages are usually more accurate and the cost to receive and record them is less. People who call me and find that I can't answer the phone can simply leave a message with a specific question or answer. Without a receptionist running interference, there is little chance of miscommunication or misunderstanding. However, many people just hate talking to a machine and hang up, even though they would leave a message with a person.

I suggest that you handle this person/machine decision in this way. First start with a live person (i.e., you) answering your main phone line and monitor the number of messages you receive every day. Then try using the voice mail to answer telephone calls. Finally, compare that average number of live messages received with the number received with an answering machine or voice mail system. If you normally receive 30 calls, and only find five messages on the machine on the days you are out of the office, then you are losing 25 caller contacts during those times. That usually means lost revenue. Make sure to subtract any telemarketing calls from the analysis to make sure that you are only counting important calls. As with many things in business, experimentation is the key.

> **Hot Tip**
>
> Don't expect your computer fax software to replace a fax machine. You will have paper documents to send, such as those requiring a signature or corrected with a pen. You need a regular fax machine in these cases.

To ensure that you rarely lose any calls, consider getting a cellular phone with voice mail as one of the calling features. Use today's technology to keep in touch with your clients and suppliers. Forward your business line to your cellular phone when you are not in the office. When your cellular phone is on, you receive calls without the caller knowing the difference. When your cellular phone is off, callers are forwarded to your voice mail system where they can leave you a message. Cellular technology is so developed now that you can have calls automatically forwarded to you even if you are in another city. The advantage is freedom, but the disadvantage is that it is harder to get away from clients, which is rarely a real problem.

For people who want to respond immediately to calls, you can also add a pager to the list of communication tools. Pagers can be set up to buzz or beep when a message is left in your voice mailbox so that you know to check it right away. You can then use your cellular phone to return the call.

Each new phone line and feature costs money, but the telephone is not a place to skimp financially. One lost call can mean a lost customer. How much is one sale worth to your company? How many new customers are needed to pay for this investment in technology? If the number is small (one or two in a month), then it is probably a good investment. If it is too large, look for another solution.

E-Mail and Faxing

E-mail is now available at little expense to everyone with a computer. In addition to sending and receiving customer and client e-mail, you can also install electronic mail as a part of your internal computer network at your company. Assume that you have a few computers in your offices. You can connect them to each other using some type of local area network (LAN) product, and your employees can share printers and files. This is an improvement on the "sneaker-net" system that many companies have, in which you copy the file to a disk and run down the hall in your sneakers to print it on another person's machine.

As you know, e-mail allows you to send a message (such as an electronic letter) to another person who also has an electronic mailbox. You can also send whole files from computer to computer. In this way, you can share information with others without using paper or overnight delivery services. The process is much faster and often less expensive.

A great way to maintain contact with your local clients and save money is through effective use of facsimile, or fax, technology. It costs you at least 34 cents in postage, plus printing costs, to mail something via the U.S. Postal Service to your local clients. It costs you nothing more than the charge for a phone call (which could be zero, zip, if your customers are local and you have unlimited local phone service). The only cost you'll incur is that for the fax paper for the faxes you'll receive. Instead of 100 customer contacts costing you $34 or more, it is now practically free!

When choosing to lease or purchase a fax machine, consider the convenience versus cost factors carefully. You want to be able to read what comes through the fax. Plain-paper fax machines are really the way to go so that you avoid having to photocopy faxes that come in on thermal paper. (If you don't, you'll end up with curled-up memos and sticky fingers.) If you go with a thermal fax machine, make sure that it has a paper cutter and takes a long (98 foot) length paper roll, or you will drive yourself, or someone else, crazy cutting the fax pages and changing paper.

> **That's the Spirit**
>
> "It is our best work that God wants, not the dregs of our exhaustion. I think he must prefer quality to quantity." —George MacDonald

Software packages on the market such as WinFax Pro automate the fax procedures. You create the documents that you want to fax and decide who should receive them. Start the program and go home while the documents are faxed to everyone. The fax program also sends documents overnight while you sleep. The following morning, your clients receive this new information from your company and you got a good night's sleep … for free if you have unlimited local service! Yes, this is definitely worth investigating.

Of course, you should check out your state's "junk" fax laws before deciding to send unsolicited information by fax. Some laws in place prohibit you from sending information by fax that someone has not requested. Although companies can send junk mail through the U.S. Postal Service, they generally can't do the same by fax.

Automating Your Sales Procedures

Contact management software is to sales management what the word processor was to the typewriter. You can completely automate your sales contact procedures using one of the many contact management software packages currently on the market. Some popular packages are ACT!, Lotus Organizer, and Microsoft Outlook. They are available at almost any computer software store.

There are other packages, such as GoldMine, that enable you to automate customer-related processes such as sending pamphlets, e-mail, faxes, and other routine activities that take up an employee's time. The entire company can use GoldMine as a centralized data resource. This all sounds pretty good but realize that nothing is free and these benefits do not come without a price. First, GoldMine is more expensive than the previous packages listed and second, it is far more complicated to use. But, if you are someone who wants to squeeze as much capability as possible out of their automation and is willing to invest the time and money to meet that goal, GoldMine might be right for you. For more information contact GoldMine Software at www. goldmine.com.

These packages allow you to keep a complete record of customer addresses, telephone numbers, fax numbers, and e-mail addresses. In addition, you can keep all contact information in one file. For example, you note when you last spoke with a customer, what you talked about, and when you are supposed to make your next contact. This is all done automatically once you enter the information. Keeping such detailed notes helps you stay on top of valuable customer relationships.

Automating the Payroll

As I mentioned in Chapter 18, you shouldn't even think about trying to become a payroll specialist. You don't have the time and probably don't have the expertise to do all the bookkeeping properly. Computer programs already exist that can do this for you in a simple and accurate way. Automated accounting is the way to go if you don't plan to hire an outside company to perform this service.

When evaluating bookkeeping, payroll tax, and accounting packages, be sure they include, as a minimum, the following features:

- A flexible chart of accounts that you can set up and modify at a later date to fit your business requirements.

- Easy-to-use reporting features (income statement and balance sheet preparation as bare minimums). You might benefit from budget versus actual reporting, or cash flow reports, so don't choose a software package that limits your reporting options too much.

- Options that meet your business needs. If you manage payroll or inventory accounting, for example, you need software that can handle those requirements.

This tax stuff is easy and painless, once the initial Social Security, unemployment, and state tax rates are set. Get help in the beginning to set up your accounts properly, and then use the program to track your financial success. You can also run financial statements from these financial packages, so there is no reason for you not to know the state of your company finances.

Accounting software packages are now very powerful and fairly inexpensive. You will likely be well-rewarded for taking the time to learn the details of what these packages can do for you.

Other Useful Software

As I mentioned in Chapter 6, there are software packages available to help you create legal corporate documents, such as employee policy manuals, corporation articles, and bylaws that you need when starting your business. I mention a couple here that I'm familiar with, but there are other packages. As always, be sure that professionals review the documentation you generate from a legal standpoint:

- You can use It's Legal (Parson Technology) for generating your corporation articles and bylaws. It's Legal also provides a standard subcontractor agreement, along with tons of other legal forms. (www.parsonstech.com)

- Try Employee Manual Maker (JIAN Tools) for generating employee policy manuals and business planning documentation. (www.jian.com)

As I mentioned in Chapter 10, the Internet offers an even wider network of communications activities than do the commercial online services. However, you can gain access to the Internet through commercial services as well.

In a Nutshell

Just to keep software information in one place for you, I created a handy table (see below) that summarizes numerous packages with some phone numbers and price ranges to get your automation investigation on the right track.

Business Planning–Related Software Products

Product	Company	Cost	What It Does	Phone
Employee Manual Maker	JIAN Tools	$139	Personnel manuals	1-800-346-5426
Policies Now!	KnowledgePoint	$95	Custom policies	Contact your local retailer.
Biz Plan Builder	JIAN Tools	$129	Business plan development assistance	1-800-346-5426
Product	Company	Cost	What It Does	Phone
Marketing Builder	JIAN Tools	$45	Marketing campaign assistance	1-800-346-5426
QuickBooks	Intuit	$129	Business accounting	1-800-4INTUIT
ACT!	Symantec	$190	Contact management	Contact your local retailer.
GoldMine	GoldMine Software	$190	Contact management	Contact your local retailer.
WinFax	Symantec	$99	Fax management	Contact your local retailer.
FrontPage	Microsoft	$99	Website development	Contact your local retailer.

Fully automated and ready to go? Then it's time to analyze your production plans, the topic of Chapter 21.

Chapter 2

Defining Your Production Plans

No matter what you plan to do, whether it is produce products or provide services, some type of process will be involved. The more efficiently you plan and manage this process, the more easily you will be able to grow as your sales grow and the lower your costs of production will be.

If you plan to sell gizmos, then whoever funds your project must be convinced that you can build the gizmo you plan to sell. As a result, it is important to understand the production aspects of your business because if you can't produce, you won't get paid.

Production in Product and Service Environments

Think of production as the process of combining raw materials, labor, and manufacturing equipment into a finished good that can be sold.

For example, if you are producing music CDs, you have a few components that add up to your finished product: the CD itself, the jewel case in which the CD is shipped, the paper inserts, and a plastic wrapper. You must combine all these pieces so that the final product can be sold in a music store. The process does not vary from one CD to the next. As a result, you can look for ways to streamline the assembly process and develop processes that make assembly as efficient as possible.

This type of production involves routine tasks that do not vary from one CD to the next. The more CDs that are produced, the better the assembly people become with the process and the more efficient the production process becomes. This increased efficiency translates into decreased manufacturing costs, which provide higher profits if you can keep your prices constant.

This process seems pretty straightforward for a product-based business, but what happens when you provide services, which is what most small business owners start out doing? The equation shifts: Materials become a very small portion of the process and the expertise and labor portion becomes dominant.

Product businesses are based on a process that is relatively independent of the people performing the tasks; service businesses often get their work because the client wants a specific person performing the task. The process and ingredients are different, but some similarities make the analysis of the production process easier to handle.

Service businesses rely heavily on the expertise of the personnel. The jobs typically performed by service personnel are nonroutine in nature, meaning that each job is potentially different from the next. This doesn't mean that there aren't similarities, but to use the CD-packaging analogy presented earlier, the jewel case might be a different color, the CD a slightly different shape, and the cover literature might need to be edited for each CD. The overall process of putting it together is the same, but the specific steps required in making it all fit will likely involve tweaking for each CD.

Hot Tip

Next time you're at another company or office, observe the blending of routine and nonroutine tasks. For example, in a doctor's office, taking temperature, blood pressure, and weight are handled by a nurse, whereas the nonroutine tasks—the examination and evaluation of each patient—are performed by the doctor. The patient might be in the office for an hour, but the doctor might only be with the patient for 15 minutes. In this way, the doctor can see four patients in an hour instead of only one, which would be the case if she performed all the routine tasks on her own.

The similarity in developing product and service processes is that you always want to find the common tasks involved in each process. This commonality presents an opportunity for applying automated, money-saving strategies to this stage of the process. Of one thing you can be sure: You will never reach high production volumes if everything you produce is a custom act of creation.

Here are some key points to remember when defining your production process:

- The more times you do something, the more efficient you become at doing it.

- Increased efficiency usually translates into reduced costs and can mean increased profits.

- The more routine (repetitive) the task, the less skilled the personnel must be to perform it.

- The more tasks vary each time performed, the higher the personnel skill level required.

- Production in product-based businesses tends to be more routine where mass volume efficiencies are the goal.

- Service-based businesses tend to be more time-dependent because the overall project variations can fluctuate from one time a task is performed to the next.

- Service-based businesses should look for a methodology that makes the non-routine tasks more routine, allowing less skilled personnel to perform the tasks without compromising quality.

- Personal customer contact is critical to a service business (would you go to a doctor you don't like?), whereas product quality is critical in a product business. (Have you ever met the designer of your Sony Walkman?)

That's the Spirit

In the frenzied activity of running your own business you risk losing the place of quiet rest in your soul where you commune with God. Here are two good reminders: "A pure, honest, and stable spirit is not distracted by a lot of activity. He does everything to honor God and is at rest within Himself." –Thomas A. Kempis

"Until we have learned to be satisfied with fellowship with God, until he is our rock and our fortress, we will be restless with our place in the world." –Erwin Lutzer

Are You a Mass Producer or a Job Shop?

It's time to add another level to the analysis process. This section compares *mass producer* to *job shop* environments. If you are continually producing the same thing, you are a mass producer. For example, a company that produces candles is a mass producer in that once set up to make candles, the process might make thousands, or even millions, in a single run. Can you imagine how good you get at something after you have done it a few million times?

Job shop environments require more customization to complete each job. This doesn't mean that the same underlying technologies are not used. It only means that they are used in a different way for each job. For example, creating a custom software package is a job shop environment in that the software is developed once for a specific customer. You are not going to take the same software and resell it to others since few other people will need EXACTLY what you developed for earlier customers. You might still perform the software programming operations using a specific programming language, but the software application itself is customized for each customer. Now, if you create the software and then package it for sale on retail shelves, the software creation process is nonroutine, but the process of packaging the software and shipping it to Wal-Mart is routine for each software box shipped.

 Business Buzzword

Mass producers continually produce the same products. **Job shop** operations require more customization to produce each product.

Certain parts of your company's operation will be routine, but others will be nonroutine. You need to match the right people with the right tasks and "routinize" tasks wherever possible to take best advantage of the highly skilled personnel needed for the nonroutine tasks. Performing this blend properly is one critical aspect of successful operations management. Notice that it affects your hiring decisions, personnel requirements, and the overall confidence you have in the quality of your offering.

Bankruptcy Alert

Be sure to build *all* of your set-up costs into any customized processes that are not mass production. I have some friends who run a small business that specializes in custom injection plastic molding of very large parts. Once the process is set up, they might produce only one, two, or three parts for a customer. This is clearly not a mass production environment, but they have a unique process methodology that allows them to create the required parts in a reliable fashion. If they based their pricing model on mass production economies, they would be out of business. They realize that their offering is unique and charge the appropriate premiums.

Linking Purchasing, Production, and Marketing Forecasts

Get ready; here comes another automation speech. If you have ever worked in a product manufacturing environment that did everything by hand, you understand the importance of automating your purchasing and inventory processes.

This can get pretty complicated, but it is really important, so bear with me. You need to order parts from your vendors before you can build your product. This means that you must have quantity projections about the products to be built. In addition, each of the components that you include in your product has some delivery lead time requirement from your vendors. This lead time can be as short as overnight for a standard part, such as a screw, or as long as several months for a custom casting part, such as the frame of a bicycle. This means that before the components can be purchased, you must know how many you plan to build, which means that you must know how many your sales and marketing people plan to sell.

The service equivalent is finding a person with the proper skill set to address your customer needs. You must either hire a person with the required skills, hire a person and train her to have the required skills, or train one of your internal personnel to have the proper skills. In any case, you have a lead time involved. You even have a lead time involved if you already have an employee with the proper skills on staff. Why? Because if you are operating profitably, that person is already busy on another project and might have to finish it before he can start on the new one.

Most of the accounting software packages I have seen, such as QuickBooks, allow you to track purchasing, inventories, and sales but don't integrate forecasting. Most of the canned sales support packages I have seen, such as ACT!, allow you to track contacts but really don't allow you to track forecasts.

![definition book icon] **Business Buzzword**

Software packages that link sales forecasts to production and purchasing requirements are generally referred to as **manufacturing requirement packages (MRP).**

How can you manage the critical gap between your sales forecast and your production and purchasing requirements? You either need to handle this gap manually, pay someone to develop custom software, or scour the industry for a software package that addresses your specific company needs. These packages are out there, but you might pay thousands of dollars finding the package that is right for you. They are generally referred to as *manufacturing requirement packages (MRP)*.

Is an MRP package worth the initial investment? It depends on how large you plan to grow and how substantial your initial funding is. Paying a lot for the right production control software package could deplete your cash reserves to the point that you jeopardize the company. Clearly not a good idea.

In keeping with my "automate from the beginning" philosophy, I suggest that you either buy the package (if possible) or train yourself to think of your company as a process from sales, through purchasing, through production, through shipping, to receipt of the product by the customer, to receipt of the payment check from the customer, to the final cashing of the check.

Create a Production Flow Chart

You don't have to become a process engineer to build many products, but you should have an idea of how the process flow works and what sections need special attention. This involves a big sheet of paper, or the use of a software package such as CorelFLOW, Microsoft Project, or other flow charting and project management software packages.

Map out the entire process on a piece of paper, and note which steps are routine or nonroutine. Also map out the weak links, or *gating items,* in the process. These are the items that restrict your ability to produce in higher volumes (mass production) or produce in less time (job shop). Making these gating items more efficient always pays huge dividends later, and you need to watch them like a hawk, for these are the items that can also put you out of business.

def·i·ni·tion Business Buzzword

A **gating item** is an item that limits the overall efficiency of the process. If this item's efficiency is increased, the overall process generally becomes more efficient. Track these carefully.

For example, a large airplane manufacturer recently went through a huge sales growth spurt where its sales and marketing people sold many new planes to several foreign governments. Good news? Not for this company. They couldn't get many of their critical parts from their vendors in time to meet the production schedules. They had to shut down their plant for a few weeks in 1997 while they waited for the gating item parts to arrive. Here is a company with a stellar sales record and a black eye simply because it outsold its production capability due to gating item parts.

Finally, look at your process map, and determine the amount of space needed for each stage of production. Don't forget that the raw inventory parts you receive from your vendors need storage space along with the finished products. In addition, products that go through many stages of production need interim storage space along with those products rejected during the production process. If you don't take a detailed look at the space requirements early, you might end up like our friend in the opening story who had employees literally climbing the walls.

That's the Spirit

If anyone does not know how to manage his own family, how can he take care of God's church? (1 Timothy 3:5)

A small business owner I know created a product for holding snow skis while people traveled from their home to a ski resort. It was a hard plastic shell with end caps. He had an outside company build the products, but then he had no place to put them. He ended up dedicating a room in his house to finished goods storage, which did not please his wife. It kept his overhead down but wasn't very good "family management."

Successful Project Management

I am not going to go into the details of project management in this chapter, other than to point you in the direction of understanding basic project charts and tools. A *Gantt chart* shows you the relationship between the various project components and their required orders of completion (see the following figure). I create my Gantt charts on a spreadsheet package with the tracked items listed in the left column and the column headings labeled as the weeks, or days, on which each stage of the project is to be completed.

Business Buzzword

A **Gantt chart** is a method of displaying and tracking project items where one item's completion is dependent upon the prior completion of another item.

A **critical path analysis** is a project management technique that maps a process flow and then determines the items that limit production. These items become **gating items.**

The *critical path analysis* allows you to determine the process bottlenecks so that you can keep an eye on them. Project management software packages perform this critical path analysis for you. You don't have to go overboard on all this stuff in the beginning, but if you don't get a realistic picture of your space and time requirements, you can be seriously hit later when you get into actual production.

There are few better feelings in the world than creating a process flow on paper and then seeing it work in action, just as you planned it. Do it once, and you might be hooked. I was.

By the way, the more detail you have in your planning, the more likely you are to get money from your investors. The details show them that you have thought through the steps and understand what you are doing. Without the details, you are winging it with their money. Think about it. Would you rather give money to someone who has spent the time thinking about the details or to someone who says, "Trust me; it will be okay"?

Maintaining Quality

Nothing will put you out of business faster than being a new company that gets a reputation for bad quality. Happy customer referrals are critical to the success of your business, and if you let the quality suffer, your referrals will become negative instead of positive.

I recently gave a speech to a group of quality professionals on the importance of instilling quality in small business environments. It forced me to formalize some of my thoughts on the topic. The talk was well received, so here is a synopsis of the high points for your consideration and specific application to your company environment:

- Know what you sell and what your customers buy. Make sure that you or someone you trust inspect the critical qualities that your customers expect from your product or service before your customers see your offering. This applies to both product and service companies. If your company offers massage services, get a massage by each of your massage personnel every now and then to ensure that they meet your standards.

- Don't ever let your customers become your final product inspection team. Make sure your product or service meets your expectations before you let them see it. They won't ever forget that you sold them deficient goods.

- *Under-promise* and *over-deliver*. This is where I see many small business owners suffer. Because you are small, you might feel that you have to over-promise to compete with a larger company. You know that you are over-promising when your evenings and weekends are tied up doing extra stuff for a customer, and you are cursing yourself for having promised things that are not part of what you normally offer. If what you promised must be there as part of the standard offering, then make the proper production changes and set up for it. If not, do not over-promise unless you have a lot of free time.

- Never *over-promise* and *under-deliver.* You can deliver exactly what all of your brochures promote and still have an unhappy customer if the customer was promised additional items that were not delivered. This is an easy problem to fix. Only promise what you can deliver or know that you and the company will continually be jumping through hoops complying with "loose lips" promises.

- Personally spot-check the products or services—before they leave your business, and let everyone know that you do it. This tends to keep employees on their toes and ensures that your toes don't get stepped on.

That's the Spirit

Successful businesses thrive on having a good grasp on the future. So it's easy for the future to be a source of anxiety and preoccupation. Listen to the wise words of George MacDonald: "It is when tomorrow's burden is added to the burden of today that the weight is more than a man can bear. Never load yourself so. If you find yourself so loaded, at least remember this: it is your own doing, not God's. He begs you to leave the future to him, and mind the present." –George MacDonald

- Work with customers up front to set their expectations. This is particularly true for service agreements, or you can find yourself working for a client forever, with the best of intentions, not getting paid for it, and still having an unsatisfied customer even though you delivered what you thought they wanted. For example: "My Company agrees to supply Your Company with a draft of the document, circulate the draft to the client for comments, and then incorporate those comments into the final draft." Notice how only one level of revision is included in this agreement; this means you do not waste time and resources endlessly revising your work.

- Define concrete expectations, and do not leave them general. (General: "To deliver a product or service to the customer's satisfaction." Concrete: "To deliver a product that meets the specifications as outlined on product specification sheet 01-A, dated 09/27/2000.")

Hopefully, this chapter has given you some solid advice and methods related to your production planning. Now, if you're feeling like a total success, you may be asking what's next. There is life even after success, so move ahead to Chapter 22!

A sample Gantt Chart.

CIG to Starting Your Own Business, First Edition
Project writing schedule - Gantt Chart
cigtimng.xls

	12/23	12/27	12/29	1/2	1/5	1/9	1/12	1/16	1/19	1/23	1/26	2/2	2/6	2/9	2/13	2/16	2/19	2/22	2/25
Milestones																			
25% Completion				MM															
50% Completion										MM									
100% Completion																MM			
Author Review																	XX	----	XX
Chapter No. Introduction																			
1 So, why go into business....		▓																	
2 Preparing the business plan	▓																		
3 Strategic vs. tactical planning			▓																
4 Which business form to choose								▓											
5 Additional corporation considerations																			
6 Effective marketing makes selling easier								XX											
7 Dealing with competition									XX										
8 Without sales, nothing happens									XX										
9 Making sure that you are making money					▓														
10 Working with banks....											XX								
11 Cash is more important than you mother												XX							
12 Setting up for credit card sales						SS													
13 What to do if they don't pay				▓			▓												
14 Complicating life by adding employees													XX						
15 Simplifying payroll....														XX					
16 Other stuff....																			
17 Using automation															XX				
18 Dealing with success															XX				
Appendix A An actual business plan																XX			
Appendix B Glossary																		XX	
Legend:																			
Milestone	MM																		
Proposed Completion Date	XX																		
Duration of Completion	XX	----	XX																
Completed Item	▓																		
Slipped Item	SS																		

The Secrets of Your Success

"Rick does seem a little disoriented lately," said Jennifer to Emily. She had started working for Rick and Emily five years ago and had never seen Rick like this. "It's weird. This just isn't the boss I once knew. He shows up late for meetings, signs checks weeks after they are written by the accountant, and just doesn't seem to care. I hope that he's okay."

Emily remembered her husband's energy during the early years of the company, as they succeeded in growing 200 percent a year. Now he just seemed bored with the daily routine. What could she do to help?

She wanted to see that energy and enthusiasm return. Maybe Rick could focus on the new publishing side of the business, leaving her to manage the training side that had become the company's bread and butter. That would be a win for all concerned. But how would Rick react?

Do you remember that, right from the beginning, I promised you one of the most exciting rides of your life? Well, here you are, a resounding success. Bask in the glory of your new situation, but know that success has its own sets of traps that can undo all your hard work and achievements. This chapter is designed to introduce you to life after success and to help you decide what comes next in your business venture.

Dealing with the Personal Aspects of Success

As you built your business, you undoubtedly put in long hours, suffered through numerous trials, and dug deeper into your soul than you ever thought possible. Otherwise, you would not be where you are now. As a business owner, you recognize all the hard work and commitment it takes to keep a business going. Business life is different for you now, and your new insight is well earned.

They All Love You When You Are Successful

Who helped you when you first started out? Think about it. Were there many colleagues and advisers or just a few? Were they old friends or new acquaintances who saw that what you were trying to achieve had merit? Many people who know you today probably did not know you back when things were tough.

That's the Spirit

Thankfulness is always appropriate when you reach goals in life. Celebrate your successes, and celebrate the one who upholds you through them all!

Shout for joy to the LORD, all the earth.
Worship the LORD with gladness;
come before him with joyful songs.
Know that the LORD is God.
It is he who made us,
and we are his;
we are his people, the sheep of his pasture.
Enter his gates with thanksgiving
and his courts with praise;
give thanks to him and praise his name.
For the LORD is good. …

(Psalm 100)

Nothing breeds business interest faster than the smell of money. Your business success makes you a desirable business partner, dinner date, speaker, and financial planning client. You will soon appear on everybody's mailing list. You will be invited to parties and other social functions. You might even be the guest of honor. (Can you believe it?) These acknowledgments are well deserved, and I encourage you to enjoy them while they last. I also encourage you to remember that you can become an unknown again as quickly as you became a success.

People who helped you along the way might need help themselves from time to time. Supporting competent people who stood by you in the past almost always pays positive dividends. Remember: Unless you are extremely blessed, you and your business will have a wide array of ups and downs. Business associates, family, and personal friends are the people who will get you through the tough times and allow you to prosper when times are better.

Success breeds success, but it also brings out opportunists who try to benefit from all your hard work and offer nothing in return. Determine early in your business relationships whether someone is trying to offer help, take help, or use you—and respond accordingly.

Watch Your Ego and Your Pocketbook

Have you ever known someone whose emotional state was linked to his credit cards? The better his mood, the more money he spent. Now multiply that effect several times over and you have the potentially dangerous situation of a successful business owner whose ego is linked with the financial success of the company.

Once the business gets to a certain point, you will be tempted to dip into the till and spend for personal gratification instead of for business. Sure, it is your business; nobody doubts that. The issue revolves around your need to spend company resources for personal gratification. Several thousand dollars is a lot to an individual, but a nominal amount to a business. Beware when you start to spend business money for items the business doesn't really need. You can spend your company right out of business if you're not careful.

Pat yourself on the back for your successes, but leave the business checkbook at work. Even the United States Constitution requires a separation of powers. You should have the same, even if only in your mind. Don't treat your business as your personal checkbook.

> **Bankruptcy Alert**
>
> You might be tempted to look at your company's profits as a means for you to enjoy yourself. This is a scary situation. Before you spend, ask yourself this: "If this were other people's money and I were the president of their company, would I still spend the money this way?"

That's the Spirit

"Humility is recognizing that God and others are responsible for the achievements in my life." —Bill Gothard

May the words of my mouth and the meditation of my heart be pleasing in your sight, O LORD, my Rock and my Redeemer. (Psalm 19:14)

Instinct Is Good, but Planning Makes It Work

Thinking on your feet is a great talent for both boxers and business people to have. Here is the potential problem: How do you maintain the quick decision-making techniques that got you through the early times while still moving in a smart direction today? I have seen successful business people violate their own plans because they thought a new direction was better than the one previously evaluated. Don't move too quickly to change company direction or switch strategy just for the sake of change.

> **Hot Tip**
>
> Know that slow times happen as part of the start-up phase, and don't let them get you down. Use these times to invest in more marketing, develop new products and services, train to improve your skills, and plan for the future. Once things get rolling, you will probably have less time for these activities.

Now that the company is really doing well, avoid the tendency to think that you are always right. Your instincts obviously are good, but rely on input from your staff regularly to ensure that you don't miss opportunities. In many cases, your employees might have excellent suggestions and strategies to propose that could be better than your initial plans. Don't leave them out of the decision-making process. Get others involved so the company can grow and prosper.

Even When It's Going Great, You Still Get Nervous!

Old habits die hard, and this is one of those tough situations for people who survive hard times. When you become used to difficult times, it is hard to adjust to good times. It might become so stressful that you wonder, "When will the situation go back to normal—back to those hard times?"

I don't think you ever let go of the fear that things can go back to the way they were in the slow, old days. I remember days in a row when my phone did not ring. My training lab often felt more like a tomb than a thriving business. In the very early days of the company, during the late '80s, economic times in Austin were tough, few people knew who we were, and our product mix was untested. Marketing efforts were underway, but it just took time for them to work. Things were slow. When I thought we might go under, I was physically ill.

Things are better today. Much better! (Whew!) But I still have this nagging fear that activity will suddenly drop off for no reason and we will be back where we were. I use this fear to keep me moving forward with new ideas, marketing approaches, and business concepts.

Take a Reality Check

Keep people around who can act as a sounding board. Sometimes you need to make important decisions and your employees cannot give you the feedback you need. In many cases, you need to consider whether to invest more of your personal funds to grow the company or how to improve your personal life without damaging the business. Only you can make some of these decisions, and other business owners are often the best advisors to consult for those issues.

I have a team of fellow businesspeople who know me, know my business, and bring tremendous business expertise to the table. They act as my reality check when I make major decisions. I encourage you to keep a sharp eye out for such people so you can form your own personal network of business advisors. They are invaluable resources as rapid growth and its associated opportunities arise. Setting up an informal business advisory or discussion group can be an invaluable way of getting regular feedback from trusted colleagues.

Dealing with the Financial Aspects of Success

You must be making money or you would be out of business. Congratulations! Now that you have all that cash floating around, take a look at some potential pitfalls associated with the financial aspects of success.

When Small Expenses Turn into Big Bucks

I have several coffee cans at my house filled with pennies, nickels, dimes, and quarters. A friend recently visited and noted that there was probably a lot of money in those cans. Funny how all of those little coins add up to some major savings.

Likewise, in your business, little expenses here and there can add up to big cash drains. This is particularly true when you allow your employees to order products, inventory, and office supplies without your approval. You have to let go of many tasks for the company to grow, which includes some purchasing functions. However, a surprise bill for thousands of dollars is never fun. Set up procedures for tracking or approving expenses over a certain threshold (for example, $200). Review your accounting on a monthly basis and always review your financial statements to ensure that your expenses aren't way out of line. It is your job to keep the company financially healthy. If you can't do that job, you should find someone such as an accountant or book-keeper who can.

> **That's the Spirit**
>
> "A great many people go through life in bondage to success. They are in mortal dread of failure. I do not have to succeed. I have only to be true to the highest I know—success or failure are in the hands of God."
> —E Stanley Jones

Watch Your Overhead

Overhead is a revenue-eating shark. Every month it requires the same, if not more, cash feeding than the month before. This is the nature of overhead items. They occur every month, and you must pay them or you are out of business. Generally, these include office rent, utilities, phones, and employees. If sales drop off, you still have to pay these. It is scary to write checks for each of these expenses during months when sales are low. If the situation continues for long, you need to take steps to correct it, which often means reducing overhead through layoffs and downsizing the operation. These are tough decisions for any business manager.

> **Bankruptcy Alert**
>
> Spending $200 here, $300 there, and another $700 on a new piece of equipment adds up to $1,200. Would you have spent $1,200 on that particular combination of items? If so, the money was well-spent. If not, then you need to start considering all expenses above a certain dollar amount in terms of their total impact on the company and not as separate, unrelated purchases.

Avoid the situation by only adding to overhead when absolutely necessary. Avoid spontaneously adding people, space, or equipment unless you know that the expense is justified for the long-term.

By keeping your overhead low and your relationships with contractors and temporary agencies in good standing, you have the ability to provide your clients with the services they need. That is your advantage when competing against the big guys: You are nimble enough to adapt to a client's particular situation and can charge less because of lower overhead expenses. The big guys have a lot of inertia and overhead, which can seriously get in the way of change. By the time they realize that they should change, you have already won some of their customers.

Justifying New Employees

When you are lean and hungry, your tendency is to watch where every penny goes and squeeze as much performance out of your personnel as possible. When things start to go better and you feel a little more comfortable, you might be tempted to hire that additional person or two who will take some of the load off you or your staff.

This might be a solid business decision, or it might be a decision driven by your personal desire for a little less pressure. If you aren't careful, you can end up increasing your salary costs to the point that your currently solvent business becomes top-heavy. It is sometimes gratifying to the ego to have a large number of employees, but all of that gratification goes away in a second when you can't pay your bills.

Make your hiring decisions based on sound financial judgment. If the numbers work out, then you have an employee who can pay for himself. If not, and you still hire this person, then you know it is a speculative arrangement that eventually might have to end if business takes a downturn. After all, nonessential personnel are the first to go. Right?

Follow this procedure to determine whether you need another employee:

1. Determine the salary range of a person with the needed skills. Ask what other business owners pay for people performing the same work to get a benchmark.

2. Add between 15 and 30 percent to that number to account for payroll taxes and other benefits such as vacation and sick time.

3. Outline the current costs the business incurs, which are associated with the tasks that this new person would perform.

4. Add to that additional revenues the company would gain as a result of freeing up the current personnel or the actions of this particular person. This is especially important in the case of a sales or marketing person.

5. Subtract the new employee cost from the sum of the new revenues and anticipated cost savings. If the difference is positive, then this is a reasonable personnel slot. If not, then you might either expand this new person's duties or hold
off for a while.

You might find your own variations on this evaluation procedure, but the net
result must come up the same. You cannot hire people who do not pay for themselves either by reducing costs (such as hiring a person full-time instead of using
more expensive contractors) or by generating adequate new revenues so that the
gross margin pays their employment costs.

Handing Over the Checkbook

Afraid to hand over the checkbook to your most trusted assistant? You should be! It
is a big deal and you should treat it as such. Once you turn it over, it is tough to take
it back without hard feelings.

You can stall passing the checkbook by taking a few steps to get you out of daily
activities while still maintaining some control:

1. Set up credit accounts with your suppliers and let your assistant be the one
who approves purchases while running them past you at the end of the month.

2. Start to involve your assistant in your financially related business decisions.
Show him how you analyze different purchases and situations so he knows
how you would handle a situation. This doesn't mean he must give up his own
perspective, but he must understand that it is your money he is spending.

That's the Spirit

Bring the whole tithe into the storehouse, that there may be food in my house. Test me in
this," says the LORD Almighty, "and see if I will not throw open the floodgates of heaven and
pour out so much blessing that you will not have room enough for it. (Malachi 3:10)

A number of very successful Christian business people have given a tithe, or one-tenth of their
gross income, to the Lord's work. There are many wonderful testimonies of how God then pros-
pered their business to an even greater degree.

3. Be sure this is the right time to let go; you might be going through a semi-personal crisis that will pass. If so, you might be back to normal in a short period of time. If not, and you are ready to remove yourself from the day-to-day operation of the business, then it's time to pick a successor and begin the training program.

Reporting and budgeting becomes critical when you hand over the checkbook. Set up the financial reports and budgeting process so you can closely track the company's overall financial performance at least monthly. Otherwise, things can get out of hand without your knowledge. Look at all the celebrities who lost their shirts when they turned over their financial dealings to another person. You are right to be cautious in this regard. Don't rush this decision, but make it when you think it's the right move for the company.

Dealing with Ups and Downs

This section covers a tough topic. Every business goes through its high and low points. When the highs are more frequent than the lows, everyone is happy. When the lows hang on for a while, interesting personnel dynamics start to happen.

You are going to see good and bad times, especially if you're in a seasonal business, such as retail or, say, sprinkler system installations in New England. You have to plan the rest of the year to accommodate these lows or you won't be able to start business when your high season starts again—and it will start again! You have to believe that or you should find another career.

I have seen a few different reactions to down times and they seem to mostly depend on the personality type of the person involved:

1. Some managers deny that anything is wrong and keep going with business as usual, even when critical depletion of company funds is happening. This ostrich approach to management is rarely a good idea.

2. The over-reaction managers see two days of low income as a terminal illness. These people often turn the organization upside down for the simple reason that they weren't patient enough to let things turnaround on their own. This approach causes mayhem, depletes employee morale, and drains company resources in paying for the changes.

3. Some people see that something is wrong and believe that it will turn around, so they keep hocking their heart and soul to keep the dying business alive. When this kind of business finally dies, it is really a heart breaker.

4. Some people see a few months of downturn and close up shop. Take the money and run. These people suffer the next time they start a business because their clients from the previous company know that they have minimal staying power.

Which is the right approach? You will only know the answer to this question in retrospect. You, as the manager, get paid to decide the proper course for the company. I suggest that you take a combined approach from the preceding types, and look at things this way:

- Know how much you are willing to risk before closing up shop.

- Talk to your customers and find out why things are slow. They might be in a special budget cycle that will clear itself up in 60 days, and they already have money budgeted for your company's offerings.

- Ask employees if they want to take some time off either without pay or to use up vacation. Either way you win.

- Protect yourself by never allowing reserve cash to drop below the point where you can still pay your bills, salaries, and payroll taxes and get out with your skin. It is painful enough to close a business. It is even more painful to close a business and pay off its debts for the next few years.

- Talk to other business owners to determine whether they are seeing the same downturn. (However, beware of talking to competitors because they will always tell you things are great, especially if they think that you are having problems.)

- Make whatever decisions you make for your own reasons. Be fair to your employees, customers, and yourself, and you will either weather the storm or close up shop with your reputation intact for your next round.

Unless you are in a business segment that has become obsolete, such as the steel manufacturing business, any downturn you see is probably only temporary. Whoever has the deepest financial pockets wins in this situation. You can't stop selling and you have to keep on doing what you do best while you walk through what might seem like a tunnel. Know that it will turn around eventually, and have preset safety limits to ensure that you don't bankrupt yourself in the process of waiting for the turn-around.

Use the high periods to stash three to six months of liquid assets so that you can weather the lows. When things slow down, she who has the most cash wins.

Don't Believe Your Own Hype

You really have three faces when your company is small: the face your company presents to the outside world of prospects and customers, the face you present to your staff and other company personnel, and the face you present to confidants and family. The one you present to the outside world is essentially your "advertising" face and should not be confused with reality.

You would never advertise that your company is struggling with a particular issue or problem. This doesn't mean the problem doesn't exist, just that you are dealing with it quietly and internally. You might advertise that your services are the best in town, but if customer feedback indicates satisfaction problems, you need to address them or you are out of business. If you believe your advertising, you might think things are fine when they are really in trouble.

Keep your ego out of the way and monitor company performance with a keen eye on reality. Make your external promotions as positive, upbeat, and benefit-oriented as possible, but don't deceive yourself or your staff in the process. There are always internal struggles that you must handle for your company to continue to be successful.

When Is It Time for You to Step Aside?

When is it time to let go and turn the reins over to someone else? You won't run into this problem in the early stages of your company but you should prepare yourself for the later possibility. Every situation is different, but here are a few points to consider:

1. Are you doing what you want to do? Just because you started the business doesn't mean that you must still like it. Would you rather be doing something else on a daily basis?

That's the Spirit

If you're a baby boomer, you may remember the song by the Byrds—Turn, Turn, Turn. The principle relates to the cycles of highs and lows in business and originally came from the Book of Ecclesiastes. It begins with Chapter 3, verse 1: "There is a time for everything, a season for every activity under heaven." There are a few other verses that relate to business: "A time to tear down and a time to rebuild." "A time to search and a time to lose." "A time to keep and a time to throw away." Check out this poem in Ecclesiastes 3:1–8.

2. Would you serve the company better in another capacity? Perhaps the temperament that served the company in start-up mode no longer applies to a maturing business. Should you turn over the day-to-day operations to your more consistent associate who likes the daily grind?

3. Should you merge the company with another so that the joint skills and marketing capabilities together can be more powerful? The president of the other company could become president of the new company. This takes care of your people, clients, and you.

4. Do your employees want to own the company? Perhaps you should sell the company to them, freeing yourself for other entrepreneurial ventures. There are very attractive Employee Stock Ownership Programs (ESOPs) that enable an owner to sell a corporation to the employees while simultaneously enabling the owner to enjoy some excellent tax benefits.

5. Have a heart-to-heart talk with your children if your intention is to pass the company on to them. They may not want it. You may find that the quality of your own life, and that of your children, improves once you have an understanding on this very important point. Sell the company. Take the money. Enjoy your early retirement.

You will know when the time is right to get out of the way. If you have a corporation with a board of directors, they will probably let you know when you become more of a liability to the company than an asset. This isn't a personal insult, just a recognition that different skills might now be needed to grow the company. Your business is now at the point where professional management needs to take over and the entrepreneur needs to look for new business and growth opportunities.

Instead of treating opportunities for change and transition as a negative, I encourage you to view them as an opportunity. You were successful before, and you will be successful again. Sharing that success is a treat rarely experienced; consider yourself blessed to have the opportunity.

Appendix A

The Kwik Chek Auto Evaluation Business Plan

Recommendations for Using This Business Plan

What follows is an actual business plan I wrote back in the late 1980s for a used car evaluation service business called Kwik Chek. When I wrote this business plan, I was trying to determine whether the idea would fly as an independent investment with national franchise potential or whether I should go back to the drawing board and find a new idea.

I didn't include the plan as an incentive for you to start a used car evaluation business. I included it as a model to help you write your own business plan for your own business. You will clearly need to do your own research, write your own content, and fill in the sections in a way applicable to your particular business idea. The data included in the plan is from the 1980s, but once again, this should be of no importance to you. The flow, format, style, analysis process, and presentation are what you should be looking at when you review this plan. Please make sure that you do not take any of the presented market information as irrefutable truths. The overall presentation of that data is still very applicable in the modern marketplace, and that is where you want to focus your attention.

Although I did not implement the plan, it served its purpose at the time it was written. The plan showed that the idea wasn't right for me since I did not want to be doing the work on the cars myself, and the analysis shows that owner/operator management was the way to go. Notice that the plan did what was expected of it. It told me that this idea did not fit my criteria for a business venture that I wanted to sink my time and money into. For the right person who is willing to do the work required, this plan could easily be modified for presentation to investors or could be self-funded. (Make sure that you update the numbers for the current marketplace and verify that it still makes money before taking the plunge. Many of the referenced sources are still in existence and provide contemporary data.)

I encourage you to review this plan as a road map for the development of your own plan and don't take the specific plan content literally. You might notice that the exact section titles and flow do not exactly match those shown on the tear card or within Chapter 4. Don't let this throw you either. A plan should address the questions of the intended readers which means that sections can be added or deleted as needed. Your plan should always include an executive summary along with the business description, competition, marketing plan, organization personnel, operations, funding requirements, and financial statements sections. The industry analysis, market analysis, and conclusion section contents will vary based on the market familiarity of the intended readers.

These final points are very important. The appendix should support the overall plan contents. The overall plan contents should support the conclusions outlined in the executive summary. Write the executive summary after you have completed the plan to avoid writing something that meets your picture of how things should be as opposed to how they really are as supported by plan data and analysis.

This Kwik Chek plan should serve as a model as you prepare your own business plan but it should not, as written here, become your business plan. Your levels of detail, section flows, and writing style will differ from that presented in the Kwik Chek plan. That is okay. It is YOUR plan for YOUR company. No single plan can do justice to the numerous business opportunities and entrepreneurial styles that exist. Read this plan as a guide, and make your plan your own. Good luck and start writing.

Executive Summary

This plan presents the Kwik Chek used automobile inspection service to determine whether it is a profitable business venture to pursue. The report begins with a brief description of the service concept and then proceeds with an in-depth look at the services proposed, an in-depth look at the used car market for purchasing characteristics, an operational analysis of the requirements for providing the service, and a financial analysis of the cash flows expected over the first three years of operation.

The results of the study show that Kwik Chek, when treated as an absentee owner investment only, requires over $100,000 in cash to accommodate negative cash flows in the first year of operation and doesn't show a positive return on investment until Year 3 of operation.

Further analysis shows that Kwik Chek, when treated as an owner/operator business, still requires $70,000+ in cash, but it shows a positive return on investment in only two years instead of three and shows a substantial positive cash flow in Year 3 and beyond. The return on investment time period is reduced by one year.

There is already competition in the used automobile inspection area, but there is substantial market share to be had by each entrant. The Kwik Chek analysis assumes that only 20 percent market penetration is achieved by Kwik Chek to achieve the goals outlined.

Because the owner/operator scenario requires less initial investment, shows a positive return in two years instead of three, and also provides increased cash flow in Year 3 and beyond, Kwik Chek should be offered to mechanic/investor groups who want to own and operate the business while establishing themselves for the long term as a service to the used car industry. The number of used car customers will continue to grow as the number of licensed drivers continues to grow, and the expected life of automobiles continues to be extended through higher quality manufacturing.

It is not recommended that Kwik Chek be pursued as strictly an investment by an absentee owner because the return on investment period is over three years and the longer-term cash flows are nominal. It is, however, recommended as an investment for an owner/operator who can serve as both owner and inspection technician with another family member working as dispatcher.

Table of Contents

Market Need Definition

The automobile marketplace has been in a state of transition since the beginning of the 1980s. There has been a trend in recent years away from purchasing new automobiles and toward purchasing an automobile on the used car market.

It has recently become common knowledge to the general public that a new car purchased from a dealer loses a tremendous amount of its resale value almost immediately. This amount of initial loss is generally financed and paid for by the owner over a three- to five-year period and consequently does not get amortized as quickly as the car loses its money. A used car, on the other hand, does not lose value as quickly after purchase because the bulk of the "new car" depreciation has already occurred by the time of purchase.

Data from the 1988 Motor Vehicle Manufacturers Association Facts and Figures, as seen in the following table, shows that the total number of registered vehicles on the road today has increased steadily from 1980 to 1988, and the mean and median ages have also increased.

Registrations and Vehicle Ages

	1980	1988
Registered vehicles	150 million	180 million
Mean age of vehicles	6.6 years	7.6 years
Median age of vehicles	6.0 years	6.8 years

There are many possible reasons for this recent trend. The increased need for fuel-efficient cars, combined with difficult financial times for the public at large, have made people more cautious about how they spend their money. They are tending to treat an automobile purchase as an investment decision, rather than an impulse buy.

The major problem with a used automobile is that the buyer generally purchases the vehicle in "as-is" condition. The buyer is typically unaware of the mechanical condition of the vehicle and consequently purchases the vehicle on faith that it does not have major mechanical or electrical problems that will substantially increase the overall cost of ownership.

The current alternative to buying on faith is to take the car to a mechanic for a complete mechanical review. This action takes time and money on the part of the buyer, and the scheduling of the mechanical inspection is typically done during the day when the buyer is at work. In essence, it is a hassle. Consequently, even though everyone agrees that an independent inspection is a good idea, few people actually have the inspection done.

From the seller's perspective, it is valuable to have an independent inspection report of the mechanical condition of the vehicle to assure potential buyers that there are no hidden defects in the vehicle.

This procedure is similar to that done when a person buys a house and arranges an inspection of the physical condition of the house. In some states, it is a legal requirement to have a house inspection before the house can be sold. Because a house and a car are typically the two largest purchases the average person makes in a lifetime, it stands to reason that they should both be treated with the same level of care.

It makes intuitive sense that a service that offers reliable mechanical inspection of vehicles in a convenient way and for a reasonable price would be well received by the public.

An analysis of the business potential of such an offering is the subject of this report. The proposed company name is Kwik Chek, and the company would initially be based in Austin, Texas. The business will be analyzed from a marketing, operations, and financial perspective to determine whether it is viable in Austin only and whether it has potential for being nationally franchised.

A Description of the Kwik Chek Service Proposed

The customer calls a local number and schedules an appointment to have an inspection performed on an automobile he or she is considering buying. The inspection is performed at the car's location, and a complete report of the mechanical and electrical condition of the car is provided.

The next section contains a listing of the inspections performed during a Kwik Chek inspection.

In total, approximately 90 points are inspected. The customer can be assured that the major components will be inspected and that any major defects will surface during the inspection.

The inspection time takes around 40 minutes once the mechanic is set up. Each Kwik Chek technician is an experienced mechanic. The equipment in the Kwik Chek van is designed to streamline the inspection process as much as possible. (See Exhibit X for a detailed listing of van equipment.)

The primary benefit being purchased by the user is the peace of mind associated with an objective, informed, third-party opinion of the purchase. Most people want to know what they are buying and not be surprised by major defects later when the vehicle is theirs. The Kwik Chek information can also be used as a negotiating tool to achieve a more equitable price for the vehicle.

A major benefit of using Kwik Chek over the existing method of inspection (that is, bringing the car to a mechanic) is the convenience of having the car inspected without borrowing the car or interrupting the customer's day to have the car inspected.

In essence, the benefits associated with the Kwik Chek service are peace of mind and convenience. The major questions are how many people are willing to pay for the service, and at what price? The next section addresses these marketing-related issues.

Kwik Chek Tests Performed

Engine Diagnostics

Compression

Rotor

Cap

Capacitor (as required)

Points (as required)

Electronic ignition

Oil leakage

Spark plug fouling

Spark plug wires

Belts

Exhaust for age and leaks

Oil consumption/burning

Suspension and Steering

Tire wear

Shock absorbers

Alignment (from tire wear in front)

Torsion bars tightness

Cracked leaf springs

Spare tire condition

Brakes

Check pads/shoes for wear

Check one rotor/drum for wear

Check for pulling when breaking

Check emergency brake

Accessories

AM/FM radio/cassette

Power windows

Power locks

Power seats

Air conditioning

Heater and fan speeds

Gauges

Speedometer/odometers

Cigarette lighter

Windshield washer

Windshield wiper operation and blade condition

Transmission

All speeds

Clutch slip and adjust (manual)

Reverse

Lights

Headlights (low/high)

Turn signals

Hazard lights

Backup lights

License plate lights

Dome lights

Instrument cluster lights

Outside lights

Fluid Levels and Condition

Oil

Transmission

Differential

Clutch

Brake

Coolant plus hoses for leaks

Battery

Washer fluid

Steering

Hydrometer test of coolant for anti-freeze

Electrical

Alternator charging

Battery load test

Slow leak test

Body

Undercoating

Accident repairs

Rust

Fading/peeling paint

Proper closure of doors and windows

Mirrors (inside and out)

Trailer hitch hook-up residuals

The Market and Industry Revenue Potential Analysis

The Scarborough Report on Austin Automobile Purchases for 1988 shows that 31 percent of all adults in Austin are planning to purchase an automobile, and 47 percent of those are planning a used car purchase. This implies that 14 percent of all adults in Austin are planning a used car purchase. (See Exhibit I.)

It is assumed that the Kwik Chek service proposed would be most applicable to used car purchases because new car purchases come with a warranty. This report will concentrate on the used car market as the potential opportunity for Kwik Chek.

There are 569,000 adults in the Austin SMSA. Fourteen percent of this number indicates that it can be expected for 81,190 used cars to be purchased each year. (See Exhibit I.)

On a national basis, 23,386,400 used cars were purchased in 1988. Of these, 7,607,172 (33 percent) were purchased from dealers. It is then assumed that the remaining 15,779,228 (67 percent) were purchased on the open market. (See Exhibit I.)

For purposes of analysis, it is assumed that the 33 percent dealer/67 percent open market ratio outlined in the previous paragraph of used car purchases is indicative of the entire nation, including Austin, in determining the number of used cars purchased from dealers or on the open market.

Referring to Exhibit II, it can be seen that Austin should be purchasing more used automobiles than indicated in Exhibit I because the total purchases divided by the total registrations indicates a holding period of 4.6 years per purchased vehicle. This is more than the 3 to 4 years indicated by the *Medical Economics Journal*, February 6, 1989, page 174.

The estimated new car purchases are assumed accurate because they come from manufacturer data. An increase in the total number of used cars purchased would decrease the holding period for vehicles and indicate a larger turnover than estimated for this analysis. A larger turnover would decrease the holding period and make it closer to the 3 to 4 years estimated. Consequently, it is assumed that this analysis is conservative and reflects a slightly pessimistic case for analysis.

Pricing of Kwik Chek Inspections

Exhibit III reflects the price demand curve for the Kwik Chek service at different prices. The curve is derived from data obtained from a survey of prospective purchasers of the service. They indicated that only 70 percent would use the service at any price and that with a service price of more than $110, none would use the service. The curve is most flat in the $40 to $60 range, with most people saying that $49 sounded "about right." It should also be noted that some mentioned a tendency to price the evaluation service at a percentage of the purchase price of the vehicle in question.

Verification of the $49 price came from the Credit Union National Association *Guide to Buying and Selling a Used Car*. The guide indicates that "If you think this is a car you want, hire a mechanic or car care center to evaluate the car. You can usually do so for $40 or less."

Based on the added convenience of performing the evaluation on site, a $49.95 price seems reasonable and justifiable. Exhibit III also indicates that with a price of $49.95, the available market of potential users of the Kwik Chek service becomes 37.5 percent of the total number of used car purchasers.

It should also be noted that purchases are seasonal in nature, as indicated in Exhibit IV. The peak buying season appears to be March (9.6 percent of purchases) through August, with the end of the year and the beginning of the year relatively slow (with 6.98 percent of purchases according to Exhibit V). It is recommended that Kwik Chek be introduced to the buying public in January to allow familiarity with the concept in time for the March to August buying peak.

As mentioned previously, 33 percent of all used cars are purchased from dealers. Kwik Chek can provide a similar service to the dealers as it intends to provide on the open market. The dealers will probably want a discount off the retail price of 20 to 25 percent, based upon past experience. This discount can be justified by Kwik Chek because of the ease of inspection of many vehicles in the same location, instead of many locations all over the city.

It is assumed that there will be two classes of service: 1) the dealer service at $39 per inspection, and 2) the open market at $49.95 per inspection.

Market Sales Potential

Exhibit V indicates that at the $49.95 price, and with 37.5 percent of the used car buyers as potential customers, the total U.S. revenue potential is $438M and that a 20 percent national penetration of the potential market will generate $87.6M in sales for Kwik Chek. It is assumed that Kwik Chek cannot obtain more than 20 percent penetration due to competition.

Exhibit VI indicates that the Austin market alone has a total potential market of $1.5M at the $49.95 price and that a 20 percent penetration of that market will generate $304,000 in annual revenues.

Exhibit VII indicates that the national potential revenues with 20 percent penetration of both the dealer and open markets is $81M, slightly down from the previous estimate but still a substantial number.

Exhibit VIII outlines the same breakdown as mentioned in the previous paragraph, but for the Austin area. It is seen that Austin can be expected to generate $282,000 in revenues and perform 6,090 inspections per year with 20 percent potential market penetration.

Competition

Kwik Chek already has two competitors in the Austin area: Auto Chek and No Lemons. In addition, a potential competitor named CheckOut may be about to launch a national franchise.

Auto Chek

Auto Chek has been in business for almost one year. The president is a successful entrepreneur who recently sold another company and started Auto Chek a short time afterward.

The president has every intention of making Auto Chek a national franchise and has already sold the franchise rights to an organization in Dallas and San Antonio.

Auto Chek wants an initial franchise fee of $25,000 and an 8 percent royalty on sales. It has advertised a great deal in Austin, but an informal survey of people regarding the service showed that there is awareness of the service but not the name of the company. There is a potential free rider opportunity available to Kwik Chek.

Auto Chek charges $49.50 for its services and checks 90 points on each car.

No Lemons

No Lemons has come onto the market in the last month. It charges $59.50 for its service and claims to inspect 120 points, but it inflates the number a little (by treating each tire as an inspection point, wipers as two inspection points instead of one, and so on).

Rumor around town is that many dealers are shying away from doing business with No Lemons. It is definitely in the market and already out there with a van and providing the service. No Lemons is planning to franchise nationally. Fees and royalty information was not available.

CheckOut

CheckOut is an inspection company in New Jersey that has been providing services for over five years but is confined primarily to the New Jersey/New York area. It charges $59 for its service and checks around 90 points.

CheckOut is rumored to have started a national franchise, but to date, I haven't found evidence of that.

The Management Team

John Doe is the author of this plan and the proposed president of the new company. He has worked as a mechanic for over ten years and has experience repairing both domestic and imported automobiles. He has served as the shop foreman for the local Ford dealership for the last two years. His foreman duties also include profit and loss projections for the service segment of the local dealerships operation. Mr. Doe would be the initial test technician with others hired as business grows.

His wife, Judy, intends to work as the secretary/dispatcher to make the initial Austin, Texas operation a success and to improve their income from the business. She has experience as both a switchboard operator for a large corporation and as an executive secretary.

Mr. Doe has a wide network of mechanic colleagues who are interested in working with Kwik Chek once the idea proves successful.

Operations Plan

Exhibit IX outlines the logistical analysis used to determine the total number of vans that would be required to address Austin at the 20 percent penetration rate. Twenty percent was used to determine the state of the company when working at its peak efficiency.

It is assumed that inspections are provided 11 hours per day, 7 days per week. Dealer inspections will occur during the week, and open market inspection will occur on the weekends and evenings.

It is assumed that a dealer inspection will constitute 33 percent of inspections. Using the estimated 40-minute inspection time per vehicle, dealer inspections are expected to take .67 hours. The open market inspections cannot be scheduled closer than 1.5 hours (90 minute) intervals due to travel times and other unforeseen circumstances.

Based on these assumptions and the 33 percent dealer/67 percent open market split mentioned previously, a maximum of 272 inspections can be performed by one van. The chart indicates that at the 20 percent penetration rate, an average of 1.9 vans will be needed to meet demand in Austin.

It is recommended to start out with one van with Mr. Doe performing the inspections and then add a technician along with progression to a second van when the number of inspections warrants the addition. (See Exhibit XI.)

Marketing and Sales Strategy

The most powerful tool for promoting Kwik Chek's success is positive word of mouth where one satisfied user tells several friends about the value received from using the service. This applies equally well for the dealer and open market segments. The most difficult initial problem is increasing the public's awareness about the service availability and benefits. A special referral reward system should be established where a person can earn a free inspection for recommending ten people for the service. Vouchers can be used to track the referrals.

Monthly marketing expense of $2,500 is assumed and it should be spent in the following areas:

Monthly Yellow Pages advertising	1/2 page ad at $1,200 per month = $1,200
Direct-mail pieces to dealers	200 pieces at $1 each = $200
Direct-mail pieces to households	$400 as an insert in a bulk mailing pack
Commissions for part-time sales	$700 per month at 10 percent of partial revenues

It is also assumed that around $10,000 will be spent during the first few months on radio and newspaper advertising. In addition, special promotions should be set up with the dealers around town in conjunction with radio simulcasts where free used car inspections are provided if you bring your car in for inspection while the radio station is present.

Financial Analysis

This section presents a detailed financial analysis of the Kwik Chek business idea. It first looks at the variable and fixed costs associated with the business operation. This section includes a profit analysis for each van, determines the break-even number of inspections needed to support the van and its driver, and then ties the pieces together into a complete profit and loss analysis over a three-year period.

Fixed- and Variable-Cost Analysis

Exhibit X outlines the fixed and variable costs associated with the operation of Kwik Chek.

It can be seen that the van with its equipment has a cost of $24,140. If financed over a three-year period, this becomes a payment of $779 per month. It is also assumed that a technician/mechanic is dedicated to the van with a salary of $1,800 per month, which is initially paid to Mr. Doe. Adding in paging, service, and maintenance, the costs associated with operating a van are expected to be $2,925 per month.

The general overhead cost is outlined in Exhibit X to be $7,191 per month. This number assumes that most equipment such as computers, copiers, and so on is financed over a three-year period at 10 percent. It also assumes a secretary who doubles as an appointment scheduler and earns $1,500 per month and $2,500 in monthly marketing expenses. The General Overhead number also includes a $417 monthly amortization of a franchise fee of $15,000 that is equally divided over 36 months. All appointments for inspection are scheduled through the main office dispatcher.

Exhibit X also shows that the variable costs associated with dealer inspection is $10, and it is $11 for the open market inspection because gas mileage is involved. Included in this cost is a $5 incentive to the mechanic for each inspection performed and paid for by the customer. This is to keep the drivers motivated to complete as many inspections as possible while assuring quality work.

It can be seen from Exhibit X that total contribution to overhead for operations when at 20 percent (and working with 2 vans) is $16,475 per month. The total overhead is expected to be $13,040, which leaves the net profit before taxes at $3,435. Up to this point, there has not been any allowance for owner income other than the income earned by Mr. Doe as the test technician. At this point, it appears that the maximum before-tax income to the owner of the Austin Kwik Chek franchise would be $3,435 per month or $41,220 per year. If the franchise were owned as a subchapter S corporation, the owner would still need to pay taxes on this amount.

It is also seen from Exhibit X that the inspection break-even for the entire operation with 2 vans is 402 inspections and that the incremental costs associated with another van are covered with 90 inspections.

Overall Financial Analysis

Exhibit XI shows the financial results expected from Kwik Chek operation when the owner is not involved with the inspections. Exhibit XII shows the expected financial results when the owner actually performs inspections from one of the vans. The owner/operator actually makes the $20,000 allocated to the van operator and retains whatever profits are left over at the end of the year.

It is assumed that Kwik Chek acquires 1 percent additional market share for each month it is in operation. At the end of the second year, Kwik Chek is assumed to be at the 20 percent penetration target.

The chart also indicates that there is a substantial negative cumulative cash flow during the first year. The peak negative value is $102,026 for absentee owners and $72,000 for the owner/operator. The profits derived by the second year of operation begin to erode the negative cumulative cash situation. Kwik Chek is still in a negative cumulative cash flow situation by the end of Year 3 for the absentee investors but shows a positive turn for owner/operators. Absentee owner/investors begin to show a return on their investment beginning in Year 4.

The chart shows that the company operates with a negative net operating income over the first year of existence for absentee investors and turns slightly positive for the owner/operator and turns positive for both scenarios in Year 2. The owner/operator stands to make substantial money after the first year should business plan projections be accurate.

An additional van is required during the second year to meet market demands. When included in the expenses of the second and ongoing years, Kwik Chek can be expected to yield a net profit before tax of $41,208 for absentee owners and $89,808 for owner/operators.

Anyone who invests in a Kwik Chek franchise must be willing to risk between $70,000 and $100,000 in cash and wait between 2 and 4 years for a positive return on that investment.

Conclusion

It can be seen from the previous discussion that the investment potential of a Kwik Chek franchise is not a viable option for a person who treats it exclusively as an investment.

Exhibit XII shows what happens to the financials of the project if the owner is also the mechanic for the first van. This creates a saving on two counts: 1) The $5 incentive per inspection is not needed to motivate the mechanic because the mechanic is the owner, and 2) there is an $18,000 savings per year in the salary paid the mechanic.

It can be seen from Exhibit XII that there is still a substantial negative cumulative cash flow for the first year, but the cash flow drain reverses direction in Month 11 as opposed to early in Year 2. We see that the project becomes a positive cumulative cash flow project by the end of Year 2 and becomes a generator of substantial cumulative cash ($107,841) in Year 3.

It still requires $75,000 (plus living expenses) to assure minimum cash reserves for the business. If the marketing penetration ramp-up is greater than expected, then the business will generate cash faster.

Kwik Chek is not a viable investment for someone who does not intend to operate the business and perform inspections in one of the vans. It does not generate a positive return on investment until Year 3 and requires over $100,000 in cash reserves to start.

If a person wants to invest his own time in the project and operates one of the vans, then there is substantial future revenue-earning potential after Year 3. There is still over $75,000 in cash required to fund the business, but the long-term prospects for return are much improved over treating the project as only an investment.

Kwik Chek should be started in Austin by a mechanic who wants to start his or her own business. If it begins to show the returns expected, then the project should be set up for national franchising to mechanic/investor groups who want to provide the service. At that time, additional funding can be obtained based upon the company's successful track record.

Exhibits

Exhibit I: Scarborough Report on Automobile Purchases

From the Scarborough Report on Austin automobile purchases (1988)

Percent of adults planning to purchase a car:	31%
(This fact implies that people change cars every 3.2 years)	
Percent of adults planning a used car purchase:	14%
Total number of Austin SMSA Adults:	569,355
Percent of woman adults buying used cars:	69%
Total number of planned used car purchases:	81,190
Women planning to buy a used car:	56,021
Men planning to buy a used car:	25,169

Notes:
1) The median price range for women's purchases is $6,900
2) The median price range for men's purchases is $10,300
3) The bulk of those buying used cars have median incomes of $27,000

4) The total number of licensed drivers in the U.S.=	164,000,000
There are Number of male drivers=	85,000,000
Number of female drivers=	79,000,000

Assuming the Austin ratios for adults purchasing used cars is valid for the
the entire U.S., then we can assume that the total number of used car
in a year are:

Total number of drivers:	164,000,000
Percent buying used cars:	14%
Percent buying new cars:	16%
Total used car purchases:	23,386,400
Cars purchased by women:	16,136,616
Cars purchased by men:	7,249,784
Cars purchased from dealers:	7,607,172 [from Wards, p. 166]
Cars purchased on open market:	15,779,228

Exhibit II: Validation of Conservative Estimates

To determine whether Austin is representative of the U.S. in general, we
can compare the new car purchases nationally to those expected in Austin.
Austin is expecting new car percentage purchases of 15.5%.

New car information:

1988 new vehicle purchases:	15,245,843
Percent of licensed drivers:	9%

This information indicates that the national average of used car
purchases may actually be higher than that seen in Austin.

Total new car purchases:	15,245,843
Used car purchases:	23,386,400

Total annual purchases:	38,632,243
Total registered vehicles:	179,000,000
Percent purchases to registration:	22%
Average holding period:	5

The national average for holding a car is 3-4 years. These numbers
indicate that the numbers used for analysis are conservative and that
more used cars are probably sold annually than predicted.

Sources:
Motor Vehicles Manufacturers Association Facts and Figures (1988)
Wards Automotive Yearbook, 1989

Exhibit III: Price Demand Curve

Price ($)	Demand	Tot Rev ($)
0	100	0
20	70	1,400
40	50	2,000
50	38	1,875
60	25	1,500
110	0	0

Exhibit IV: Seasonality of Buyer Purchasing Habits (1988/1988)

Month	1987	% of total	Cumulative %	1988	% of total	Cumulative %
1	1,001,879	5.99%	5.99%	1,211,704	6.98%	6.98%
2	1,249,911	7.48%	13.47%	1,412,058	8.14%	15.12%
3	1,527,827	9.14%	22.62%	1,667,601	9.61%	24.73%
4	1,554,248	9.30%	31.92%	1,493,641	8.61%	33.34%
5	1,464,754	8.76%	40.68%	1,629,931	9.39%	42.74%
6	1,584,114	9.48%	50.16%	1,634,603	9.42%	52.16%
7	1,478,519	8.85%	59.01%	1,426,720	8.22%	60.38%
8	1,522,813	9.11%	68.12%	1,446,218	8.34%	68.72%
9	1,413,512	8.46%	76.58%	1,339,803	7.72%	76.44%
10	1,330,895	7.96%	84.54%	1,381,685	7.96%	84.40%
11	1,231,478	7.37%	91.91%	1,313,526	7.57%	91.97%
12	1,352,231	8.09%	100.00%	1,392,945	8.03%	100.00%
	16,712,181			17,350,435		

Exhibit V: National Potential Sales in Units and Dollars at 5, 10 & 20% Penetration

Month	1988 Percent	Used Car Sales (Units)	Total KwikChek Market @ $49.95 (Units)	Total KwikChek Revenues @ $49.95 (Dollars)	At a 5% Penetration of Total Market (Units)	At a 5% Penetration of Total Market (Dollars)	At a 10% Penetration of Total Market (Units)	At a 10% Penetration of Total Market (Dollars)	At a 20% Penetration of Total Market (Units)	At a 20% Penetration of Total Market (Dollars)
January	6.98%	1,633,238	612,464	$30,592,594	30,623	$1,529,630	61,246	$3,059,259	122,493	$6,118,519
February	8.14%	1,903,293	713,735	$35,651,048	35,687	$1,782,552	71,373	$3,565,105	142,747	$7,130,210
March	9.61%	2,247,735	842,901	$42,102,891	42,145	$2,105,145	84,290	$4,210,289	168,580	$8,420,578
April	8.61%	2,013,257	754,971	$37,710,821	37,749	$1,885,541	75,497	$3,771,082	150,994	$7,542,164
May	9.39%	2,196,960	823,860	$41,151,814	41,193	$2,057,591	82,386	$4,115,181	164,772	$8,230,363
June	9.42%	2,203,258	826,222	$41,269,771	41,311	$2,063,489	82,622	$4,126,977	165,244	$8,253,954
July	8.22%	1,923,055	721,146	$36,021,228	36,057	$1,801,061	72,115	$3,602,123	144,229	$7,204,246
August	8.34%	1,949,336	731,001	$36,513,505	36,550	$1,825,675	73,100	$3,651,351	146,200	$7,302,701
September	7.72%	1,805,901	677,213	$33,826,784	33,861	$1,691,339	67,721	$3,382,678	135,443	$6,765,357
October	7.96%	1,862,353	698,382	$34,884,203	34,919	$1,744,210	69,838	$3,488,420	139,676	$6,976,841
November	7.57%	1,770,483	663,931	$33,163,353	33,197	$1,658,168	66,393	$3,316,335	132,786	$6,632,671
December	8.03%	1,877,530	704,074	$35,168,491	35,204	$1,758,425	70,407	$3,516,849	140,815	$7,033,698
		23,386,400	8,769,900	$438,056,505	438,495	$21,902,825	876,990	$43,805,651	1,753,980	$87,611,301

Notes:
1) 1988 percentages taken from Exhibit IV: Seasonality of Buying Chart
2) Used car sales derived from data in Exhibit II for total National used car purchases
3) Total Kwik chek market derived from Exhibit III. 37.5% demand expected at $50 pricing
4) 20% penetration is the maximum expected due to future entrants and other competition

Exhibit VI: Austin Potential Sales in Units and Dollars at 5, 10 & 20% Penetration

Month	1988 Percent	Used Car Sales (Units)	Total KwikChek Market @ $49.95 (Units)	Total KwikChek Revenues @ $49.95 (Dollars)	At a 5% Penetration of Total Market (Units)	At a 5% Penetration of Total Market (Dollars)	At a 10% Penetration of Total Market (Units)	At a 10% Penetration of Total Market (Dollars)	At a 20% Penetration of Total Market (Units)	At a 20% Penetration of Total Market (Dollars)
January	6.98%	5,670	2,126	$106,208	106	$5,310	213	$10,621	425	$21,242
February	8.14%	6,608	2,478	$123,769	124	$6,188	248	$12,377	496	$24,754
March	9.61%	7,803	2,926	$146,168	146	$7,308	293	$14,617	585	$29,234
April	8.61%	6,989	2,621	$130,920	131	$6,546	262	$13,092	524	$26,184
May	9.39%	7,627	2,860	$142,866	143	$7,143	286	$14,287	572	$28,573
June	9.42%	7,649	2,868	$143,275	143	$7,164	287	$14,328	574	$28,655
July	8.22%	6,676	2,504	$125,054	125	$6,253	250	$12,505	501	$25,011
August	8.34%	6,767	2,538	$126,763	127	$6,338	254	$12,676	508	$25,353
September	7.72%	6,270	2,351	$117,436	118	$5,872	235	$11,744	470	$23,487
October	7.96%	6,465	2,425	$121,107	121	$6,055	242	$12,111	485	$24,221
November	7.57%	6,147	2,305	$115,132	115	$5,757	230	$11,513	461	$23,026
December	8.03%	6,518	2,444	$122,094	122	$6,105	244	$12,209	489	$24,419
		81,190	30,446	$1,520,790	1,522	$76,040	3,045	$152,079	6,089	$304,158

Notes:
1) 1988 percentages taken from Exhibit IV: Seasonality of Buying Chart
2) Used car sales derived from data in Exhibit I for total Austin used car purchases
3) Total Kwik chek market derived from Exhibit III. 37.5% demand expected at $50 pricing
4) 20% penetration is the maximum expected due to future entrants and other competition

Exhibit VII: National Dealer/Open Market Potential Sales in Units and Dollars at 10 & 20% Penetration

Dealer Percentage: 33%
Open market Percentage: 67%

Month	1988 Percent	Used Car Sales (Units)	Total KwikChek Market @ 37.5% (Units)	Potential Dealer Sales @ 33% (Units)	Dealer Revenues @ 10% Penetrat. of Dealer Potential & $39 price (Dollars)	Dealer Revenues @ 20% Penetrat. of Dealer Potential & $39 price (Dollars)	Potential Open Market Sales @ 67% (Units)	Open Market Revenues @ 10% penetrat. of Open Mrkt. Potential & $49 price (Dollars)	Open Market Revenues @ 20% penetrat. of Open Mrkt. Potential & $49 price (Dollars)
January	8.14%	1,903,293	713,735	232,165	$905,443	$1,810,887	481,570	$2,405,441	$4,810,882
February	9.61%	2,247,735	842,901	274,180	$1,069,303	$2,138,607	568,720	$2,840,758	$5,681,517
March	8.61%	2,013,257	754,971	245,579	$957,756	$1,915,512	509,393	$2,544,417	$5,088,835
April	9.39%	2,196,960	823,860	267,987	$1,045,148	$2,090,297	555,873	$2,776,587	$5,553,175
May	9.42%	2,203,258	826,222	268,755	$1,048,144	$2,096,288	557,467	$2,784,546	$5,569,093
June	8.22%	1,923,055	721,146	234,576	$914,845	$1,829,690	486,570	$2,430,418	$4,860,835
July	8.34%	1,949,336	731,001	237,781	$927,348	$1,854,695	493,220	$2,463,632	$4,927,265
August	7.72%	1,805,901	677,213	220,285	$859,112	$1,718,224	456,928	$2,282,354	$4,564,709
September	7.96%	1,862,353	698,382	227,171	$885,967	$1,771,935	471,211	$2,353,700	$4,707,401
October	7.57%	1,770,483	663,931	215,965	$842,262	$1,684,525	447,966	$2,237,592	$4,475,183
November	8.03%	1,877,530	704,074	229,022	$893,188	$1,786,375	475,051	$2,372,882	$4,745,764
December		0	0	0	$0	$0	0	$0	$0
		23,386,400	8,157,436	2,653,466	$10,348,517	$20,697,034	5,503,970	$27,492,329	$54,984,657

Notes:
1) 1988 percentages taken from Exhibit IV: Seasonality of Buying Chart
2) Used car sales derived from data in Exhibit II for total National used car purchases
3) Total Kwik chek market derived from Exhibit III. 37.5% demand expected at $50 pricing
4) 20% penetration is the maximum expected due to future entrants and other competition
5) It is assumed that dealers will want a 20% discount off of retail to use the service
6) The breakdown of dealer to open market sales percentages is taken from Exhibit I.

Exhibit VIII: Austin Dealer/Open Market Potential Sales in Units and Dollars at 10 & 20% Penetration

Dealer Percentage: 33%
Open market Percentage: 67%

Month	1988 Percent	Used Car Sales (Units)	Total KwikChek Market @ 37.5% (Units)	Potential Dealer Sales @ 33% (Units)	Dealer Revenues @ 10% Penetrat. of Dealer Potential & $39 price (Dollars)	(Units)	Dealer Revenues @ 20% Penetrat. of Dealer Potential & $39 price (Dollars)	(Units)	Potential Open Market Sales @ 67% (Units)	10% penetrat. of Open Mrkt. Potential & $49 price (Dollars)	(Units)	Open Market Revenues @ 20% penetrat. of Open Mrkt. Potential & $49 price (Dollars)	(Units)
January	6.98%	5,670	2,126	692	$2,697	69	$5,395	138	1,435	$7,166	143	$14,332	287
February	8.14%	6,608	2,478	806	$3,143	81	$6,287	161	1,672	$8,351	167	$16,702	334
March	9.61%	7,803	2,926	952	$3,712	95	$7,425	190	1,974	$9,862	197	$19,724	395
April	8.61%	6,989	2,621	853	$3,325	85	$6,650	171	1,768	$8,833	177	$17,667	354
May	9.39%	7,627	2,860	930	$3,628	93	$7,257	186	1,930	$9,639	193	$19,279	386
June	9.42%	7,649	2,868	933	$3,639	93	$7,278	187	1,935	$9,667	194	$19,334	387
July	8.22%	6,676	2,504	814	$3,176	81	$6,352	163	1,689	$8,438	169	$16,875	338
August	8.34%	6,767	2,538	825	$3,219	83	$6,439	165	1,712	$8,553	171	$17,106	342
September	7.72%	6,270	2,351	765	$2,983	76	$5,965	153	1,586	$7,924	159	$15,847	317
October	7.96%	6,465	2,425	789	$3,076	79	$6,152	158	1,636	$8,171	164	$16,343	327
November	7.57%	6,147	2,305	750	$2,924	75	$5,848	150	1,555	$7,768	156	$15,536	311
December	8.03%	6,518	2,444	795	$3,101	80	$6,202	159	1,649	$8,238	165	$16,476	330
		81,190	30,446	9,904	$38,624	990	$77,248	1,981	20,543	$102,610	2,054	$205,221	4,109

Notes:
1) 1988 percentages taken from Exhibit IV: Seasonality of Buying Chart
2) Used car sales derived from data in Exhibit II for total National used car purchases
3) Total Kwik chek market derived from Exhibit III. 37.5% demand expected at $50 pricing
4) 20% penetration is the maximum expected due to future entrants and other competition
5) It is assumed that dealers will want a 20% discount off of retail to use the service
6) The breakdown of dealer to open market sales percentages is taken from Exhibit I.

Exhibit IX: Operations Breakdown for Austin to Determine the Number of Vans Required

Dealer Price:	$39.00
Open Market Price:	$49.95
Number of inspection hours per day:	11
Number of days per week:	7
Inspection hours per week:	77
Inspection hours per year:	4,004
Average inspection hours per month:	334
Maximum Inspections per van/month:	272
(Assuming 33%-67% dealer-open market split)	
Inspect time (Hrs.):	1.50 (Open market inspection time including 30 minutes travel)
Inspect time (Hrs.):	0.67 (Dealer inspection time of 40 minutes)

Month	20% Penetrat. of Dealer Potential & $39 price (Dollars)	(Units)	Inspection Hours Required	20% penetrat. of Open Mrkt. Potential & $49 price (Dollars)	(Units)	Inspection Hours Required	Total Num. Inspt.	Total Van Hours Needed	Total Vans Needed
January	$5,395	138	92	$14,332	287	430	425	523	1.6
February	$6,287	161	107	$16,702	334	502	496	609	1.8
March	$7,425	190	127	$19,724	395	592	585	719	2.2
April	$6,650	171	114	$17,667	354	531	524	644	1.9
May	$7,257	186	124	$19,279	386	579	572	703	2.1
June	$7,278	187	124	$19,334	387	581	574	705	2.1
July	$6,352	163	109	$16,875	338	507	501	615	1.8
August	$6,439	165	110	$17,106	342	514	508	624	1.9
September	$5,965	153	102	$15,847	317	476	470	578	1.7
October	$6,152	158	105	$16,343	327	491	485	596	1.8
November	$5,848	150	100	$15,536	311	467	461	567	1.7
December	$6,202	159	106	$16,476	330	495	489	601	1.8
	$77,248	1,981	1,320	$205,221	4,109	6,163	6,089	7,483	1.9

Exhibit X: Fixed and Variable Cost Breakdown per Van and Inspection

Van Equipment		Cost
The Van		$15,000
Test Equipment:		$290
Compression	$50	
Calipers	$50	
Depth Gauge	$50	
VOM	$125	
Hydrometer	$15	
Scope and Analyzers		$3,500
Portable Personal Computer		$3,000
Other Equipment:		$1,350
Generator	$200	
Hydraulic jack	$200	
Jack Stands	$150	
Scooter	$50	
Misc hand tools	$750	
Van Cusutomization		$1,000
Total Van Cost:		$24,140

Van Fixed costs:		$2,925
Monthly payment	$779	(Finance over 3 years at 10%)
Technician Wages	$1,800	($20k per year + benefits)
Paging Service	$25	
Insurance	$220	
Maintenance (@ 5%)	$101	

General Overhead Costs:		$7,191 (Including 20% buffer for error)
Office rent	$450	
Postage	$150	
Marketing	$2,500	
Insurance/benefits	$500	
Franchise fee ($15K)	$417	(Divided over 36 months)
Telephone	$140	
Secretary/appointment	$1,500	(Includes appointment scheduling)
Office Equipment:	$336	(Finance over 3 years at 10%)
Computer	$5,000	
FAX	$900	
Copier	$1,500	
Furniture	$1,500	
Telephone	$500	
Misc	$1,000	
Total	$10,400	

Fixed cost per van Assuming Two Vans are in Operation: $6,520

Van Fixed Cost	$2,925
Office Overhead (pro-rated)	$3,595

Fixed Cost per Van-Hour of Operation (the scarce item): $20

Pro-rated cost per dealer inspection	$13
pro-rated cost per Open Market Inspec	$29

Variable costs per Inspection: $11

Gasoline	$1	(Assume 10 miles/call @ 10mpg & $1/gal.)
Misc consumables	$5	
Incentive to tech	$5	

Profit Margin Analysis for Dealer and Open Market Inspections

	Open Market	Dealer	
Revenue	$49.95	$39.00	
7% Franchise fee	($3.50)	($2.73)	
Variable cost	($11.00)	($10.00)	(No gas for dealer insp.)
Contribution	$35.45	$26.27	
Inspections per month:	342	165	
Segment contribution:	$12,138	$4,336	

Monthly Expected Total Contribution:	$16,475
Less: Total Fixed Cost	($13,040)
Net Total Profit Before Tax:	$3,435

Assuming a 33% Dealer/67% Open market breakdown in inspections:

Breakeven Monthly Inspections Quantity:		402
Total 2-van fixed cost:	$13,040	
Dealer inspections:	133	
Open market Inspections:	269	

Breakeven Quantity for Justifying Another Van Purchase:

Van Breakeven for 33%/67% split:		90
Van incremental fixed cost:	$2,925	

Exhibit XI: Summary Financial Analysis for Kwik Chek in Austin

	Start	Mo. 1	Mo. 2	Mo. 3	Mo. 4	Mo. 5
Market Share	0%	1%	2%	2%	3%	3%
Dealer Inspections	0	8	17	17	25	25
Open Market inspects	0	17	34	34	51	51
Total Inspections	0	25	51	51	76	76
Number of Vans needed	1	1	1	1	1	1
INCOME FROM PRODUCTION ACTIVITIES						
Dealer Sales ($)	0	322	644	644	966	966
Open Mkt Sales ($)	0	855	1,710	1,710	2,565	2,565
Less: Cost of Good Sold						
Variable Costs	0	(271)	(542)	(542)	(813)	(813)
Franchise Royalty	0	(82)	(165)	(165)	(247)	(247)
Gross margin	0	824	1,647	1,647	2,471	2,471
OPERATING EXPENSES						
General Fixed costs	(7,191)	(7,191)	(7,191)	(7,191)	(7,191)	(7,191)
Van fixed costs	(2,925)	(2,925)	(2,925)	(2,925)	(2,925)	(2,925)
Net Operating Income	(10,116)	(9,292)	(8,469)	(8,469)	(7,645)	(7,645)
ADDITIONAL EXPENSES						
Promotion cost	(10,000) [Initial advertising, public relations, etc.]					
Misc. Start-Up Cost	(5,000)					
Net Profit Before Tax	(25,116)	(9,292)	(8,469)	(8,469)	(7,645)	(7,645)
CUMULATIVE CASH FLOW	(25,116)	(34,408)	(42,877)	(51,345)	(58,990)	(66,635)

Assumptions:
1) There is a 33%/67% quantity split between dealers and open market inspections
2) Dealer inspections cost $39.00 and Open Market inspections cost $49.95
3) The maximum number of inspections per van is 272 per month.
4) Office fixed expenses can handle up to 4 vans without expansion.
5) Demand will never exceed 37.5% of all used car purchases.
6) Kwik Chek can achieve a 20% share of the demand within 2 years.
7) More than 20% share may not be possible due to competition.
8) Available market for Dealers and Open Market inspections in Units is:

        Dealers: 9,904 (From Exhibit VIII)
        Open Mkt: 20,543 (From Exhibit VIII)

Mo. 6	Mo. 7	Mo. 8	Mo. 9	Mo. 10	Mo. 11	Mo. 12	Year 2	Year 3
4%	4%	5%	6%	7%	8%	9%	20%	20%
33	33	41	50	58	66	74	1,981	1,981
68	68	86	103	120	137	154	4,109	4,109
101	101	127	152	178	203	228	6,089	6,089
1	1	1	1	1	1	1	2	2
1,288	1,288	1,609	1,931	2,253	2,575	2,897	77,251	77,251
3,420	3,420	4,276	5,131	5,986	6,841	7,696	205,225	205,225
(1,083)	(1,083)	(1,354)	(1,625)	(1,896)	(2,167)	(2,438)	(65,003)	(65,003)
(330)	(330)	(412)	(494)	(577)	(659)	(741)	(19,773)	(19,773)
3,295	3,295	4,119	4,942	5,766	6,590	7,414	197,700	197,700
(7,191)	(7,191)	(7,191)	(7,191)	(7,191)	(7,191)	(7,191)	(86,292)	(86,292)
(2,925)	(2,925)	(2,925)	(2,925)	(2,925)	(2,925)	(2,925)	(70,200)	(70,200)
(6,821)	(6,821)	(5,997)	(5,174)	(4,350)	(3,526)	(2,702)	41,208	41,208
(6,821)	(6,821)	(5,997)	(5,174)	(4,350)	(3,526)	(2,702)	41,208	41,208
(73,456)	(80,277)	(86,274)	(91,448)	(95,797)	(99,323)	(102,026)	(60,818)	(19,610)

Exhibit XII: Owner/Mechanic Summary Financial Analysis for Kwik Chek in Austin

	Start	Mo. 1	Mo. 2	Mo. 3	Mo. 4	Mo. 5
Market Share	0%	1%	2%	2%	3%	3%
Dealer Inspections	0	8	17	17	25	25
Open Market inspects	0	17	34	34	51	51
Total Inspections	0	25	51	51	76	76
Number of Vans needed	1	1	1	1	1	1
INCOME FROM PRODUCTION ACTIVITIES						
Dealer Sales ($)	0	322	644	644	966	966
Open Mkt Sales ($)	0	855	1,710	1,710	2,565	2,565
Less: Cost of Good Sold						
Variable Costs	0	(144)	(288)	(288)	(432)	(432)
Franchise Royalty	0	(82)	(165)	(165)	(247)	(247)
Gross margin	0	951	1,901	1,901	2,852	2,852
OPERATING EXPENSES						
General Fixed costs	(7,191)	(7,191)	(7,191)	(7,191)	(7,191)	(7,191)
Van fixed costs	(1,125)	(1,125)	(1,125)	(1,125)	(1,125)	(1,125)
Net Operating Income	(8,316)	(7,365)	(6,415)	(6,415)	(5,464)	(5,464)
ADDITIONAL EXPENSES						
Promotion cost	(10,000) [Initial advertising, public relations, etc.]					
Misc. Start-Up Cost	(5,000)					
Net Profit Before Tax	(23,316)	(7,365)	(6,415)	(6,415)	(5,464)	(5,464)
CUMULATIVE CASH FLOW	(23,316)	(30,681)	(37,096)	(43,511)	(48,975)	(54,439)

Assumptions:
1) There is a 33%/67% quantity split between dealers and open market inspections
2) Dealer inspections cost $39.00 and Open Market inspections cost $49.95
3) The maximum number of inspections per van is 272 per month.
4) Office fixed expenses can handle up to 4 vans without expansion.
5) Demand will never exceed 37.5% of all used car purchases.
6) Kwik Chek can achieve a 20% share of the demand within 2 years.
7) More than 20% share may not be possible due to competition.
8) Available market for Dealers and Open Market inspections in Units is:

        Dealers: 9,904 (From Exhibit VIII)
        Open Mkt: 20,543 (From Exhibit VIII)

Mo. 6	Mo. 7	Mo. 8	Mo. 9	Mo. 10	Mo. 11	Mo. 12	Year 2	Year 3
4%	4%	5%	6%	7%	8%	9%	20%	20%
33	33	41	50	58	66	74	1,981	1,981
68	68	86	103	120	137	154	4,109	4,109
101	101	127	152	178	203	228	6,089	6,089
1	1	1	1	1	1	1	2	2
1,288	1,288	1,609	1,931	2,253	2,575	2,897	77,251	77,251
3,420	3,420	4,276	5,131	5,986	6,841	7,696	205,225	205,225
(576)	(576)	(720)	(864)	(1,008)	(1,152)	(1,296)	(65,003)	(65,003)
(330)	(330)	(412)	(494)	(577)	(659)	(741)	(19,773)	(19,773)
3,802	3,802	4,753	5,704	6,654	7,605	8,556	197,700	197,700
(7,191)	(7,191)	(7,191)	(7,191)	(7,191)	(7,191)	(7,191)	(86,292)	(86,292)
(1,125)	(1,125)	(1,125)	(1,125)	(1,125)	(1,125)	(1,125)	(21,600)	(21,600)
(4,514)	(4,514)	(3,563)	(2,612)	(1,662)	(711)	240	89,808	89,808
(4,514)	(4,514)	(3,563)	(2,612)	(1,662)	(711)	240	89,808	89,808
(58,953)	(63,466)	(67,029)	(69,642)	(71,303)	(72,014)	(71,775)	18,033	107,841

Legal Considerations

The primary legal issues that should be considered in establishing Kwik Chek as a national franchise are (1) franchiser liability for franchisee actions, and (2) termination of franchise agreement by either the franchiser or the franchisee.

The principle way that the franchiser can be held liable for the actions of a franchisee is if the franchisee represents itself as an agent of the parent company. To avoid this agency issue, all collateral literature published by the franchiser should indicate that all Kwik Chek operations are independently owned and operated. In this way, there can be no mistake on the part of the customer that the local franchisee is working their own business and on their own behalf.

A clear definition of the agency relationship will protect the franchiser from liability related to injury or accidents resulting from improper inspection and also from any financial liabilities that the franchisee may incur.

To address the termination of franchise agreement issue, it should be clearly delineated in the franchise agreement what the required payment procedures and time frames should be from the franchisee to the franchiser. In addition, the level of support that the franchisee can reasonably expect from the franchiser should also be clearly defined. In this way, there is less likelihood of misunderstanding by either party, and the franchiser is protected from having a franchisee who is not performing up to expectations bring down the rest of the organization.

In addition, if the franchiser has agreed to supply credit to the franchisee to start the business, then the franchiser should protect the investment by having strict reporting procedures as to the actions being taken by the franchisee to meet the required revenue goals.

Franchising agreements are being treated more as "relational contracts" that extend over a longer period of time than as individual contracts that have a clearly defined duration and outcome. Many courts are treating franchise agreements as a sort of marriage, and many of the precedents established for divorce law in community property states are being incorporated into termination of franchise agreements. The relationship is treated as a type of partnership, and the parties involved are compensated for their "expected" returns from the venture should it be terminated.

In this way, it should be clearly understood by the franchisee that should the franchisee lose the right to operate under the Kwik Chek name, the business is returned to the franchiser. An equitable settlement for the return can be established at the time of transfer.

Appendix
B

Resources

The following list offers you extra resources on a variety of business and entrepreneurial subjects. I included website addresses where possible.

Small Business—General

American Chamber of Commerce Executives
4232 King Street
Alexandria, VA 22302
703-998-0072
www.acce.org

The American Institute for Small Business
Educational Materials for Small Business and Entrepreneurship
7515 Wayzata Blvd.
Minneapolis, MN 55426
1-800-328-2906

American Success Institute
www.success.org

Business Resource Center
www.morebusiness.com

CCH Business Owner's Toolkit
www.toolkit.cch.com

eWeb: Education for Entrepreneurship
www.slu.edu/eweb

Howard University Small Business Development Center (SBDC)
2600 Sixth Street NW, Room 125
Washington, DC 20059
202-806-1550
www.sbaonline.sba.gov/SBDC

The National Association for the Self-Employed
1023 15th Street NW, Suite 1200
Washington, DC 20005-2600
202-466-2100
www.nase.org

National Business Incubation Association
20 East Circle Drive, Suite 190
Athens, OH 45701
www.nbia.org

National Organization of Business Opportunity Seekers (NOBOSS)
8281 Northwind Way
Orangevale, CA 95662
916-723-0344
www.noboss.com

Service Core of Retired Executives (SCORE)
www.score.org

Small Business Development Center Research Network
www.smallbiz.suny.edu

U.S. Chamber of Commerce Small Business Institute
201 E. Dundee Rd.
Palatine, IL 60067
1-800-429-7724
www.usccsbi.com

U.S. Department of Commerce
14th & Constitution Avenue NW, Room 5053
Washington, DC 20230
202-482-5061
www.mbda.gov

U.S. Small Business Administration (SBA)
409 3rd Street, SW
Washington, DC 20416
202-205-7701
www.sba.gov

U.S. SBA/Business Information Center
1110 Vermont Ave. NW, 9th Floor
Washington, DC 20059
202-606-4000, ext. 279

Special Topics

The following are specialized resources that may be of use to you in your business.

Census Information

Here is an excellent place to obtain information regarding general population characteristics in your area of question.

U.S. Bureau of the Census
Public Information Office
Washington, DC 20233-8200
301-763-4040
www.census.gov

Financing

Here are several locations you can review for information on preparing for financing, or actually obtaining financing for your venture.

Business Loan Center
1301 N. Hamilton Street
Richmond, VA 23230
804-358-6454

Datamerge Financing Sources
1-800-580-1188
www.datamerge.com

FinanceNet

www.financenet.gov

National Financial Services Network

www.nfsn.com

Franchises

Don't buy a franchise before talking to these people to determine as much as possible about the parent company of your possible franchise purchase.

American Association of Franchisees & Dealers

PO Box 81887

San Diego, CA 92138-1887

1-800-733-9858

www.aafd.org

International Franchise Association

1350 New York Avenue NW, Suite 900

Washington, DC 20005-4709

202-628-8000

www.franchise.org

International Business

Business Network International

199 S. Monte Vista, Suite 6

San Dimas, CA 91773-3080

www.bni.com

International Chamber of Commerce

156 Fifth Avenue, Suite 308

New York, NY 10010

212-206-1150

International Small Business Consortium

2015 Martingale Dr.

Norman, OK 73072

www.isbc.com

U.S. Agency for International Development (USAID)
Public Inquiries
320 21st Street NW
Washington, DC 20523-0016

U.S. Council for International Business
www.uscib.org

Marketing

Marketing Resource Center
Concept Marketing Group, Inc.
115-B Mark Randy Pl.
Modesto, CA 95350
1-800-575-5369
www.marketingsource.com

Minorities in Business

National Minority Business Council
235 E. 42nd Street
New York, NY 10017
212-573-2385

National Minority Supplier Development Council
1040 Avenue of the Americas, 2nd Floor
New York, NY 10018
212-944-2430
www.nmsdcus.org

SBA Office of Minority Enterprise and Development
www.sba.gov/MED

Patents

U.S. Patent and Trademark Office
Office of Public Affairs
2021 Jefferson Davis Highway
Arlington, VA 20209
703-557-4636
www.uspto.gov

Women in Business

Interagency Committee on Women's Business Enterprise
National Economic Council
The White House
Washington, DC 20500
202-456-2174

National Association of Women Business Owners
1411 K Street, Suite 1300
Washington, DC 20005
301-608-2590
www.nawbo.org

National Foundation for Women Business Owners
1100 Wayne Avenue, Suite 830
Silver Spring, MD 20910-5603
www.nfwbo.org

U.S. Small Business Administration Office of Women's Business Ownership
409 Third Street SW
Washington, DC 20416
202-205-6673
www.sbaonline.sba.gov/womeninbusiness

Christian Resources

Capstone Asset Planning Company
5847 San Felipe, Suite 4100
Houston, TX 77057
1-800-262-6631
www.servfunds.com

Investment opportunities for the socially responsible investor, in harmony with Christian ethics.

Christian Management Association
1-800-727-4262
P.O. Box 4090
San Clemente, CA 92674-4090

Serves more than 3,500 leaders and managers of Christian organizations, helping equip its member organizations with management information, leadership training, and strategic networking relationships.

Executive Ministries
864-370-3115
201 West McBee Avenue, Suite 201
Greenville, SC 29601
www.execmin.org

Reaches out to the executive, professional, and leadership community to provide help for increasing Christian witness in the workplace.

Full Gospel Businessmen's Fellowship, International
(001) 949-461-0100
27 Spectrum Pointe Drive, Suite 312, Lake Forest,
CA 9263 USA

Holds meetings for breakfast, lunch, and dinner, to provide encouragement, fellowship, outreach, and personal ministry among Christian men in business.

International Christian Chamber of Commerce, USA
202-824-0770
ICCC-USA
Washington DC 20004
www.icccusa.net

Stimulates the development of member businesses and services through development of an interactive network of mature, dedicated Christian business and governmental leaders.

National Christian Business Referral Network
1-888-747-5673
5226 Edgemont Circle
Cypress, CA 90630
www.christianreferrals.com

Seeks to bring Christians together for business relationships, with a focus on real estate and loan businesses.

Christian Resources Online

Christian CareerNet

www.christian-careers.com

Guides to job search resources and home business opportunities.

Christiancoaching.com

christiancoaching.com

Provides personal "coaches" or mentors and trainers, for those who need help in the various aspects of life, including help in business and ministry.

Christian Top Sites

www.christiantopsites.com

Provides links and search engines to Christian websites appropriate for your family.

Christiansinbusiness.net

www.christiansinbusiness.net

Provides ways for Christian start-up projects to get in front of potential funding resources.

Ichristianweb.com

ichristianweb.com

Provides a search engine dedicated to Christian website searches.

scruples.org

scruples.org or scruples.net

A social-conscience oriented approach to business, filled with resources for business professionals and Christian entrepreneurs, including forums on small-business creation and development along with a library of teaching resources.

Ultimate Christian Resources

www.chritech.com

Provides links to hundreds of Christian and family-friendly resources and businesses.

Wealthwalk.com

wealthwalk.com

Provides financial services designed for Christians of any age who want to manage their money wisely.

Appendix C

Bibliography

The Complete Idiot's Guide to Buying and Selling a Business. Ed Paulson. Macmillan, 1999, ISBN: 0-02-862903-5.

The Complete Idiot's Guide to Personal Finance with Quicken. Ed Paulson. Macmillan, 1998, ISBN: 0-7897-1751-4.

Almanac of Business and Industrial Financial Ratios. Prentice Hall, 1992, ISBN: 0-13-038282-5.

The Best Home Businesses for the '90s. Paul and Sarah Edwards. Jeremy P. Tarcher/Putnam Books, 1994, ISBN: 0-87477-784-4.

The Complete Communications Handbook. Ed Paulson. Wordware Publishing, 1992, ISBN: 1-55622-238-6.

Creating the Successful Business Plan for New Ventures. LaRue Hosmer. McGraw-Hill, 1985, ISBN: 0-07-030452-1.

The Essence of Small Business. Colin Barrow. Prentice Hall, 1993, ISBN: 013285-362-0.

Getting Paid in Full. W. Kelsea Wilber. Sourcebooks Inc., 1994, ISBN: 0-942061-68-3.

The Internet Roadmap. Bennett Falk. Sybex, 1994, ISBN: 0-7821-1365-6.

Job and Career Building. Richard Germann and Peter Arnold. 10 Speed Press, 1980, ISBN: 0-89815-048-5.

"A Liability Shield for Entrepreneurs." Ripley Hotch. Nation's Business, August 1994.

The Little Online Book. Alfred Glossbrenner. Peachpit Press, 1995, ISBN: 1-566609-130-6.

Nobody Gets Rich Working for Somebody Else: An Entrepreneur's Guide. Roger Fritz. Dodd, Mead & Company, Inc., 1987, ISBN: 0-39608877-5.

The Personnel Policy Handbook for Growing Companies. Darien McWhirter. Bob Adams, Inc., 1994, ISBN: 1-55850-430-3.

Small Claims Court Without a Lawyer. W. Kelsea Wilber. Sourcebooks Inc., ISBN: 0-942061-32-2.

Books Quoted in "Advice from Above"

12,000 Religious Quotations. Frank S. Mead, ed., Baker Book House, 1992, ISBN: 0-8010-6253-5.

The Complete Book of Christian Prayer. Continuum, 1995, ISBN: 0-8264-0872-9.

Don't Worry, Make Money. Richard Carlson. Hyperion, 1997, ISBN: 0-7868-8360-x.

Greeting the Day: Morning Prayers and Meditations from around the World. Brian Wright. Adams Media, 1999, ISBN: 1-58062-121-x.

Illustrations for Preaching and Teaching. Craig Brian Larson, ed. Baker Book House, 1993, ISBN: 0-80100-5691-8.

Illustrations of Bible Truths. Spiros Zodhiates. AMG Publishers, 1991, ISBN: 0-89957-079-8.

The Treasury of Inspirational Anecdotes, Quotations, and Illustrations. E. Paul Hovey, ed., Fleming H. Revell, 1994, ISBN: 0-8007-5539-1.

Wishful Thinking: A Seeker's ABC. Frederick Buechner. HarperSanFransisco, 1983, ISBN: 0-0606-1139-1.

Women's Wisdom through the Ages. Mary Horner and Vinita Hampton, eds. Harold Shaw Publishers, 1994, ISBN: 0-8778-8900-7.

Your Work Matters to God. Doug Sherman and William Hendricks. NavPress, 1987, ISBN: 0-8910-9372-9.

Recommended Reading

Business Basics from the Bible, More Ancient Wisdom for Modern Business. Bob Briner. Grand Rapids, MI: Zondervan, 1994, ISBN: 0310213207.

Business by the Book: The Complete Guide of Biblical Principles for Business Men and Women. Larry Burkett. Nashville, TN: Thomas Nelson, 1990, ISBN: 0785271414.

High-Wire Mom: Balancing Your Family and a Home Business. Kendra Smiley. Chicago, IL: Moody Press, 2002, ISBN: 0802443419.

Jesus CEO, Using Ancient Wisdom for Visionary Leadership. Laurie Beth Jones. New York, NY: Hyperion, 1995, ISBN: 0786881267.

Prosperity & the Christian-Owned Business. Os Hillman. Fairfield, CT: Aslan Publishing, 1996, ISBN: 1888582030.

Succeeding in Business as a Christian: The Application of Christian Principles to Business Ventures. Theodore V. Foster. Clarion Publishing Corporation, 1993, ISBN: 1883866014.

The People Skills of Jesus: Ancient Wisdom for Modern Business. William Beausay. Nashville, TN: Thomas Nelson, 1997, ISBN: 0785271643.

Additional Reading

The 7 Habits of Highly Effective People. Stephen Covey. Fireside/Simon & Schuster, 1989, ISBN: 0-671-70863-5.

1000 Things You Never Learned in Business School. William Yeomans. Mentor, 1985, ISBN: 0-451-62810-1.

Beyond Entrepreneurship. James Collins and William Lazier. Prentice Hall, 1992, ISBN: 0-13-085366-6.

Business Owner's Guide to Accounting and Bookkeeping. Jose Placencia, Bruce Welge, and Don Oliver. Oasis Press, 1991, ISBN: 1-55571-156-1.

The Complete Idiot's Guide to Business Management. Hap Klopp. Macmillan, 1997, ISBN: 0-02-861744-4.

The Complete Idiot's Guide to Marketing Basics. Sarah White. Macmillan, 1997, ISBN: 0-02-861490-9.

The CompuServe Yellow Pages. Rob Tidrow. New Riders Publishing, 1994, ISBN: 1-56205-396-5.

The Entrepreneur's Business Law Handbook. Sean Melvin. Macmillan, 1997, ISBN: 0-02-861751-7.

Essentials of Media Planning. Arnold Barban, Steven Cristol, and Frank Kopec. NTC Business Books, 1989, ISBN: 0-8442-3018-9.

Exporting, Importing and Beyond. Lawrence Tuller. Adams Media Corporation, 1994, ISBN: 1-55850-777-9.

Financing the Small Business. Lawrence Tuller. Prentice Hall, 1991, ISBN: 0-13-322116-4.

Free Money for Small Businesses and Entrepreneurs. Laurie Blum. John Wiley, 1992, ISBN: 0-471-58122-4.

Home Based Mail Order. William Bond. Liberty Press, 1990, ISBN: 0-8306-3045-7.

How to Advertise and Promote Your Small Business. Connie McClung and Connie Siegel. Wiley Press, 1978, ISBN: 0-471-04032-0.

How to Start a Service Business. Ben Chant and Melissa Morgan. Avon, 1994, ISBN: 0-380-77-77-6.

How to Think Like an Entrepreneur. Michael Shane. Bret Publishing, 1994, ISBN: 0-9640346-0-3.

Inc Yourself. Judith McQuown. Harper Business, 1992, ISBN: 0-88730-611-X.

Insider's Guide to Growing a Small Business. Peter Richman. Macmillan, 1997, ISBN: 0-02-861176-4.

The Internet Business Guide. Rosalind Resnick and Dave Taylor. Sams, 1994, ISBN: 0-672-30530-5.

Internet Yellow Pages. New Riders Publishing, 1997, ISBN: 1-56205-784-7.

One Minute for Myself. Spencer Johnson. Avon, 1985, ISBN: 0-380-70308-4.

Start, Run and Profit from Your Own Home-Based Business. Gregory Kishel. John Wiley, 1991, ISBN: 0-471-52587-1.

Starting an Import/Export Business. Entrepreneur Magazine Group. John Wiley and Sons, Inc., 1995, ISBN: 0-471-11059-0.

Starting Right in Your New Business. Wilfred Tetreault and Robert Clements. Addison-Wesley, 1988, ISBN: 0-201-07795-7.

Strategic Planning for the Small Business. Craig Rice. Bob Adams, Inc., 1990, ISBN: 1-55850-858-9.

The Strategy Game. Craig Hickman. McGraw-Hill, 1993, ISBN: 0-07-028725-2.

The Successful Business Plan. Rhonda Abrams. Oasis Press, 1993, ISBN: 1-55571-194-4.

Tax Deductions for Small Business. Barbara Weltman. J.K. Lasser, 1997, ISBN: 0-02-860313-3.

Using CompuServe. Matthew Ellsworth. Que, 1994, ISBN: 1-56529-726-1.

West's Business Law. Gaylord Jentz, et. al. West Publishing Company, 1989, ISBN: 0-314-47214-2.

Your Income Tax. J. K. Lasser. Macmillan, 1998, ISBN: 0-02-861996-X.

Appendix
D

Business Buzzword Glossary

accounting period   A period of time used to correlate revenues and expenses usually defined as a day, week, month, quarter, or year.

accrual basis of accounting   A method of accounting that relates revenues and expenses based on when the commitments are made as opposed to when the cash is spent or received.

action plans   The steps needed to achieve specific goals.

advisory board   A group of business associates who act as advisors to your company on an informal basis.

analysis statement   A statement provided by your bank that details the various deposits and charges associated with your business account.

articles of incorporation   A set of documents that are filed with the secretary of state's office that formally establish your corporation in that state.

assets   Those items of value the company owns, such as cash in the checking account, accounts receivables, equipment, and property.

authorized shares   The total number of shares of stock the corporation is permitted to issue.

bad debt ratio   The amount of money you believe customers will never pay (also called uncollectible funds), divided by total sales and expressed as a percent.

balance sheet   One type of financial statement that you (or your accountant) create to show all the company's assets and all the liabilities and equity owned by investors.

benefit   What the customer gains by using your product or service.

board of accountancy   The group of accountants that make decisions regarding generally accepted accounting principles.

board of directors   A group of experienced business leaders who are asked or elected to serve as advisors to a company.

bookkeeping   A system for tracking where your money is coming from and where it is going.

break-even analysis   An analysis technique used to determine the quantity of an item that must be produced and/or sold to cover the fixed expenses associated with the time period in question.

break-even point   The quantity point where the gross margin equals the fixed expenses for the period in question. Above the break-even point, the company makes money and below the break-even point, the company loses money.

business inertia   The inability of a company to change its thinking or ways of doing business.

business judgment rule   A concept that protects members of corporate boards of directors from lawsuits filed by shareholders, customers, or others if the decision that caused the lawsuit was made in the best interests of the corporation.

business plan   A document that outlines your overall business objectives, their viability, and the steps you intend to take to achieve those objectives.

bylaws   The overall rules for operation of a corporation. Bylaws are an integral part of the corporation filing procedure.

C corporation   The business structure used primarily by major corporations so they can sell shares of stock to the public. Other forms of a corporation have restrictions on the number of shareholders that can exist, but a C corporation does not.

calendar fiscal year   A company which has its financial year start on January 1 and end on December 31.

card processing company   A company that processes the credit card transactions for the retailers by verifying the account validity, the credit amounts available, and the transfer of funds into your company checking account.

cash basis of accounting   A method of accounting where expenses and revenues are tracked based on when cash is received or actual checks are written.

cash flow analysis   A financial statement that shows how much money the company had at the beginning of the month, how much money came in through sales and payments, how much went out in the form of payments, and what was left at the end of the month.

chain style franchise   A franchise arrangement where the franchisee pays a fee for an established chain store outlet like Midas or McDonald's.

chart of accounts   A list of all the categories a business uses to organize its financial expenditures and sales.

class of stock   Corporations can issue different types of stock that each have different legal rights with regard to dividends, voting, and other rights. Each of these different stock categories is called a class of stock.

clipping services   Companies such as Bacon's and Luce Clipping Services that read thousands of newspapers and magazines on the lookout for articles about or references to specific companies.

close   A request by the salesperson for a specific action on the customer's part.

close corporation   A company where owners or shareholders are active in the daily management of the corporation, which has no public investors.

commodities   Products that have no distinguishing features or benefits, such as flour, salt, and pork bellies, so that there is little or no difference in pricing between competitive products.

company policy manual   A manual that outlines the overall company policies that apply to all employees.

consideration   Something of value, such as money or a right to do something, that is usually given at the signing of a contract.

content (website)   The information included in a website that is viewed by Internet visitors.

corporation   A legal entity that is created as an umbrella under which business operation can occur. Corporations are chartered with the state and come in various forms such as the S corporation and the Limited Liability Corporation (LLC).

cost of sales   The costs directly linked to the production or sale of a product or service, also called the Cost of Goods Sold (COGS).

cost plus profit pricing   Calculating your price using the cost to the company plus your desired profit margin. A widget that costs $1 to produce with a desired 50 percent profit margin would sell for $1 + ($1 \times 5) = 1.50

credit card transaction processing company   An organization that processes the typical credit card transaction and handles the transfer of funds from a credit card account into yours.

current assets   Company assets that are liquid or can be converted to cash in less than one year.

debt financing   A means of securing funding to start or expand your business by way of a loan of some sort.

demographic profile   Usually refers to a specific set of demographic characteristics used by sales and marketing to target likely sales prospects. Sometimes called an ideal customer profile.

demographics   A set of objective characteristics, such as age, home ownership, and marital status, that describe a group of people.

depreciation   An accounting procedure that deducts a certain amount of an asset's worth for each year of its operation.

direct competitors   Companies that sell the same product or service your company does, going after the same customers.

direct shareholder vote   A voting procedure where the shareholders personally cast their votes instead of voting by proxy.

distribution channel   However your product or service gets from your facilities into the hands of customers.

distributor franchise   A franchise arrangement where the franchisee actually acts as a distributor for a major manufacturer's products, such as with a large auto dealership.

dividends   Money paid to shareholders out of the corporation's net income (after taxes are taken out).

doing business as (d/b/a)   When you start a sole proprietorship that is named something other than your given name, you must complete some forms to officially use that name. The form you complete is a doing business as, or d/b/a, form.

domain name   A unique name used to define an Internet location.

double taxation   Where the business pays tax on its annual profits and then passes the income to you, the majority shareholder, who again gets taxed at the personal level; thus, the same dollar is taxed twice.

earned income   Income attributed to business operations during a specific period of time.

employee manual   A document prepared by the company and issued to all employees, indicating the company's policies and procedures.

employer identification number (EIN)   A number issued by the IRS to any company with employees.

entrepreneur   Someone who is willing to take personal and financial risks to create a business out of a perceived opportunity.

equity financing   When someone gives you money in return for ownership of a portion of your company. You are giving up equity in the business in return for capital, which is equity financing.

exchange rate   The rate at which one form of currency is converted into another.

exchange rate liability   The uncertainty that comes from holding a purchase/sale agreement that is not in your home country's currency in an environment where exchange rates change.

factoring   The process of receiving money now for payments your customers are expected to make to you in the next few weeks. There is a cost to having that money now, which is paid in the form of a percentage fee to the factoring company or factor.

feature   The different characteristics of a product or service.

federal tax deposit coupon   Coupon issued by the IRS for collection of employee withholding taxes on a regular basis.

fictitious name statement   *See* doing business as (d/b/a).

fiscal year   The period of time over which you track your annual business accounting operations.

fixed expenses   Business expenses that do not vary each month based on the amount of sales, such as rent, equipment leases, and salaries.

float   The time period during which you have to cover expenses that should have been paid out of money received from customers.

forum   A site on a computer service in which people with similar interests can post and read messages.

franchiser   A company that has created a successful business operation and concept that offers to sell the rights to the operation and idea on a limited geographic or market basis.

freelancer   An individual who works for several different companies at once, helping out on specific projects.

freight forwarder   A company that specializes in shipping, duties, customs, and other administrative complexities related to international commerce.

gating item   The section of a process that limits the overall process speed. Increase the gating item's throughput and you increase the overall process throughput.

Gantt chart   A method of tracking project items so that their order of completion, time frame, and status are easily monitored.

gross profit   The amount of money left after you cover the cost of sales. Out of gross profit, you pay your operational expenses. Gross profit = revenue ÷ cost of sales.

Hypertext Markup Language (HTML)   The programming code embedded in a website's pages that is interpreted by a browser for display on the user's computer.

IBM clone   A personal computer that uses technology similar to that used for the IBM personal computers.

income   The amount of money left over after expenses are deducted from the sales revenue amount.

income statement   A type of financial statement that reflects all the income and expenses for a particular period of time, which is generally a year.

independent contractor   Another word that the IRS frequently uses for a freelancer.

industrial espionage   The practice of collecting information about competitors through devious methods.

inertia   Indisposition to motion, exertion, or change; resistance to change.

initial public offering (IPO)   A stock trading event where the stock for a corporation is offered to the general public for the first time.

Internet   An electronically connected network of computers that spans the globe. Once you are connected to it, the usage is typically provided at a flat fee for unlimited usage.

Internet service provider (ISP)   A company that provides access to the Internet for users with a computer, modem, and the proper software.

job description   A detailed listing of the duties to be performed by the person filling the job in question; a listing of the required skills, education, certification levels, and other criteria directly related to the job.

job shop operation   A company which has a process flow that creates unique items at lower production volumes for each of its customers, as opposed to producing a standardized product in high volumes.

letter of credit (L/C)   A financial note that is set up through international banks by buyers and sellers who reside in different countries. Establishes a third-party, bank-to-bank handshake to ensure that both sides of the transaction are executed properly.

liabilities   Amounts that you owe. Typical liabilities include loans, credit cards, taxes owed, and other people to whom you owe money.

life cycle   The four general phases that a product or service goes through between being introduced to the market and being discontinued or taken off the market.

limited liability company (LLC)   A new type of business structure available in almost every state that has many of the advantages of a partnership or subchapter S corporation but fewer of its disadvantages.

limited partnership   A special form of partnership in which a partner invests money and does not participate in the daily operation of the business.

link   A technological tool used to connect one Internet site's pages with website pages either on the home site or on another.

liquid assets   Anything the company owns that can be quickly sold and turned into cash, such as accounts receivables, computer equipment, or stocks and bonds.

logistics   The set of activities that deal with making the daily routine effective.

long-term goals   Goals that extend beyond the next twelve months.

maintenance temperament   Someone who enjoys keeping established systems running like a well-oiled machine.

managerial accountants   People who help you use your financial information to make business decisions.

manipulation   When customers feel that they are not in control of the sales process—that they will be encouraged and persuaded to purchase something they don't really need.

manufacturing franchise   A franchise arrangement where the franchisees are licensed to manufacture a specific product, such as Coca-Cola.

manufacturing requirement package (MRP)   A software package that integrates production forecasts with purchasing volumes to ensure that component parts needed to assemble a final product are available to meet production schedules.

market maker   A company with the clout to create an entire market opportunity simply by its involvement.

market niche   A segment of the market that has an existing need for a product or service that nobody currently offers.

market penetration   The percent of prospective users of your products and/or services who are already existing customers.

market positioning   Creating a positive image in the minds of potential and existing customers.

market segmentation   Dividing the total available market (everyone who may ever buy) into smaller groups, or segments, by specific attributes such as age, sex, location, interests, industry, or other pertinent criteria.

market value   The value of a product or service as determined by what the market will pay for it.

market-based pricing   Where offerings are priced at a level set by what everyone else is charging, rather than by costs.

marketing   Selecting the right product, pricing strategy, promotional program, and distribution outlets for your particular audience or market.

marketing theme   The overall thought that pops into people's minds when they think of your company and its offerings.

markup   The amount of money over and above the cost of producing a product or service that is added to pay for overhead expenses and profit.

mass producers   Companies that produce the same product(s) in very high volume as opposed to a large number of products with very small production runs.

merchant number   A number given to your company that is used to identify which account should be credited when a customer makes a credit card purchase. It also verifies that you're allowed to accept credit cards in payment.

mind share   The portion of a person's thinking processes that includes perceptions of your company's offerings.

mission statement   A simple statement that clearly defines the overall goals, or mission, of the company.

momentum   Describes the direction in which things are naturally moving and implies the amount of work or energy that would be needed to change the natural course of the business as it is currently operating.

net income   Money left over after all company expenses have been paid out of revenues.

noncompete clause   An agreement that employees or suppliers sign indicating they won't steal your ideas or business methods and go to work for a competitor or become competitors by starting their own firm.

nonsolicitation clause   A statement included in most noncompete agreements that restricts former employees from contacting prior customers with the intention of soliciting business from that customer for the employee's current employer.

objectives   Goals that define the overall direction of an organization, which can be divided into a number of shorter-range action items.

officers   Senior members of a management team or board of directors elected to serve as secretary, treasurer, president, and vice president of the corporation or board.

operational expenses   Those expenses associated with just running your business.

opportunity cost   The profit that would have been gained by pursuing another investment instead of the one currently in process.

outsourcing   Corporate-speak for hiring outside consultants, freelancers, or companies to provide services that in the past have been provided by employees.

over-promise   When you promise more to a customer than you actually deliver.

over-deliver   Delivering more to the customer than was agreed to, or more than the customer expected. It is usually a good idea if you can afford it.

owner's equity   What is left over when the liabilities are subtracted from the assets. Take what you have, subtract what you owe, and you are left with owner's equity.

partnership   When you and one or more people form a business marriage; your debts and assets are legally linked from the start.

pending event   A future event with a specific date that forces business people to make decisions that they would otherwise put off until later.

perceived value   The overall value the customer places on a particular product or service.

percentage markup   The amount of money a business adds into a product's price, over and above the cost of the product, expressed as a percent. A piece of candy costing $.05 to produce that has a markup of $.10 (meaning that the price to the consumer is $.15) has a percentage markup of 200 percent.

performance to plan   A measurement tool used by investors to determine how close an organization is to performing according to the initial business plan goals.

potential sale revenue   A measurement of the total amount of money that can be made from a specific customer or event.

pretax profit   The amount of money left over after all the business expenses and costs of goods sold are subtracted from total sales, but before taxes have been subtracted and paid.

price erosion   When competitive sales present enough alternative product selections to your customers that you must drop your price to keep their business.

price war   When all competitors compete based on price and keep undercutting their competitors to get sales.

probationary period   A time frame within which an employee is evaluated by the company, and vice versa.

product positioning   A conscious attempt on the part of your company to differentiate between your offering and those of your competitors.

professional corporation   A type of corporation, such as the subchapter S and subchapter C used by professionals such as attorneys and accountants. Such corporations have P.C. after the company name to indicate the company is a professional corporation.

pro-forma balance sheet   A balance sheet comprised of numbers that are calculated based on historical performance and known future events.

prospectus   A formal legal document a company prepares before being able to sell shares of stock to the public.

proxy statement   A form distributed to shareholders who will not be attending the company's annual meeting so their votes regarding the election of the board of directors, or other issues, can be counted.

publicity   Working with the media to have your company covered by the professional media such as magazine, newspaper, TV, and radio.

pull and push marketing strategy   A pull strategy convinces your potential customers to request your offering through their suppliers. In essence, the end user pulls your offering through the distribution channel by putting pressure on suppliers to carry it in their inventory. A push strategy sells your product to distributors, who then promote it to their customers. A pull strategy is driven by customers. A push strategy is driven by distributors.

registered agent   The official contact point for all legal matters.

retained earnings   Earnings from the company that are reinvested in operating the business. An item usually found on a company's balance sheet.

revenue   Money you receive from customers as payment for your services or the sale of your product. Some people also call it sales.

routine tasks   Things you do that are pretty much the same as the last time you did them, except for minor variations.

sales   Begins where marketing leaves off and involves all the steps you take to get the customer to buy your product or service.

sales revenue targets   The sales goals you set that affect all the other financial figures.

scattergun marketing   Marketing information sent everywhere in the hopes that someone will hear it and buy—the opposite of target marketing.

Securities and Exchange Commission (SEC)   A regulatory body that monitors and defines policy for the exchange of stock on the public markets.

scope of work   A highly recommended section of a proposal that defines the overall intent of the work to be performed.

search engine   Internet technology that allows a program to categorize website information in such a way that a search can be performed on the site based on specific key words.

secured line of credit   A line of credit that has some form of asset such as account receivable or equipment as collateral for the loan.

shareholders   Any individual or organization that owns shares of stock in a company.

short-term goals   Goals that occur within a short period of time and, ideally, lead to the completion of a long-term goal.

short-term loan   A loan that is to be paid off within one year.

shrinkage   The loss of product due to any number of means including loss in shipment or theft.

sole proprietorship   You transact business without the legal "safety net" associated with a corporation. You are personally responsible for all the business's obligations.

start-up temperament   Someone who thrives on new and exciting projects and challenges.

strategy   A careful plan or method; the art of devising or employing plans toward a goal.

S corporation   A type of corporation that has a limited number of shareholders, and the profits are passed directly through to the owner.

suite   A term used in relation to software where a number of different application programs are sold under the same name, so that purchasing a single product actually provides a variety, or suite, of other software packages.

sunk cost   Money already spent that you cannot recover.

superstore   An organization that provides a little, or a lot, of everything as opposed to specializing in a specific area.

tactics   Relating to small-scale actions serving a larger purpose, such as a strategy.

target marketing   A marketing approach involving focusing your marketing efforts on those potential customers most likely to buy your products or services.

tax accounting   A type of accounting concerned solely with how much money you will have to pay in taxes.

under-deliver   Delivering less to the customer than you promised.

under-promise   Promising less to a customer than you actually plan to deliver.

underwriter   A company responsible for marketing and selling shares of stock in a company to outside investors.

unearned income   Payments made by a customer for work that has not yet been performed that show up as income on the financial statements.

unqualified prospect   An individual who says he needs your product or service but who has not yet confirmed that he is able to make the purchase decision.

unsecured line of credit   A line of credit such as a credit card that a company can turn to for cash and that is not backed by some form of collateral.

variable expenses   Those costs that vary according to how much of a product or service is produced.

Index